Human Resource Management in the Nonprofit Sector

NEW HORIZONS IN MANAGEMENT

Series Editor: Cary L. Cooper, CBE, *Distinguished Professor of Organizational Psychology and Health, Lancaster University, UK*

This important series makes a significant contribution to the development of management thought. This field has expanded dramatically in recent years and the series provides an invaluable forum for the publication of high quality work in management science, human resource management, organizational behaviour, marketing, management information systems, operations management, business ethics, strategic management and international management.

The main emphasis of the series is on the development and application of new original ideas. International in its approach, it will include some of the best theoretical and empirical work from both well-established researchers and the new generation of scholars.

Titles in the series include:

Handbook of Managerial Behavior and Occupational Health
Edited by Alexander-Stamatios G. Antoniou, Cary L. Cooper, George P. Chrousos, Charles D. Spielberger and Michael William Eysenck

Workplace Psychological Health
Current Research and Practice
Paula Brough, Michael O'Driscoll, Thomas Kalliath, Cary L. Cooper and Steven A.Y. Poelmans

Research Companion to Corruption in Organizations
Edited by Ronald J. Burke and Cary L. Cooper

Self-Management and Leadership Development
Edited by Ronald J. Burke and Mitchell G. Rothstein

Handbook of Employee Engagement
Perspectives, Issues, Research and Practice
Edited by Simon Albrecht

Human Resource Management in Small Business
Achieving Peak Performance
Edited by Cary L. Cooper and Ronald J. Burke

Research Handbook of Comparative Employment Relations
Edited by Michael Barry and Adrian Wilkinson

Psychological Ownership and the Organizational Context
Theory, Research Evidence, and Application
Jon L. Pierce and Iiro Jussila

Handbook of Stress in the Occupations
Edited by Janice Langan-Fox and Cary L. Cooper

The New Knowledge Workers
Dariusz Jemielniak

Narcissism in the Workplace
Research, Opinion and Practice
Andrew J. DuBrin

Gender and the Dysfunctional Workplace
Edited by Suzy Fox and Terri R. Lituchy

The Innovation Imperative in Health Care Organisations
Critical Role of Human Resource Management in the Cost, Quality and Productivity Equation
Edited by Peter Spurgeon, Ronald J. Burke and Cary L. Cooper

Human Resource Management in the Nonprofit Sector
Passion, Purpose and Professionalism
Edited by Ronald J. Burke and Cary L. Cooper

Human Resource Management in the Nonprofit Sector

Passion, Purpose and Professionalism

Edited by

Ronald J. Burke

Emeritus Professor of Organizational Studies, Schulich School of Business, York University, Toronto, Ontario, Canada

Cary L. Cooper CBE

Distinguished Professor of Organizational Psychology and Health, Lancaster University, UK

NEW HORIZONS IN MANAGEMENT

Edward Elgar

Cheltenham, UK • Northampton, MA, USA

Published by
Edward Elgar Publishing Limited
The Lypiatts
15 Lansdown Road
Cheltenham
Glos GL50 2JA
UK

Edward Elgar Publishing, Inc.
William Pratt House
9 Dewey Court
Northampton
Massachusetts 01060
USA

A catalogue record for this book
is available from the British Library

Library of Congress Control Number: 2012940704

ISBN 978 0 85793 729 2

Typeset by Columns Design XML Ltd, Reading
Printed and bound by MPG Books Group, UK

Contents

Contributors

Jeanette Blackmar University of Kansas, USA

Ronald J. Burke York University, Canada

Heather L. Carpenter Grand Valley State University, USA

Susan M. Chandler University of Hawaii, USA

Cary L. Cooper Lancaster University, UK

Chris W. Coultas University of Central Florida, USA

Ian Cunningham University of Strathclyde, UK

Dail Fields Regent University, USA

Stacy Landreth Grau Texas Christian University, USA

Whitney E. Hein DePaul University, USA

Morgen Johansen University of Hawaii, USA

Joy Jones Regent University, USA

Breanne Kindel University of Central Florida, USA

Susan Bardi Kleiser Texas Christian University, USA

Nathalie Laidler-Kylander Harvard Univesity, USA

Kelly LeRoux University of Illinois at Chicago, USA

Mary McDonald University of San Diego, USA

Roseanne Mirabella Seton Hall University, USA

Thomas R. Packard San Diego State University, USA

John C. Ronquillo DePaul University, USA

Eduardo Salas University of Central Florida, USA

Stephanie Zajac University of Central Florida, USA

Acknowledgements

We believe that 'the people make the place' so it should come as no surprise that Cary and I have tried to raise the appreciation and importance of people in the success of organizations in all sectors – private, public, health care and nonprofit.

Thanks to Gerry Wood at Lancaster University, UK for again riding hard on Cary, me and our contributors, and managing our relationship with Edward Elgar. And to Carla D'Agostino for making the path smoother for us here in Toronto. We value all the support given to Cary and me over the past several years by our friends at Edward Elgar, with a special thanks to Fran O'Sullivan. It was always a joy to work with them. We acknowledge the co-operation of our international contributors. My contributions to this collection were supported in part by York University, Canada.

Finally, appreciation to my immediate and extended family for making life joyous: Susan, Sharon, Rachel, Jeff, Liane, Brendan, Jay and Christie.

Ronald J. Burke
Toronto

PART I

Setting the stage: human resource management in the nonprofit sector

1. Human resource management in the nonprofit sector: setting the stage

Ronald J. Burke

There has been considerable writing on the critical role human resource management plays in the performance of private sector organizations (e.g. Burke & Cooper, 2006; Becker, Huselid & Beatty, 2005; Lawler, 2003; Lawler & Worley, 2006; Pfeffer, 1998; Sisodia, Wolfe & Sheth, 2007; Ulrich & Smallwood, 2003; Katzenbach, 2000), with less attention devoted to the public sector (see Burke, Noblet & Cooper, 2012), the small business sector (Cooper & Burke, 2011), the health care sector (Spurgeon, Burke & Cooper, 2012) and the nonprofit sector. This volume addresses this gap by considering human resource management in the nonprofit sector.

In the 1980s, governments began to downsize and download services and responsibilities to the private and nonprofit sectors. At the same time, more individual citizens have come to rely on these products and services. These factors increased competition among nonprofits for funding support, supported the use of human resource management practices from the private sector into the nonprofit sector, as well as increasing pressures on nonprofits to be accountable and demonstrate their value (Alexander, Brudney & Yang, 2010).

Nonprofit organizations now play a growing role in most societies (Evers & Leville, 2010). These include the provision of critical services to citizens, advocacy for change in government policies and priorities, and the conduct of original research (Balassiano & Chandler, 2010). The nonprofit sector is being called upon to provide public goods and services that previously had been provided by various levels of government. Nonprofit organizations also need to demonstrate results in order to survive, they need to meet the needs of citizens and government regulators, and meet the expectations of various external stakeholders (Alexander, Brudney & Yang, 2010). This raises important issues for nonprofits: do they have the capacity to deliver these goods and services, to whom are these organizations accountable, and who are their constituencies?

The nonprofit sector then fills a critical need in society. It addresses issues that are low priority for profit-making organizations. They fill a gap that governments would address if governments had more resources. Given the large deficits facing all governments, nonprofit sector organizations will increasingly be called upon to meet these needs. In addition, as the population in many developed countries age, governments will be harder pressed to address these needs (health care, home care, Alzheimer's, etc.) making it more important than ever that the voluntary sector steps up to these challenges. Nonprofit organizations then exist in various areas: mental health, supporting the poor, assisting immigrants, assisting in hospitals, supporting cultural organizations and raising money to support health-related research (e.g., cancer). Balassiano and Chandler (2010) noted an increasing role for nonprofit organizations in advocacy and participation in community decision-making.

Individuals have become cynical about governments and this cynicism may rub off on nonprofit organizations as well. Nonprofits need to ensure that they can deliver what they promise by setting clear priorities and assessing their resources. Nonprofit organizations are facing important challenges such as meeting the needs of diverse groups of clients, reducing waste and inefficiencies, and using the latest management techniques.

SIZE OF THE NONPROFIT SECTOR

There were more than 1.9 million nonprofit organizations in the United States (US) as of 2005. These organizations received 8.1 billion volunteer hours from more than 61 million individuals. In 2001, nearly 60 million Americans 16 years or older (28 percent of this population) volunteered in at least one organization and spend 52 average annual hours at this. Volunteers contribute billions of dollars in terms of their time spent with their organizations (see Bowman, 2009).

There has been a growth in nonprofits of 54 percent from 1980 and 1997 in the US (US Census Bureau, 1998) and their contribution to gross domestic product (GDP) rose from 2.9 percent to 4.3 percent during this same period (Bureau of Economic Analysis, 1998). Nonprofit organizations use the majority of volunteer labor, and nonprofit organizations comprise the majority of paid employment in some sectors (Ruhm & Borkoski, 2003).

In Canada, nonprofit organizations represent about 10 percent of the total number of organizations with a GDP estimated at about $100 billion in 2011. In addition, nonprofit organizations employ over 1 million paid workers, about 10 percent of the Canadian workforce. As nonprofit organizations have grown, so has the appreciation of the importance of professional management.

INTEREST IN THE NONPROFIT SECTOR

There are now an increasing number of academic journals focusing on the voluntary sector. These include: *International Journal of Public Sector Management*, *Nonprofit and Voluntary Sector Quarterly*, *International Journal of Nonprofit and Voluntary Sector Marketing* and *Nonprofit Management and Leadership*.

There are also more professional associations focusing on the voluntary sector. These include the following: Association for Research on the Voluntary and Community Sector and the Association for Research on Nonprofit Organizations and Voluntary Action (ARNOVA). Professional associations, both national and international, have emerged, each holding conferences to disseminate research knowledge in this sector.

Increasing interest, both research and writing, has developed over the past decade. There are a number of academic journals that have emerged in North America, the United Kingdom (UK) and Europe that address the nonprofit sector. There have been some books written, primarily in the fund raising and marketing areas, that focus on the nonprofit sector.

Business programs (e.g. the MBA) in leading universities offer concentrations and specializations in the nonprofit sector. More business school graduates have taken employment in this sector. Some universities in North America and the UK have developed research and teaching programs in the nonprofit sector, and some academic institutions are offering diplomas or certificates in managing in the nonprofit sector.

CHALLENGES FACED BY THE NONPROFIT SECTOR

Nonprofit organizations currently face several challenges, some brought on by the worldwide economic recession. These include the following:

- competition from other sectors for qualified staff;
- increasing societal demands to do more;
- competition for funding support;
- lack of human resource management expertise;
- low staff pay and limited career advancement possibilities, limited training and development opportunities (courses, seminars);
- considerable time needed to recruit and train staff;

- a young staff prone to 'job hopping';
- an aging society and older volunteers;
- too many volunteers report a negative volunteer experience – one-third of volunteers do not continue;
- large nonprofit organizations that transcend a number of countries need to develop cultural sensitivities to people's needs in a diverse array of societies, besides developing international management capacities (Jackson, 2009);
- introducing human resource management policies and practices from the profit sector into a different context and a sometimes skeptical workforce.

DIFFERENCES BETWEEN NONPROFIT AND FOR-PROFIT ORGANIZATIONS

Oster (1995) identified five areas in which nonprofits differ from for-profit organizations: organizational culture; human resources; collaboration versus competition; complexity of their clients and customers; and the importance of mission:

- Nonprofits: decentralized, informal hierarchy, a culture of consensus, individual autonomy, flexibility, empowerment, difficulty in addressing organization-wide issues as a result.
- Nonprofit employees: intrinsically motivated, non-financial rewards.
- Nonprofits: collaboration, lots of clients and customers.
- Nonprofits: complex, a broad range of stakeholders.

Nonprofit organizations are driven by mission, typically a social mission, not a profit motive. Mission is more important for nonprofits than for-profit organizations. In nonprofits, mission fosters motivation, trust and is an important criteria for evaluating the value of internal processes (Paton & Cornforth, 1992; Parry, Kelliher, Mills & Tyson, 2005).

Nonprofit organizations differ from traditional small and large private sector organizations, and from government organizations, in important ways:

- They have a small paid professional and managerial staff and must rely heavily on unpaid volunteers, but pay levels are lower in nonprofit organizations than in the private sector.
- Their purposes are generally humanitarian, educational, social welfare and health related.

- Nonprofit organizations generally have highly educated workforces.
- They rely on financial support from various sources (e.g., government, donations from citizens, donations in kind from corporations).
- Volunteer staff generally report high levels of loyalty, job satisfaction and commitment to their nonprofit organization – though not receiving pay. They feel good about helping others and giving of their time.
- Nonprofit organizations are generally small in size. As a consequence they lack dedicated human resource professionals. Human resource management policies and practices are generally attached to a senior administrator's job (e.g., the chief executive officer, or executive director).
- Nonprofit organizations often rely on part-time staff. Haley-Lock (2006) found that most part-time employees are married women with children, not primary wage earners, and looking for work–family balance. While they may achieve these objectives, few part-time nonprofit employees realize the employment benefits of their full-time colleagues.
- Young volunteers report developing skills, knowledge, attitudes and behaviors that end up being helpful to them as they develop later careers in other types of organizations. Female volunteers indicate that their volunteer experiences often give them the confidence to pursue careers in other sectors. Retired women and men report that the volunteer experience contributed to their feelings of value later in life. Thus the volunteering experience can have large positive benefits to those who participate in it.
- Volunteers often make contacts which then lead them to part-time or full-time paying jobs; volunteering has been shown to have networking benefits.
- Volunteers have also been shown to have 'health benefits' from their volunteer experiences (Post & Neimark, 2007).

There is a potentially large number of volunteers in all countries. These include the recently retired, part-time workers and full-time home makers, individuals wanting to make the world a better place, individuals searching for greater meaning in their lives and individuals wanting to mentor the next generation.

Nonprofit organizations are different from both private organizations and government organizations in important ways, and yet similar to them in other ways. Nonprofit organizations, similar to private sector and government organizations, need effective human resource management (HRM) for long-term success. Individuals who choose to work in nonprofit organizations are typically motivated by different factors than their colleagues in the private and government sectors. Thus HRM managers in nonprofits need to address unique issues in integrating board, organizational staff and volunteer needs while building a motivated, loyal and productive workforce and effective organization. The unique characteristics of nonprofit organizations will then affect their HRM policies and practices. Yet people – paid staff and volunteers – make nonprofits (and all other organizations) work.

KEY ISSUES IN NONPROFIT SECTOR MANAGEMENT

This section briefly reviews emerging issues in nonprofit organizations as covered in the recent literature.

PRESSURES FOR CHANGE IN NONPROFIT ORGANIZATIONS

Light (2000) identified four forces for change in the nonprofit sector. These were:

- Scientific management – the emphasis on efficiency, rules, procedures and accountability.
- The war on waste – controlling costs, mergers, consolidating services, re-engineering and performance-based accountabilities.
- Liberation management – emphasizing the development of staff and a belief that they will function as adults and perform responsibly.
- Watchful eyes – making information more readily available to individuals inside and outside the nonprofit organization.

Ways that HRM practices affect individuals (attitudes, motivations, behaviors, productivity) and organizational performance:

- Few nonprofit organizations have an HR manager.
- Many HRM issues affect nonprofit organization managers.
- While profit making is not a goal of nonprofit organizations, being viable and successful over the long term is.
- The nonprofit sector is becoming increasingly complex, raising the management and organizational challenges they face.
- Nonprofit organizations have to 'do more with less'; they have to become more efficient.
- Nonprofit organizations face higher levels of evaluation and accountability to multiple stakeholders.

- Nonprofit organizations need to increase their emphasis on capacity building.

This introductory chapter identifies important issues, concepts and challenges related to human resource management in nonprofit organizations. Many of these are addressed in more detail in the chapters that follow. In addition, a summary of each contribution concludes this chapter.

The collection combines nonprofit specific functions (e.g., attracting and managing volunteers) with broader topics in human resource management, organizational behavior and organizational development. It assembles the latest research findings and thinking on the management of nonprofit sector organizations and the effective utilization of both paid staff and volunteers. These organizations, ranging in size from small to large, and local to international, exist in every country. They are numerous, pervasive and involve a large number of paid staff and an even larger number of unpaid volunteers.

Nonprofit organizations serve a number of purposes: supporting research on various illnesses and diseases (e.g., cancer, Alzheimer's), making health care more available in developing countries, supporting educational institutions such as museums and libraries, providing support to victims of AIDS, collecting and passing out food to the unemployed and to needy families, and helping immigrants get settled in their new countries. This list is only a small sample of the purposes served by these types of organizations.

TRENDS IN HUMAN RESOURCE MANAGEMENT IN NONPROFIT ORGANIZATIONS OVER TIME

Cunningham (1999) provides an overview of the nature and practice of human resource management in nonprofits over the past 50 years. Nonprofits exhibited little interest in management before 1980. Nonprofits were believed to be different from profit-making organizations; the belief that 'doing good was good enough' prevailed. In the early 1980s there was the start of a move towards more professional management. In the 2000s, more nonprofits see sound human resource management policies and practices as a competitive advantage necessary for their success and survival. Cunningham identifies several reasons why human resource management is now more important for nonprofit organizations. These include:

- a more important role for nonprofit organizations in society today;
- growth in the 'contract culture' in which nonprofit organizations

'contract' with governments to provide particular products and services in an efficient manner;
- nonprofits now face more complex tasks;
- use of these human resource management policies and practices raises the status of nonprofit organizations;
- volunteer and staff dissatisfaction with their current training and development;
- increases the likelihood of attracting and retaining more highly qualified staff.

But Cunningham identifies some obstacles to the use of private-sector-developed human resource management policies and practices in nonprofit organizations. These include internal resistance to change (managing volunteers is different and democracy makes it difficult to get consensus on specific changes), a lack of resources and funds to incorporate these successfully (cannot pay, little training and development and limited promotion prospects), the expectations of clients, employees and the general public (not a competitive business organization but rather a participative culture) and, in some recent cases, union resistance to these changes.

HRM FUNCTIONS

HRM policies and functions have been fairly well identified and addressed in the nonprofit writings (Bambeito, 2004; Herman & Associates, 2005; Hudson, 2005; Letts, Ryan & Grossman, 1999; Pynes, 2008). These functions typically include: job analysis, recruitment, selection, orientation, performance management with a focus on increasing and maintaining levels of motivation, pay, benefits, training and development, collective bargaining with employee associations of unions, strategic HRM and challenges to HRM in the nonprofit sector.

Research findings and attempts to 'professionalize' the management of voluntary sector organizations have raised at least two critical issues. Both of these will be addressed in this volume. Firstly, some of the research findings have produced inconsistent results (e.g., Herman & Renz, 2008). There are some things we seem to know now for sure in explaining voluntary sector effectiveness, but other things are still in play. Secondly, efforts to translate HRM practices from the private (for-profit) sector into the voluntary sector sometimes fail to produce the expected benefits.

PASSION AND PROFESSIONALISM

As the nonprofit sector has grown, there has been an increasing realization of the importance of leadership and management skills to complement the passion of those working and volunteering in the nonprofit sector (Rothschild & Milofsky, 2006; Nickson et al., 2008).

MISSION ATTACHMENT

Mission attachment, associated with employee passion for the mission and a willingness to remain to accomplish it, was found to be related to employee retention in a study by Kim and Lee (2007). They studied 198 employees of a nonprofit community health center from ten counties in a southeastern US state. They found that positive attitudes towards the organization's mission and dissatisfaction with working conditions (pay, advancement) were related to employee retention, with dissatisfaction having a stronger effect. But the positive correlation between mission attachment and working conditions indicated that mission attachment still played a role in staff retention by reducing dissatisfaction with working conditions. An earlier study by Brown and Yoshioka (2003) found that dissatisfaction with working conditions influenced employee retention while mission attachment had no effect. The results of both these studies indicates convincingly that making efforts to address negative aspects of working conditions within nonprofit organizations is likely to pay large dividends.

GOVERNANCE IN NONPROFIT ORGANIZATIONS

Jegers (2009) contends that we know less about governance in nonprofit organizations than in for-profit organizations, and governance is more complex in nonprofit organizations. It is important to consider why boards of directors are important, their role and functions. It is vital that nonprofits attract and select the right members. These individuals need to know their roles and responsibilities, and boards need to work on their discussion and decision-making processes (Weisman, 2003). There is emerging evidence that particular board processes are associated with more competent board members which in turn is associated with more effective organizational performance. These processes and competencies will be reviewed below.

Bradshaw (2009) proposes that nonprofit organizations would improve their governance by incorporating contingency factors in their choice of a governance pattern. Contingencies that might be included are: age, size, structure, strategy, and environmental contingencies such as stability and complexity. An organization's governance pattern that fits with its internal and external contingencies will (should) perform more effectively. She provides considerable detail on how these factors might be considered in developing a governance pattern.

Francis and Kelleher (2011) believe that too many nonprofit organizations employ outdated or subpar governance practices. They offer ten questions that nonprofit directors should raise at the next board meeting.

1. Why is our board so big? They suggest that an effective size is about nine members.
2. Is this an oversight board or a fundraising board? Boards should provide oversight in their view.
3. Have all board members reviewed the executive directors' contract? They need to do this.
4. Has the board reviewed the organization's detailed expense policies? This is critical to prevent financial abuse.
5. Is the board chair elected openly by the full board? Too many board chairs select their successor or nominate committee chairs and members.
6. Are committees providing all of their work to the full board? Board members need to see all the work done by every committee.
7. Has the board set clear expectations about attendance and preparation and how to deal with poor performance? Attendance of board members should be published.
8. Does the board ask and encourage tough questions and value different opinions?
9. Does the board spend enough board time together without the presence of management? Having the executive director or chief executive officer (CEO) present at all board meetings tends to limit questions about their organization's strategy, plans and performance. The executive director or CEO should be invited to attend some meetings however.
10. Does the board candidly evaluate its performance in a confidential meeting? About half of nonprofit boards conduct no self-evaluations. Evaluations should be both formal (conducted annually) and informal (undertaken more often).

Zimmerman and Stevens (2008) undertook a study of board governance among nonprofit organizations in South Carolina. Boards of directors are legally responsible for the nonprofits they work with. BoardSource (2004) identified four board functions of nonprofit boards: legal and fiduciary oversight; fundraising; representation of stakeholders; and their own opinions and viewpoints. BoardSource then identified more specific responsibilities of nonprofit boards. Zimmerman and Stevens collected information from 948 nonprofit organizations and found that most nonprofits indicated that their board members followed 'best practices'.

Brown (2007), using data from 1051 CEOs and board chairs from 713 nonprofit credit unions, investigated the relationship of three board development practices (recruitment, board member orientation, evaluation practices) with more competent board meetings and better board performance. The results indicated that use of the three board development practices was associated with more capable board members, and board member capacity was associated with better board performance.

The board is an important asset for nonprofit organizations. Effective boards are associated with more successful nonprofit organizations (Bradshaw, Murray & Wolpin, 1992; Brown, 2005; Carver, 2006; Green & Griesinger, 1996). Thus there is an great need today for high-quality board members. Some suggestions, based on research evidence, have emerged on ways to develop an effective board. These include recruitment and selection, training and preparing board members for service, monitoring performance, removing board members who fail to contribute. The process must begin however by first identifying the skills that are needed for a particular board, recruiting, attracting and selecting an individual(s) that has these skills, orienting, coaching and mentoring new board members, and monitoring and evaluating the contribution of all board members.

Brown and Guo (2010), using content analysis of descriptions of board member roles from 121 nonprofit CEOs, identified 13 different roles. CEOs from larger nonprofits identified more board member roles than did CEOs from smaller nonprofits. These roles were (in descending order): fund development, strategy and planning, financial oversight, public relations, board member vitality, policy oversight, relationship to executive, provide guidance and expertise, facilitate granting, generate respect, be a 'working board', board membership, and become knowledgeable.

Ostrower and Stone (2010) tested a model of nonprofit board governance in 5111 public charities. The model considered three categories of independent variables: board attributes, internal nonprofit organization characteristics and external environmental characteristics. Boards varied in how active they were in 11 different roles. They were active in providing financial oversight, setting policies, planning and evaluating the CEO, and less active in influencing public policy, evaluating the board and educating the public.

Variables in all three categories were associated with how actively board members engaged in particular roles. Internal nonprofit characteristics and board attributes had the widest relationships with level of board member engagement. Nonprofit organization size was associated with many indicators of board member engagement. Each independent variable was associated with performance of some board roles and not others, with the direction also varying from positive to negative. The influence of the external environmental factors was more focused and less widespread.

PAY IN THE NONPROFIT SECTOR

In general, nonprofit workers earn less than similar employees in the for-profit sector (Preston, 1989; Handy & Katz, 1998; Leete, 2001). The nature of both the distribution of jobs and worker characteristics play a role in these pay differences as well (Ruhm & Borkoski, 2003). Joslyn (2002) reported that motivation for nonprofit service was found to be more norm-based (emotional, compassionate) than rational (pay, self-centered).

JOB SATISFACTION IN THE NONPROFIT SECTOR

A number of research studies comparing employees in the nonprofit sector with employees in private or public sectors have shown that job satisfaction is almost always higher among nonprofit sector employees (see Borzaga & Tortia, 2006; Almond & Kendall, 2000; Leete, 2000; Levine, 1991; Mirvis, 1992; Benz, 2005; Light, 2002a; DeCooman, DeGieter, Pepermann & Jegers, 2011).

Employee Turnover

Employee turnover is an important challenge for nonprofit organizations. There are both direct costs (e.g., financial replacement costs) and indirect costs (potential negative impact on remaining employees who now have to do more work; lower quality of service to clients) making it vital that nonprofits do whatever they can to increase their employee retention rates.

PERSON–ENVIRONMENT FIT

Vigoda and Cohen (2002) examined the relationship of person–organization fit (P–E fit) and met expectations (ME) on attitudes and performance of nonprofit employees in two samples (244 public sector, 155 nonprofit sector). Job satisfaction and organizational commitment were higher among employees with greater P–E fit and ME. Higher ME was also associated with more effort to solve organizational problems, higher in-role performance and higher organizational citizenship behaviors. Thus better matching of individuals and organizations, both in selection and orientation, have value to both parties. Vigoda and Cohen believe that both P–E fit and ME may be more important in the nonprofit sector as well. Nonprofit organizations would benefit from selecting employees that share the organization's values.

LEADERSHIP

Suarez (2010) investigated the professional backgrounds and nonprofit experience of 200 leaders of nonprofit organizations. Most were female (54 percent), white (86 percent), and had a college degree (89 percent), and most were between 40 and 59 years of age (75 percent). Some had management credentials and management experiences, most advanced in the nonprofit sector through nonprofit experiences. He concludes that having a 'nonprofit ethic' was a critical path to nonprofit leadership; nonprofit experiences enhanced individual credibility.

Leadership succession can be a complex process in organizations in all sectors (Dym & Hutson, 2005). Interesting case studies providing guidance for nonprofit organizations can be found in both Neville and Murray (2008) and McKee and Driscoll (2008).

Leadership concepts from research on for-profit organizations have, not surprisingly, been used in nonprofit organizational research (Agard, 2010; De Hoogh, 2005; Ronquillo, 2010). Rowald and Rohmann (2009a, 2009b), for example, investigated the relationship of transformational and transactional and volunteer emotional experiences and effectiveness in German choirs. Greater use by leaders of transformational leadership was associated with more positive emotional experiences whereas greater use of transactional leadership was associated with more negative emotional experiences. Higher use of transformation leadership by conductors was associated with greater singer satisfaction, extra effort and higher levels of singer effectiveness. Ulrich and Smallwood (2007, 2003) also demonstrate the importance of leadership and particular leadership competencies.

Ritchie, Kolodinsky and Eastwood (2007) explored the relationship of CEO intuitive decision style and financial measures of nonprofit organization performance. Data were collected from 144 CEOs using a questionnaire while financial information was taken from their organization's IRS data. Six financial performance measures were included. They found that CEO intuition was significantly and positively related with three of the six financial measures.

LEADERSHIP DEVELOPMENT VIA EDUCATION AND TRAINING

Voluntary sector programs have an impact on the practice of voluntary sector leadership and management. Various programs are currently available (college and university-based, association-based, government-based) designed to improve leadership of voluntary and nonprofit sector organizations, their organization, management and fund raising, and their effectiveness.

LEADERSHIP DEVELOPMENT VIA EXECUTIVE COACHING

Increasing use is being made of executive coaching including in the nonprofit sector. Bell, Moyers and Wolfred (2006) in a survey of nonprofit executives found that 25 percent had used executive coaches and 8 percent were being coached at the time of their survey. Fischer and Beimers (2009) report the evaluation of a six-month executive coaching program involving nine executive directors and five coaches. They present a coaching model used as a framework for their evaluation. Data were collected from participants using both questionnaires and structured interviews. The results showed high levels of both executive director and coach satisfaction with the experience, wanting it to continue, and indicated that progress was made in their leadership skills, in their relationships with both boards and staff, and in their ability to move their nonprofit organization toward its goals.

Executive coaching may be particularly useful in nonprofit organizations since given the way that nonprofit executives obtain their leadership jobs, the absence of transition plans, the limited preparation and support for this now role generally available to incumbents, and the high levels of turnover among senior management (Bell, Moyers & Wolfred, 2006).

SKILL DEVELOPMENT

How and where do executives in nonprofit organizations learn the craft? What are the challenges they fact in this learning and what are their key learnings (Paton et al., 2007)? Sherlock and Nathan (2007) undertook a qualitative study of 12 CEOs of nonprofit association organizations of what, how, and why they learned what they did on the job. CEOs have no one above them to facilitate their learning (other than their boards); they are on their own. In addition, CEOs feel isolated from their boards and their staff, so they learn on their own through personal reflection and discussions with spouses, family members and close friends. CEOs also feel vulnerable since they lacked long-term job security and/or severance arrangements. Finally, politics in their relationship with their boards of directors, and power differences with their staff, places limitations on their learning from both these sources.

Sherlock and Nathan offer the following suggestions for the development of nonprofit CEOs:

1. Highlighting and being cognizant of the ways in which their context affects their development and learning.
2. Enhancing the CEO's reflective practice.
3. Increasing CEO skill in operating in a political environment.
4. Utilizing a professional coach.
5. Working on improving their relationship with their boards of directors.

Dolan (2002) advocates on-the-job learning, training opportunities, performance management, career development possibilities and attendance at conferences. Executive coaching has proven useful in enhancing senior management skills. In addition, voluntary sector organizations need to put more thought into leadership succession and the transition among leaders.

IS THERE A LOOMING NONPROFIT LEADERSHIP DEFICIT?

Some nonprofit experts have proposed a leadership shortfall in the nonprofit sector (Salamon & Gellar, 2007). Bell, Moyers and Wolfred (2006), in their survey of nonprofit executives, reported that three-quarters of their respondents planned to leave their jobs within the next five years. Tierney (2006) estimated a shortfall of 140 000 senior managers in nonprofits over the upcoming decade. Solomon and Sandahl (2007) observed that younger nonprofit staff are unwilling to fill senior level executive jobs due to high levels of workload, making it difficult to integrate work and personal life, and job stress.

Johnson (2007), however, sees various 'adjustments' that are likely to lessen this potential leadership shortfall. These include: increases in executive pay; newer staff having higher levels of skill; attracting workers from other sectors; increased labor force participation of older workers; mergers and consolidation of nonprofits lessening the need for senior executives; the greater use of board member and volunteer expertise; and donors and funders taking a more active leadership and managerial role in nonprofits they support.

CAN THE PERFORMANCE OF NONPROFIT ORGANIZATIONS BE MEASURED?

There is increasing agreement that the performance of nonprofit organizations needs to be measured and that it can be measured (Sowa, Selden & Sandfort, 2004; Yoo & Brooks, 2005; Yoo, Brooks & Patti, 2007). Clients are now defined as customers, accountability must be shown 'upwards' to donors, funders and the board of directors and 'downwards' to clients. But it will not be easy or straightforward. Nonprofit organization's goals are numerous, complex, sometimes 'soft' (e.g., helping and changing people), and involve multiple stakeholders to whom they are accountable and must demonstrate value. Baruch and Ramalho (2006) examined criteria for effectiveness in private sector and nonprofit organizations and found that nonprofits made greater use of 'soft' evaluation criteria.

In order to start the process of measuring performance nonprofit organizations must first define and describe all of their goals, then develop multiple performance measures of them (Light, 2002b; Martin & Kettner, 2009). These measures must be flexible, adaptive and able to track accountabilities both upward and downward (Alexander, Brudney & Yang, 2010). Nonprofit organizations can then undertake research on identifying those factors that are central to their performance. Leadership is critical in dealing with accountability and performance measurement challenges.

Packard (2010) developed a model for understanding and measuring the performance of a human service organization that included inputs (e.g., community, clients, staff, managers, board of director effectiveness, resources), throughputs (e.g., program capacity including the use of best practices, clear standards and procedures, extent of program implementation, and management capacity including management processes, organizational climate and culture) and environmental relations and management outcomes (e.g., satisfaction of external stakeholders, employee satisfaction, financial health) and outputs (e.g., client outcomes, cost and cost-effectiveness). Packard's model, as you can see, is comprehensive.

Performance measurement within nonprofit organizations is necessarily multidimensional and includes many components that are perceptual in nature (Herman & Renz, 1999, 1998, 1997). Herman and Renz (2008) suggest that organizational effectiveness measures for nonprofit organizations are always comparative, must be multidimensional, are certainly related to board of director effectiveness, are social and perceptual constructs, and need to include assessments of nonprofit adaptability as an important criterion. They also argue that effectiveness measures will necessarily be different in different types of nonprofit organizations.

LeRoux and Wright (2010), in a study of 314 nonprofit organizations, found a positive relationship between range of performance measures used and levels of effectiveness in strategic decision-making. Performance measures included: workload and output indicators, unit cost and efficiency measures, client or customer satisfaction, external audits and industry standards and benchmarks. Other factors found to influence ratings of strategic decision-making were effective governance, funding diversity, and education level of the executive director.

FACTORS CONTRIBUTING TO PERFORMANCE OF NONPROFIT ORGANIZATIONS

Packard (2010) reports on staff perceptions of factors affecting performance in a California agency providing educational and workforce development for 15–21-year-old high-risk youth. Data were obtained using questionnaires from 52 managers, supervisors and line staff. Factors that emerged as important predictors of performance were: adequate program funding, positive attitudes of leaders, motivated and committed staff, an organizational structure that supported organizational objectives, and a process that supported the effective use of resources.

The American Society of Association Executives (2006) reported findings from a four-year study of 'exceptional' nonprofit organizations. They identified seven critical factors that distinguished 'exceptional' from other nonprofit organizations under three broad categories.

- Commitment to purpose:
  1. A customer-serviced culture.
  2. Alignment of products and services with its mission.
- Commitment to analysis and feedback:
  3. Data-driven strategies: collecting, disseminating and analyzing data to learn and shape future directions.

   4. Dialogue and engagement: an ongoing discussion between staff and volunteers about the nonprofit organization's mission and priorities.
   5. CEO as a broker of ideas. Engage staff and volunteers so that the nonprofits mission is influenced by their interests.
- Commitment to action:
   6. Organizational adaptability: through learning changing, dropping programs and adding programs.
   7. Audience building: acquiring partners and institutions that support the nonprofits mission and purpose.

Shilbury and Moore (2006) studied the effectiveness of ten Australian national Olympic sports organizations using eight indicators of organizational performance or effectiveness to predict an overall effectiveness rating. These were flexibility, resources, planning, productivity, availability of information, stability, skilled workforce and cohesive workforce. Data were collected from 289 members of these sporting organizations. Productivity and planning were the strongest predictors of sport organization effectiveness.

USE OF WORK TEAMS

Greater use is being made of work teams in the non-profit sector. But management needs to be clear on why, when and how to use work teams. Much of the work undertaken by nonprofit organizations is project-based, ideal for the use of work teams. Work teams provide opportunities to exchange information, ideas, issues and concerns, and ways to do the work more effectively. Work teams are also a source of social support and friendships inside and outside the workplace.

CAN EFFECTIVE HUMAN RESOURCE MANAGEMENT PRACTICES FROM THE PRIVATE SECTOR BE APPLIED TO NONPROFIT ORGANIZATIONS?

The answer to this question seems to be both 'yes' and 'no'. On the one hand, Herman and Renz (2008) conclude that the merits of using 'best practices' from the private sector in nonprofit organizations are still not yet determined. Beck, Lengnick-Hall and Lengnick-Hall (2008) identify a paradox in introducing private sector human resource management policies and practices into the nonprofit sector. On the one hand, nonprofits may benefit from adapting private sector human resource management practices; but on the other hand, the nonprofit sector is different from the private sector so these human resource management practices will be difficult to apply and may not work well. They advocate a middle ground based on their intensive study of one nonprofit organization. They advocate a configurational approach in which particular human resource management 'bundles' (groups of human resource management practices) that fit the nonprofit organization's mission be utilized.

Beck, Lengnick-Hall and Lengnick-Hall (2008) undertook an intensive case study of a single nonprofit organization focusing on its organizational culture and vision and organizational structure and size. They found that the use of private sector-based human resource management practices related to these two areas was limited, haphazard and ineffective. Hence their call for using clusters of human resource management practices that fit a nonprofit's mission be introduced.

HUMAN RESOURCE ARCHITECTURE IN NONPROFIT ORGANIZATIONS

Ridder and McCandless (2010) considered influences on human resource management policies and practices in nonprofit organizations. They identified four types of human resource management frameworks using two dimensions (high or low): a strategic orientation (nonprofit goals determine human resource management strategies and practices) and a human resource-based emphasis. The four types of human resource architectures were:

1. Administrative human resource management – low strategic focus and low human-resource-based emphasis. These nonprofits exhibited a low level of human resource management professionalism.
2. Motivational human resource management – low strategic focus and high human resource emphasis, focus on mission and satisfying diverse employee needs.
3. Strategic human resource management – a high strategic focus and a low human resource emphasis, focused on responses to external demands
4. Values-driven human resource management – high strategic focus and high human resource base emphasis, committed both to the mission and to staff and volunteer development.

Some may say that their framework argues against a 'one size fits all' approach to human resource management in nonprofit organizations.

BRINGING ABOUT CHANGE IN NONPROFIT ORGANIZATIONS

As indicated earlier, there is now more pressure on nonprofit organizations to be well managed and accountable as they take on larger roles in a more complex environment. Both internal pressures from nonprofits themselves and external pressures from funders, regulators, clients and stakeholders have increased the need for change. But some factors in nonprofits make change sometimes difficult to achieve. Kellock Hay, Beattie, Livingstone and Munro (2007) identify some of these factors: the nonprofits committed to stated values; a lack of resources; vague, multiple and difficult-to-measure goals; differing stakeholder goals; and a democratic structure making it harder to achieve consensus and reconcile differences (e.g., between paid staff and volunteers). Using a case study, they employ Lewin's three-stage model of organizational change (unfreezing, change, refreezing) to indicate how and when these factors came into play.

INCREASING USE OF THE INTERNET BY NONPROFIT ORGANIZATIONS

Organizations in all sectors are making increasing use of the internet to achieve their objectives (Waters & Lord, 2009; Waters, 2007). Nonprofit organizations are making increasing use of the internet in at least two important areas: attracting and managing their volunteers; and developing and maintaining relationships with important stakeholders (Waters & Lord, 2009). Dhebar and Stokes (2008) similarly highlight ways in ways the internet can be used in attracting and management volunteers. Waters (2007) also indicates a number of uses that nonprofit organizations are making of the internet.

GENDER AND THE GLASS CEILING

Themudo (2009) laments the limited attention given to the role of women in nonprofit organizations and calls for a gender theory of nonprfits. She notes the following: women have been shown to be more public spirited than men, volunteer more than men, and give a larger share of their income to nonprofit organizations than men. Women also make up more than half of the employees of nonprofit organizations. Yet men hold a disproportionate number of senior-level managerial jobs in the nonprofit sector, suggesting the presence of a 'glass ceiling' (Lewis, 2002; Joslyn, 2003; Oldenhall & O'Neill, 1994; Pynes, 2000; Preston, 1990). She undertook two pieces of research on the relationship of women's empowerment, voluntary activities, and nonprofit sector size and strength. She observed that countries with greater women's empowerment had larger nonprofit sectors. In addition, women's empowerment was associated with their greater participation in the nonprofit sector, again at the country level.

Some researchers have focused their attention on the 'glass ceiling' directly. Sampson and Moore (2008), in a study of salary equity among 970 women and men in fundraising and development, found that women earned smaller salaries than men, and this gap seemed to be widening over time. Women, however, comprised 83 percent of their sample. Women were less satisfied with their pay than were men. Women in development were less likely to work in larger nonprofit organizations and as a result their nonprofits had smaller budgets. More women than men had taken time off at some point during their career but even this figure was relatively modest. Women were also less likely to be on nonprofit boards. Yet the women in the Sampson and Moore study were still optimistic about their advancement opportunities, most (65 percent) seeing them the same as men's. Those women less optimistic about their advancement prospects indicated that these prospects could be improved through leadership development offerings for them, having greater recognition of different work and leadership styles, and more family-friendly polices and cultures.

Gibelman's work (2000) showed that men were disproportionately represented in senior managerial jobs in the nonprofit sector and they earned higher salaries at all hierarchical levels. At all hierarchical levels Moore and White (2000) found that women were less connected to important network elites.

UNIVERSITY AND CERTIFICATE EDUCATION PROGRAMS

University- and college-level educational programs focusing on nonprofit and philanthropic sectors are increasing (O'Neill & Fletcher, 1998; O'Neill & Young, 1988; Mirabella, 2001). Mirabella (2007) and Mirabella and Wish (2000) reviewed university-based educational programs in nonprofit management. She observed a large increase in the numbers of these programs, identifying at least 240 college and university-based programs in the US alone. These programs included graduate doctoral (PhD) programs, Master's-level programs including MBA concentrations, undergraduate, continuing education, and diploma/certificate granting offerings (Mirabella & Wish, 2001). Allison, Chen, Flanigan, Keyes-Williams, Vasavantia and Saidel (2007) reviewed PhD level programs in nonprofit education; while Dulch, Ernst, McClusky, Mirabella and Sadow (2007) examined undergraduate nonprofit education in US universities. In all cases, US universities have increased their emphasis on nonprofit education. Despite these increases, Hurrell, Warhurst and Nickson (2010) observed a shortage of nonprofit sector graduates which they attribute to students being unaware of nonprofit sector job opportunities.

Fletcher (2005) considered the relationship of obtaining a Master's degree in nonprofit management on graduate's professional lives. She administered a survey to graduates of three US universities (n = 400). The majority of nonprofit Master's graduates were satisfied with the education they had received in their programs in helping to prepare them for careers in the sector.

Tschirhart, Reed, Freeman and Anker (2008), using a sample of 688 alumni from four US Master's programs, two offering the MBA and two offering the MPA, observed that most respondents had a favorite sector and remained in that sector for their employment. Sector change was affected by perceptions of the competence of that sector and fit with an individuals career orientation. Individuals that shifted sectors were more likely to have a protean career orientation.

University students have images of nonprofit and for-profit employees. Nonprofit employees were 'scratching out a living and asked to produce with too few resources', for-profit employees were 'business employees earning high pay but working in a soulless environment of bottom-line pressures', and public sector employees were 'government employees bogged down in red tape but comfortable in secure employment' (Tschirhart, Reed, Freeman & Anker, 2008, p. 669).

Tschirhart, Reed, Freeman and Anker (2009) compared board service of MBA (for-profit focus) and MPA (nonprofit focus) from four US universities; two specializing in each. Both MBA and MPA graduates were equally likely to serve on nonprofit boards of directors. They found that nonprofit sector employment predicted service on nonprofit boards. Using a measure of 'orientation to do good', they found that this predicted service on all three types of boards (nonprofit, public sector, private sector).

INNOVATION

McDonald (2007) writes that innovation is the key to the success on nonprofit organizations. He undertook two studies of innovation in 260 US nonprofit hospitals, finding that a clear motivational mission was related to innovation focus, an innovation testing and implementation process, more innovations and the adoption and development of more innovations. Jaskyte (2004) and Jaskyte and Fressler (2005) show how nonprofit leadership and nonprofit organizational culture influence levels of innovation.

IMAGE OF NONPROFIT ORGANIZATIONS IN THE MEDIA

Hale (2007) examined nonprofit coverage in nine major newspapers in the US. Media coverage can have a powerful influence on the public's views of nonprofit organizations. The media tells readers and viewers which issues are important, how they should think about these issues and how to feel about issues. The media tends to prefer 'interesting' stories and this sometimes leads to an emphasis on problems within nonprofit organizations (e.g., fraud, and spending considerably more funds on administration than on meeting the needs of clients).

A FEW BAD APPLES

The increasing pressures on nonprofit organizations, and the inevitability of 'human frailties' has increased 'bad behavior' in the nonprofit sector (Wolverton, 2003a, 2003b). This has caused some individuals to become skeptical of their value (Goldstein, 2003). In addition there has been increasing pressure on boards of directors to hold chief executives and executive directors more accountable. Consider the following examples:

- 'Muslim charity misspent $600,000 in donations. Gifts for needy were spent on personal expenses, office costs, audit finds', *Toronto Star*, 20 January 2011, A1.
- 'Game over for shady charity', *Toronto Star*, 8 March 2011, A1, A10.
- The Organ Donation and transplant Association of Canada was closed when auditors found that most collected money went to fundraising and administrative expenses (Bruser, 2011).

Salterio (2011) notes that many nonprofits fall short in accounting for the funds given to them. Some nonprofit organizations provide limited financial information while a small minority participate in fraudulent practices. Volunteers, donors and government regulators need to know that a nonprofit is achieving its objectives and is worthy of support. Sound financial information is a solid first step. The preparation of an annual report, partly an accountability document and partly a statement of the nonprofit's mission and how the mission will be realized, is a necessity. The annual report should indicate how much money was received, how it was spent, and why it was spent this way.

FRAUD IN NONPROFIT ORGANIZATIONS

Holtfreter (2008) studied occupational fraud in 128 nonprofit organizations considering characteristics of offenders, victims and offenses. Financial loss was predicted at the individual level by gender (females responsible for larger dollar losses). Most frauds within nonprofit organizations, about 97 percent, involve misappropriation of funds (theft, stealing). More frauds were undertaken by non-management employees than by management employees but larger fraud losses result from fraud by management employees. Smaller losses from fraud were associated with male offenders, larger nonprofits, nonprofits using internal audits, nonprofits using external audits, and nonprofits having anonymous hotlines. She indicates the following as effective controls of fraud loss in nonprofit organizations: financial controls, non-financial control mechanisms, and management oversight behavior.

Greenlee, Fischer, Gordon and Keating (2007) studied 58 cases of fraud in nonprofit organizations using 2004 data. Losses ranged from $200 to $17 million, with a median loss of $100 000; four nonprofits reported losses over $1 million. Factors found to be associated with fraud were: collusion between multiple perpetrators, higher salaries, being older, having longer organizational tenure prior to fraud detection, being more highly educated and being male. Most of these characteristics were a function of being at more senior levels of management in their nonprofit organizations. Most frauds were identified by tips from various sources (42 percent), with half of these coming from other employees or volunteers. Only 25 percent of fraud were found by internal auditors. In the vast majority of instances, perpetrators of fraud were terminated (72 percent). Personal characteristics associated with fraud were being in debt, and having a lavish lifestyle.

They offer a variety of suggestions for minimizing fraud. These include: background checks on new employees, developing an anonymous reporting method (e.g., a tipline), use of internal auditing or fraud examination function, external auditing by certified public accountants, bonding key employees and having insurance to cover losses from fraud. Other suggestions include having orientations to volunteers about theft, training programs for all staff, having the board of directors set the tone at the top of the nonprofit for ethical behavior by serving as a model, communicating expectations of ethical behavior, audit committees, background checks on all employees who handle cash, and educating employees on the consequences and harm that fraud has on themselves and the nonprofit organization (see also Zack, 2003).

PUBLIC RELATIONS

Nonprofit organizations can find value in public relations, both in the short and the long term. Public relations hinge on relationships. The goal of all public relations is to build and strengthen ongoing and long-term relationships with key stakeholders and constituencies. In the short term, nonprofit organizations can measure the outputs and outcomes of specific events, programs and campaigns. The long-term benefits of public relationships, while historically being harder to assess, are now more readily measured. Hon and Grunig (1999) suggest six indicators for measuring the quality of relationships in public relations and provide examples of items used to assess the state of each of the six. These are: control mutuality, trust, satisfaction, commitment, exchange relationship and communal relationship.

Nonprofit organizations need proactively to develop, maintain and protect their reputations. This involves dealing with negative publicity (e.g., spending 50–80 percent of revenues on administrative expenses; sexual abuse of boy scouts by troop leaders) by responding to it immediately.

BUILDING A NONPROFIT BRAND

Nonprofit branding has received considerable attention in the marketing literature (Andreasen & Kotler, 2002; Andreasen, Goodstein & Wilson, 2005; Chiagouris, 2005; Gainer & Padanyi, 2005; Ritchie, Swami & Weinberg, 1999). Nonprofits need branding for several reasons: donors expect a professional approach to a nonprofit image; a stronger brand increases donor interest; a stronger brand is associated with a more positive view of the nonprofit's products and services; and a positive image spills over to other nonprofit initiatives (Webster, 2002). Quelch and

Laidler-Kylander (2006) indicate that nonprofit brandings also differentiates a nonprofit from its competitors.

Nonprofits need to understand that they are a brand, what a brand does and what values it potentially has; how to use the brand as a resource, and how to manage and protect the brand, as well as consistently communicating the brand internally and externally. In order to have real value, the brand must embody the values of the nonprofit organization (Keller, Dato-on & Shaw, 2009).

Branding is important for nonprofit organizations yet many nonprofits do not pursue building brand equity (Laidler-Kylander & Simonin, 2009). Brand equity refers to 'a set of brand assets and liabilities linked to a brand, its name and that add to or subtract from the value provided by a product or service to that firm's customers' (Aaker, 1991, p. 17). Though there is evidence that trust in nonprofits and non-governmental organizations (NGOs) is higher than trust levels in other sectors (e.g., business, government, media), nonprofit organizations reap many benefits from developing and protecting their brands (Keller, Dato-on & Shaw, 2009).

Laidler-Kylander and Simonin (2009) suggest that nonprofits may build brand equity differently than for-profit organizations. The characteristics of nonprofits discussed earlier, and how these differ from for-profit organizations, support their thesis. They developed and tested a model for building international brand equity in three nonprofit organizations. They found that four concepts emerged as critical. These were: consistency, focus, trust and partnerships. Successful development of brand equity entailed internal, external and internal–external consistency in message and tactics, a focus on developing a brand that differentiated the nonprofit from others, working on building trust with various stakeholders, and developing partnerships with some stakeholders to leverage their efforts. They, along with Keller et al. (2009), offer practical suggestions for nonprofits interested in developing brand equity. Laidler-Kylander, Quelch and Simonin (2007) undertook ten case studies of nonprofit organizations and their development of brand equity, finding again that trust emerged as a central factor.

Nonprofit organizations need strong brands (Judd, 2004), and developing a strong brand requires explicit strategies and processes. It has been suggested that the most important advantage a nonprofit has is its brand (Burke, Martin & Cooper, 2011; Bennett & Sargeant, 2005; Brunham, 2002; Keller, Dato-on & Shaw, 2009). But, again, nonprofits tend to do this poorly. A brand unifies nonprofit staff around a common mission or purpose, represents a force for change to achieve the mission better, and is a driver for increasing professionalism. Aaker (1996) identified three key steps in developing a nonprofit brand: an understanding of how to develop a brand identity, knowing what the brand stands for, and expressing the brand identity effectively.

HR DEPARTMENTS

Human resources (HR) departments only exist in relatively large nonprofit organizations. Unfortunately in many large organizations (typically in the public and governmental sectors), HR departments have acquired a negative reputation and image. They are seen as lacking in credibility, rule-bound, unaware of the needs of line managers, talking a different language than line managers, unaware of current management practices, and as a cost rather than as a contributor to organizational performance (Burke & Cooper, 2006).

Managers having HR responsibilities need to work proactively to get all other managers to appreciate HRM policies and practices, and to change those HRM policies and practices that are not helpful and develop more useful policies and practices (Burke & Cooper, 2006; Ulrich, 1997; Ulrich & Smallwood, 2003; Ulrich & Smallwood, 2007; Ulrich & Brookbank, 2005). HRM policies and practices need to support the objectives of line managers. Central functions of the HR department would include developing a human resources plan and creating a human resources advisory committee that reports directly to the CEO or executive director.

HRM FUNCTIONS

HRM policies and functions have been fairly well identified and addressed in the nonprofit writings. These functions typically include: job analysis, recruitment, selection, orientation, performance management with a focus on increasing and maintaining levels of motivation, pay, benefits, training and development, collective bargaining with employee associations or union, strategic HRM, and addressing challenges to HRM in the nonprofit sector.

Research findings and attempts to 'professionalize' the management of nonprofit organizations have raised at least two critical issues. Both of these are addressed in this volume. Firstly, some of the research findings have produced inconsistent results (e.g., Herman & Renz, 2008). There are some things we seem to now know in explaining nonprofit organizational effectiveness, but other things are still in play. Secondly, efforts to translate HRM practices from the private, for-profit sector into the nonprofit sector sometimes fail to produce the expected benefits.

NEW ROLES FOR HR DEPARTMENTS – ONE MORE TIME

The field of HRM is experiencing dramatic change, particularly to the HR function. Rothwell, Prescott and Taylor (2008) note that many HR professionals complain about not being valued, given respect, status and recognition within senior management ranks. They identify five major complaints about the HR function and HR professionals (Rothwell, Prescott & Taylor, 2008, pp. 6–7):

1. HR professionals do not possess a sufficient working knowledge of what business is all about or the strategic goals of the organization they serve.
2. HR practitioners lack leadership ability.
3. HR practitioners are reactive.
4. HR practitioners are sometimes seen as unable to take the lead to establish a vision for change and garner the support necessary to lead the change.
5. HR practitioners are fad-chasers who want to find solutions to problems in other organizations and then 'drop them in place'.

This view of the HR function and HR professionals is, unfortunately, still very much alive and well today despite efforts over the past 20 years to change the HR function into a 'strategic partner' (Pfeffer, 1998; Ulrich, 1997).

Now, once again, the HR function and HR professionals are being asked to transform HR to serve their organizations better. HR professionals can play an important role in aligning talent with organizational goals, and in bringing about organizational change. HR professionals often know how they are perceived by senior executive ranks, and what they would like to do, but too often fall short (Pfeffer & Sutton, 2000). This is a necessary requirement of HRM policies and practices and to bringing about competitive advantage to nonprofit organizations. Rothwell et al. suggest that for this to take place, some basic questions need to be addressed. Why does the HR function exist? What does our organization need from the HR function? How can HR achieve these objectives?

Rothwell, Prescott and Taylor first identify future trends in the workplace and in the general workforce and suggest that the transformation of HR should begin by focusing on these future trends. The transformation of the HR function and of HR professionals will not be easy or guaranteed. These authors, through the use of case studies of organizations on this journey, examine processes and initiatives found to be effective in creating new roles of HR leadership and the power of HR in bringing about organizational change. If the HR function and HR professionals do not meet this challenge, the value of HRM policies and practices in improving nonprofit organizational success and effectiveness will not be realized.

MANAGING A DIVERSE WORKFORCE

Many voluntary sector organizations and NGOs have staff and clients that include individuals of varying backgrounds, religions, ethnicities, races and sexual orientations. Lewis (2009), for example, has reported a disproportionate number of gays and lesbians in nonprofit organizations, raising issues of discrimination (Hostetler & Pynes, 2000a, 2000b). These factors should be reflected in their boards of directors, paid professional staff and individual volunteers. However, diversity seems to be less well represented in the boards of nonprofit organizations. Ostrower (2007), in a national survey of US nonprofit governance, found that 96 percent of board members were white (non-Latino), 7 percent were African American and 3.5 percent Latino.

Bradshaw and Fredette (2011) address these questions among others: why is it important to reflect the make-up of one's clients? What are the challenges raised by differences? And, can using these differences be an advantage? First they present results of a survey of nonprofit boards in Canada conducted in 2008 that showed that the majority of board members were between 30 and 60 years old, and 44 percent were women. About 28 percent of these nonprofits indicated at least one board member had a disability; 22 percent had a board member who was openly gay, lesbian or bisexual; and only 13 percent were considered 'visible minorities' or people of color.

There has been a suggestion that nonprofit boards should be more diverse in representing their 'communities'. In addition, it has been proposed that a more diverse board can lead to better decision-making and stronger organizational performance; other work, however, has noted increasing conflict among board members and poorer performance among more diverse boards.

Bradshaw and Fredette interviewed 18 board directors seen by their peers as leaders in diversifying their boards of directors. They identified two types of inclusion of diverse board members: inclusion to get the job done – functional inclusion; and inclusion to have different representative individuals get along well together – relationship or social inclusion They propose that combinations of the two would lead to a transformational inclusion which increases board competence and capabilities. They defined board-level inclusion as 'members of diverse and traditionally marginalized communities are present on boards and meaningfully engaged in the governance of their organizations' (Bradshaw & Fredette, 2011, p. 34). But to realize the benefits of diversity, steps must be taken. This involves balancing functional and social inclusion processes. Specific steps include: policies that support getting diverse members on boards, including diversity in assessing board performance, advertising in ethnic-specific outlets, linking with ethnic-specific organizations to fill vacancies, forming a diversity subcommittee to increase board diversity, and training members of diverse communities to succeed in their board roles. Social inclusion is fostered by mentoring and coaching, orientation sessions for newcomers, holding retreats and seminars to build work teams, holding meetings at times and places that all can attend, and catering to dietary needs of particular individuals.

Perkins and Fields (2010), in a study of the performance of Christian churches, found that top management team diversity (e.g., age, relationships with senior church leader) was associated with higher levels of church performance.

ATTRACTING AND MANAGING VOLUNTEERS

Volunteer work has been shown to have many benefits to volunteers. Besides satisfying a need to help others, volunteer work can also open career opportunities. Through helping others, volunteers develop contacts, skills and experiences. This is particularly valuable to younger volunteers and newly arrived immigrants. Volunteers also contribute considerable time and energy to nonprofit organizations, valued at over $200 billion annually.

Volunteers may have various motives for volunteering. Clary, Snyder and Ridge (1993) and Clary, Snyder and Stukas (1996) developed measures of six motives: career (gain work experience), social (obtain interpersonal interactions), values (offers an opportunity to act on personal convictions), enhancement (increasing one's level of self-esteem), protective (opportunites to protect one's ego) and understanding (a chance to practice one's knowledge and skill).

Volunteers develop both a formal and a psychological contract with their nonprofit organizations (Brudney, 1999). The formal contract includes an expectation of the length of commitment (long-term versus short-term) and the nature of expected tasks and roles. The psychological contract includes volunteer feelings about what they give or owe the nonprofit, and what the nonprofit gives or owes them in return (beyond the formal). Psychological contracts can be transactional (working for pay and advancement in return for commitment and hard work), relational (volunteer is given job security in return of loyalty and a minimum stay with the nonprofit), or balanced which includes both transactional and relational elements. Liao-Troth (2005) conducted two studies of the effects of functional motives (career, social values) and personality factors on the psychological contracts of volunteers. In the first study involving volunteer firefighters, there was no relationship between functional motives and nature of their psychological contract (transactional versus relational). In the second study involving student volunteers, personality factors (e.g., agreeableness, emotional stability) were related to a relational psychological contract preference, career motives and conscientiousness were related to preference for a transactional psychological contract.

Taniguchi (2006) observed gender differences in volunteer behavior and motivation. Among women, working part time was associated with higher levels of volunteering, whereas having eldercare responsibilities was associated with lower levels of volunteering; among men in this study, being unemployed was associated with lower levels of volunteering. Gender differences in eldercare responsibilities may signal a problem in women's volunteering in the future as the population ages.

A recent Canadian study indicated that two-thirds of volunteers reported a negative experience (Cohen, 2010). Among the complaints were not using their skills, a lack of support and organizational politics. The study highlighted a number of gaps between what volunteers look for and what organizations offer. Volunteers wanted group activities, short-term opportunities, chances to offer their own ideas and doing work that is different from their regular work lives. Sundeen, Raskoff and Garcia (2007) studied perceived barriers to volunteering in the eyes of non-volunteers and found that the most common were lack of time, lack of interest and ill health. So there are real barriers to volunteering for some individuals. Yanay and Yanay (2008), in a study of Israeli volunteers at a nonprofit organization for victims of violence, found that volunteer dropout was more a function of the gap between volunteer expectations and actual experiences than of declining motivation.

Waters and Bortree (2010) surveyed 317 teenage volunteers to study factors associated with a commitment to continue their volunteering. About one-third of teenagers volunteer with nonprofits, but teenage volunteers drop out at higher rates than adult volunteers, with over one-third of teenage volunteers discontinuing their volunteering from year to year. Four factors emerged as important:

1. Trust – the nonprofit organization does what it says it will.
2. Commitment – a belief that the nonprofit organization is worth devoting time and energy to support and promote it.

3. Satisfaction – positive feelings about the nonprofit and its mission.
4. Control mutuality – a chance to participate in discussions about the work, the mission and the future.

Tying these all together, for Waters and Bortree, is the notion of inclusion. But several factors make the inclusion of teenage volunteers a low priority, including: they have few skills, they are only temporary, they have less to contribute, they are less invested in the nonprofit, and they are less valuable as a resource. They offer practical suggestions for increasing feelings of inclusion among volunteers. These include:

- asking for their ideas and advice;
- keeping them informed about nonprofit activities, announcements and events;
- inviting them to attend some meetings and events (decision-making, information sessions, networking events, participation in work teams).

Nonprofit organizations could improve the volunteer experience by getting to know more about their volunteers, being flexible and being sensitive to gender, culture, language and age differences (Brudney, 2005a, 2005b; McCurley, 2008). Nonprofit organizations need to be aware of the changing needs of volunteers as they go thorough various life states, particularly in recruitment and retention. Use of the internet to offer volunteers opportunities, and following up with volunteers to show how their participation has helped, is likely to make the volunteer experience a more satisfying one.

ATTRACTING, RECRUITING AND RETAINING VOLUNTEER AND PAID STAFF

Volunteers and paid staff are increasingly being recruited using current employees and their networks and websites. Various levels of government have created websites designed to support the nonprofit sector. In addition, nonprofit sector employees and volunteers can work from home using the internet.

Turnover can be high among volunteers so nonprofits need to determine why they quit and what can be done about it. It is critical to improve the volunteer work experience by providing real work not make work. Volunteers need to receive early socialization in the mission of the organization and its values and challenging work from the start. Matching interests and skills of volunteers with tasks creates feelings of competence and mastery.

Follow up training should be provided, if relevant, to support feelings of successful accomplishment. Recognition and psychic rewards for jobs well done pay dividends in terms of retention. Some volunteers need flexible work arrangements to accommodate other important parts of their lives. Encouraging and supporting contacts between volunteers and paid staff fosters a sense of inclusion and ownership on both sides. Finally, conducting exit interviews with volunteers and paid staff who leave is a source of vital information on what may have gone wrong.

WORKING WITH AN AGING VOLUNTEER WORKFORCE

Einolf (2009), using longitudinal panel data, predicted that the total number of elderly volunteers would likely increase over the next decade. Are nonprofits ready for this group of volunteers and thier unique needs? Hong, Morrow-Howell, Tang and Hinterlong (2009) studied the capacity of 51 nonprofits to take advantage of an increasing number of older volunteers. They developed a model that included individual capacity (e.g., physical functioning, cognitive functioning) and institutional capacity (e.g., role specification, role availability, cash compensation).Their nonprofit sample ranked highest on capacity to recognize older volunteers and disseminate information and lowest on ability to offer cash compensation.

Some have suggested that as the aging 'baby boomers' retire, there will be a leadership gap in nonprofit organizations. Others have identified factors likely to minimize this deficit, including more retired people still working, higher levels of pay, younger women and men acquiring the skills needed for these jobs, the merging of nonprofit organizations, and board and volunteer skill sharing. In any eventuality, the development of effective leaders and committed volunteers will remain important factors in voluntary organization success.

INTERNATIONAL DIMENSIONS OF THE NONPROFIT SECTOR

Some voluntary sector organizations and NGOs work across national borders. This chapter reviews the challenges, opportunities and strategies to make such initiatives more likely to succeed. Cultural sensitivity to individual's needs and the appropriateness of interventions in other countries are competitive advantages of international voluntary sector organizations (NGOs).

CONCLUSIONS

As this chapter has indicated, nonprofit organizations are now playing a larger role in civil society. They are also facing new and significant challenges on several fronts (e.g., resources, talent, need to change and adapt). Fortunately, we are now learning much more about the ways in which human resource management policies and practices can address these challenges. It is important to note that nonprofit organizations are different from for-profit organizations in significant ways. Nonprofits have to carefully incorporate HRM polices and practices that 'fit' their circumstances. Our goal was to assist in this process by providing our readers with the latest research evidence, case study examples, and current writing and thinking in these areas.

OVERVIEW OF THE CONTENTS

Part I contains three chapters. In the first chapter, Ronald Burke reviews some of the research and writing on the roles played by human resource management practices in the performance of organizations in the nonprofit sector. He considers the mission of nonprofits, how and why they have increased in number, the roles they play in society, and how they differ from for-profit organizations. He then identifies some HRM challenges facing nonprofits. Not surprisingly, there have been trends in HRM in nonprofits over the past 50 years, with more for-profit HRM policies and practices finding their way into nonprofits. But there are obstacles to greater use of these for-profit policies and practices by nonprofits. Attention is then given to the role of mission in nonprofits, governance and the role of boards of directors, pay and other rewards, sources of job satisfaction in nonprofits, leadership and its development, concerns about a potential leadership deficit, measuring the performance of nonprofits (mission impossible or merely mission difficult?), factors associated with the success of nonprofit organizations, workforce diversity and the glass ceiling, increasing skills via university and certificate education programs, the image of nonprofits in the media, fraud in nonprofits, building of the nonprofit brand and the management of volunteers.

In Chapter 2, Ian Cunningham provides a review of HRM in the voluntary, nonprofit sector in the UK. Although there are some unique features of the UK environment, his work is generally applicable to most other countries. The sector has grown and is now facing new challenges, particularly from outsourcing, public service cutbacks and increasing attention being paid to more personalized services. He begins by defining the sector:

constitutionally independent self-governing organizations that are nonprofit and utilize volunteers. Managing HR in the voluntary sector has become more complex as these organizations face greater scrutiny with a greater reliance on government funding. These factors, among others, have made improving HRM policies and practices vital. As a result, HRM has become more disciplined and accountable, with greater attention paid to recruitment and selection of people who 'fit' the plans of various client groups, and a greater emphasis on increasing workforce skills through training. Pay levels seem to have been reduced. Voluntary sector organizations now face greater challenges in sustaining workforce commitment, with line managers having this responsibility. The author suggests specific ways in which line managers might tackle these critical needs. These factors also impact the nature of the industrial relations of employees and volunteers with their organizations.

Susan Chandler and Morgen Johansen in Chapter 3 describe and analyze changing roles that nonprofit organizations play in the United States. Their thoughts obviously apply to several other countries as well. They first define a nonprofit organization, acknowledging that the lines between nonprofits and for-profit are blurred. They outline the size and scope of the nonprofit sector, about 1.4 million in the US at present. They review ways in which nonprofit organizations benefit society. Nonprofits provide services, advocate for citizens and society by building citizen participation, building social and cultural capital by helping those in need, and instilling national values such as individualism and solidarity. The authors offer a glimpse into the founding of nonprofits and how they have evolved over the past 250 years. Nonprofit organizations today have taken on new roles and responsibilities by providing a wider array of services and programs to the public. And as governments shrink, the role for nonprofits increases. This has produced increasing competition among nonprofits for funding and clients. More nonprofits today survive through government contracts and grants. Demand for services has increased as well. There are also increasing calls for accountability and effectiveness: nonprofits now also have to evaluate their effectiveness to demonstrate value. As a result, nonprofits have become more entrepreneurial. This raises the interesting question of whether nonprofits are becoming more like their for-profit cousins and losing their mission to serve and enhance the wider society

Part II contains seven chapters. In Chapter 4, John Ronquillo, Whitney Hein and Heather Carpenter review the literature on leadership in nonprofit organizations. Leadership by executives and board members, among others, in nonprofit organizations is vital to their success. Leadership is widely discussed and written about in nonprofit journals. It is best to view leadership in the nonprofit sector as interdisciplinary. Leadership in nonprofits is different in some ways from leadership in the profit sector (e.g., less coercive, no distribution of profits, no lines of ownership) leading to both deep and subtle differences. The authors first offer a historical overview of the leadership field. They conclude that relatively little work has examined leadership in nonprofits. Nanus and Dobbs (1999), whom they cite, suggest four leadership emphases: internal organizational, external organizational, managing the present, and managing instability and the future. They then consider a political and power-oriented perspective on leadership. They tackle the 'leadership deficit' question but believe it can be successfully addressed. They see training in leadership as helping to fill this need, but that nonprofit management training needs to be updated to keep up with the changes in the sector. Nonprofit leaders can learn from profit leaders and vice versa. Leadership in many nonprofits can also be achieved by using members of the board of directors and volunteers. The authors provide suggested reading materials for those interested in a more in-depth treatment of the topic.

Chris Coultas, Breanne Kindel, Stephanie Zajac and Eduardo Salas then offer guidance in Chapter 5 on the development and use of top management teams in nonprofit organizations. Nonprofits are increasingly relying on teams to achieve their goals. Top management teams may even be more important to the effectiveness of nonprofits than to the effectiveness of for-profits, given their complexity. They review definitions of top leadership teams indicating what is different about top leadership teams in nonprofits as compared to for-profits. They then identify short-term and long-term desired outcomes from these teams, noting team inputs, mediators of the relationship of inputs and outcomes, and team outcomes. They offer seven constructs underlying effective leadership teams in nonprofits, indicating examples of 'best practice' associated with increasing levels of each. These constructs are: cohesion, conflict management, communication and debate, consensus, communication, culture and composition of the team.

In Chapter 6, Stacy Grau and Susan Kleiser contend that the brand should be at the heart of a nonprofit organization. They first define branding and show why a strong brand identity is critical for the success of nonprofit organizations. The core of a brand is the organization's vision, including its mission, purpose, values, actions and principles. But these need to be expressed in ways that differentiate one's organization from other nonprofits. How can your nonprofit stand out? A strong brand builds loyalty and commitment, reduces risk, provides insurance against negative events and increases awareness among stakeholders. A strong brand needs to be simple, clear, consistent, differentiating the nonprofit from others, emotional and inspiring, and relevant. The authors suggest that nonprofits should go about building their brands in ways that differ from those used by for-profit organizations. They emphasize consistency, focus, trust and partnerships as important variables in the building of nonprofit brands, and illustrate each with concrete examples.

Nathalie Laidler-Kylander in Chapter 7 also discusses the importance and development of nonprofit brands and brand management with particular attention given to global nonprofit brands. A large number of nonprofits however undertake little brand management activity. In addition, global nonprofits manage their brands differently than international for-profit organizations. Interestingly, nonprofit organizations are viewed as more trustworthy by citizens than other types of organizations. The author defines a brand and the potential benefits of branding. She then examines differences in nonprofit and for-profit branding. Many of the differences involve culture, human resources, collaboration, complexity and the importance of mission. She outlines a brand equity model specifically for global nonprofits. She also discusses threats to one's brand. Internal and external branding both have important benefits. The author identifies four components in nonprofit brands: integrity, democracy, ethics and affinity (IDEA), showing how these concepts interact and add value. She concludes with implications of brand management for human resources

In Chapter 8, Jeannette Blackmar and Kelly LeRoux consider ways of enhancing learning and skills development among both paid staff and volunteers. High-performing people are central to high-performing organizations. Nonprofits are now facing greater demand for their services. In addition, nonprofits are increasingly accountable for how they use their resources. Nonprofits need talented and skilled people in all positions, but historically have not devoted enough attention to staff development. A leadership gap in nonprofits makes these challenges even more difficult, particularly in a time of resource scarcity. Nonprofits have no choice but to invest in learning and skill development of staff and volunteers. The authors begin with an analysis of training in skills development, defining training; then consider questions of developing a training plan, training methods, training program design and implementation, delivery methods and program evaluation. They then review essential skills for nonprofit organizations, both 'hard' and 'soft'. Examples of formal and informal training methods are offered. Formal methods typically involve training programs offered within or outside the organization. Informal methods include mentoring, coaching and job rotation. Each is discussed in some detail, offering guidance to nonprofits interested in their implementation.

Joy Jones and Dail Fields believe that nonprofit organizations need to address a changing demographic landscape in terms of the workforce, clients and sponsors. Nearly half of all new employees in the US would now be classified as 'minorities'. In Chapter 9 the authors focus specifically on factors that affect a nonprofit leader's leadership strategies. They consider the following: perspectives on workforce diversity and their implications for nonprofit executives; ways in which employee diversity affects perceptions of leader behavior and characteristics; ways in which employee diversity gets played out in communication practices; and ways that nonprofit executives can use 'diagnostic thinking' to lead diverse employees more effectively in their settings. Employees from different cultures see leadership behaviors differently. Minorities in nonprofits suffer the same disadvantages as they do in for-profits (the glass ceiling, lower pay). Some individuals would see these environments as hostile. It is not clear that diverse work teams always perform better, but a diverse team is likely to be successful if the leader is skilled and the team has had team training. The authors highlight communication competence as a critical factor in leadership effectiveness; communicating effectively in specific and different situations. Leaders need to recognize communication differences in a diverse workforce. Members of some minority groups exhibit 'communication apprehension' – shyness. Learning about other cultures will likely help leaders here. In addition, members of some minority groups are more likely to respond to forms of reward than are others. Interestingly, both servant leadership and transformational leadership are likely to appear in nonprofit organizations.

Thomas Packard in Chapter 10 considers the association of change management in a successful nonprofit organization and the role played by HRM in this initiative. The organization, San Diego Youth Services (SDYS), realized it had to respond to new challenges it was facing: streamline management, cut administrative costs, clarify management structure and organizational philosophy, and consolidate programs. SDYS was successful in this, while maintaining morale and the continuity of programs. The author identifies common reasons why change efforts fail. He begins by reviewing challenges facing nonprofit organizations and how planned organizational change processes can help. Changes can range from small to large scale; changes can be developmental, transitional or transformational. Planned change may involve both content (what needs to change) and process (the change tactics employed). He moves then to discussing ways that HR professionals can assist. He develops a model for planned organizational change, showing how the model can be applied. In it he identifies specific phases of change: assess the present, create a sense of urgency, clarify the change imperative, garner support and tackle resistance, build a change coalition to guide the effort, implement the change, then evaluate, institutionalize and celebrate. Common organizational change methods are then considered, identifying various options for internal change leaders. Finally, the use of consultants (why, who and when) is addressed. Packard sees a broad role for HRM in facilitating change activities.

Part III, Chapter 11, considers ways of increasing skills of all nonprofit sector employees: executives, managers, professionals and front-line staff including volunteers. Roseanne Mirabella and Mary McDonald note the growth of nonprofit, non-governmental and philanthropy education programs in universities and colleges worldwide. They report on the development of these educational offerings over the 15 years to 2011. In the US, there are over 375 universities and colleges offering courses in nonprofit management and philanthropy. There have been increases in both undergraduate and graduate-level programs. The largest increases have been in schools of public affairs, with a slightly larger number of these programs based in Arts and Science faculties. Inside management functions dominate course offerings. About 100 courses address aspects of HRM, reflecting general HRM in many cases, followed by HRM in nonprofits and HRM in the management of volunteers. The authors then consider curricular categories, with special mention of HRM offerings. The largest increase has taken place in graduate-level social entrepreneurship courses, most located in business schools. The authors note that more research is needed to address the tangible contribution of these offerings. It is clear, however, that interest in university and college-based nonprofit management programs remains high.

ACKNOWLEDGEMENT

Preparation of this chapter was supported in part by York University.

REFERENCES

Aaker, D.A. (1991). *Managing Brand Equity: Capitalizing on the Value of a Brand Name*. New York: Free Press.

Aaker, J. (1996). *Building Strong Brands*. New York: Free Press.

Agard, K.A. (2010). *Leadership in Nonprofit Organizations*. Thousand Oaks, CA: Sage.

Alexander, J., Brudney, J.L. & Yang, K. (2010). Introduction to the symposium: accountability and performance measurement: the evolving role of nonprofits in the hollow state. *Nonprofit and Voluntary Sector Quarterly*, 39, 565–570.

Allison, L., Chen, X., Flanigan, S.T., Keyes-Williams, J., Vasavada, T.S. & Saidel, J.P. (2007). Toward doctoral education in nonprofit and philanthropic studies. *Nonprofit and Voluntary Sector Quarterly*, 36, 51S–63S.

Almond, S. & Kendall, J. (2000). Taking the employees perspective seriously: an initial United Kingdom cross-sectoral comparison. *Non-profit and Voluntary Sector Quarterly*, 29, 205–231.

American Society of Association Executives (2006). 7 measures of success: what remarkable associations do that others don't. Washington, DC: American Society of Association Executives.

Andreasen, A., Goodstein, R. & Wilson, J. (2005). Transferring 'marketing knowledge' to the nonprofit sector. *California Management Review*, 47, 46–67.

Andreasen, A. & Kotler, P. (2002). *Strategic Marketing for Nonprofit Organizations*, 6th edn. Upper Saddle, NJ: Prentice Hall.

Balassiano, K. & Chandler, S.M. (2010). The emerging role of nonprofit associations in advocacy and public policy: trends, issues, and prospects. *Nonprofit and Voluntary Sector Quarterly*, 39, 946–955.

Bambeito, C.L. (2004). *Human Resource Policies and Practices for Nonprofit Organizations*. New York: John Wiley.

Baruch, Y. & Ramalho, N. (2006). Communalities and distinctions in the measurement of organizational performance and effectiveness across for-profits and nonprofit sectors. *Nonprofit and Voluntary Sector Quarterly*, 35, 39–65.

Beck, T.E., Lengnick-Hall, C.A. & Lengnick-Hall, M.L. (2008). Solutions out of context: examining the transfer of business concepts to nonprofit organizations. *Nonprofit Management and Leadership*, 19, 153–171.

Becker, B.E., Huselid, M.A. & Beatty, R.W. (2005). *Workforce Success Metrics: Creating a Human Capital Scorecard for the CEO*. Boston, MA: Harvard Business School Press.

Bell, J., Moyers, R. & Wolfred, T. (2006). *Daring to Lead: A National Study of Nonprofit Executive Leadership*. San Francisco, CA: Compress Point.

Bennett, R. & Sargeant, A. (2005). The nonprofit marketing landscape: Guest editorial, introduction to a special section. *Journal of Business Research*, 58, 797–805.

Benz, M. (2005). Not for the profit, but for the satisfaction? Evidence on worker well-being in non-profit firms. *Kylos*, 58, 155–176.

BoardSource (2004). *Ten basic responsibilities of nonprofit boards*. Washington, DC: Boardsource.

Borzaga, C. & Tortia, E. (2006). Worker motivations, job satisfaction, and loyalty in public and nonprofit social services. *Nonprofit and Voluntary Sector Quarterly*, 35, 225–248.

Bowman, W. (2009). The economic value of volunteers to nonprofit organizations. *Nonprofit Management and Leadership*, 19, 491–506.

Bradshaw, P. (2009). A contingency approach to nonprofit governance. *Nonprofit Management and Leadership*, 20, 61–81.

Bradshaw, P. & Fredette, C. (2011). The inclusive nonprofit boardroom: leveraging the transformative potential of diversity. *Nonprofit Quarterly*, Spring, 32–38.

Bradshaw, P., Murray, V.V. & Wolpin, J. (1992). Do nonprofit boards make a difference? An exploration of the relationship among board structure, process and effectiveness. *Nonprofit and Voluntary Sector Quarterly*, 21, 227–249.

Brown, W.A. (2005). Exploring the association between board and organizational performance in nonprofit organizations. *Nonprofit Management and Leadership*, 15, 317–339.

Brown, W.A. (2007). Board development practices and competent board members: implications in performance. *Nonprofit Management and Leadership*, 17, 301–317.

Brown, W.A. & Guo, C. (2010). Exploring the key roles for nonprofit boards. *Nonprofit and Voluntary Sector Quarterly*, 39, 536–546.

Brown, W.A. & Yashioka, C.F. (2003). Mission attachment and satisfaction as factors in employee retention. *Nonprofit Management and Leadership*, 14, 5–18.

Brudney, J.L. (1999). *Fostering Volunteer Programs in the Public Sector: Planning, Initiating and Managing Voluntary Activities*. San Francisco, CA: Jossey-Bass.

Brudney, J.L. (2005a). *Emerging Areas of Volunteering*. Indianapolis, IN: ARNOVA.

Brudney, J.L. (2005b). Designing and managing volunteer programs. In R.D. Herman & Associates (eds), *The Jossey-Bass Handbook of Nonprofit Leadership and Management*, 2nd edn. San Francisco, CA: Jossey-Bass. pp. 310–344.

Brunham, K. (2002). What skills will nonprofit leaders need in the future? *Nonprofit World*, 20, 29–36.

Bruser, D. (2011). Game over for shady charity. *Toronto Star*, March 8, A1, A10.

Bureau of Economic Analysis (1998). *Survey of current businesses*, 79. Washington, DC: Bureau of Economic Analysis.

Burke, R.J. & Cooper, C.L. (2006). *The Human Resources Revolution: Why Putting People First Matters*. London: Elsevier.

Burke, R.J., Martin, G., & Cooper, C.L. (2011). *Corporate Reputation: Managing Opportunities and Threats*. Farnham, UK and Burlington, VT, USA: Gower Publishing.

Burke, R.J., Noblett, A. & Cooper, C.L. (2012). *Human Resource Management in the Public Sector: Achieving High Quality Service and Effectiveness*. Cheltenham, UK and Northampton, MA, USA: Edward Elgar.

Carver, J. (2006). *Boards That Make a Difference*, 3rd edn. San Francisco, CA: Jossey-Bass.

Chiagouris, L. (2005). Nonprofit brands come of age: commercial sector practices shed light on nonprofit branding success. *Marketing Management*, 14, 30–34.

Clary, E.G., Snyder, M. & Ridge, R. (1993). Volunteers' motivations: a functional strategy for recruitment, placement, and retention of volunteers. *Nonprofit Management and Leadership*, 2, 333–350.

Clary, E.G., Snyder, M. & Stukas, A.A. (1996). Volunteers' motivations: findings from a national survey. *Nonprofit and Voluntary Sector Quarterly*, 15, 485–505.

Cohen, T. (2010). Trying to do good leaves majority feeling bad. *National Post*, December 9, A2.

Cooper, C.L. & Burke, R.J. (2011). *Human Resource Management in Small Business: Achieving Peak Performance*. Cheltenham, UK and Northampton, MA, USA: Edward Elgar.

Cunningham, I. (1999). Human resource management in the voluntary sector: challenges and opportunities. *Public Money and Management*, April–June, 19–25.

DeCooman, P., De Gieter, S., Pepermans, R. & Jegers, M. (2011). A cross-sector comparison of motivation-related concepts in for-profit and not-for-profit service organizations. *Nonprofit and Voluntary Sector Quarterly*, 40, 296–317.

De Hoogh, A.H. (2005). Leader motives, charismatic leadership, and subordinates' work attitudes in the profit and voluntary sector. *Leadership Quarterly*, 16, 17–38.

Dhebar, B.B. & Stokes, B. (2008). A nonprofit manager's guide to online volunteering. *Nonprofit Management and Leadership*, 18, 497–506.

Dolan, D.A. (2002). Training needs of administrators in the nonprofit sector: what are they and how should we address them? *Nonprofit Management and Leadership*, 12, 277–292.

Dulch, N.A., Ernst, M., McClusky, J.E., Mirabella, R.M. & Sadow, J. (2007). The nature of undergraduate nonprofit education: models of curriculum delivery. *Nonprofit and Voluntary Sector Quarterly*, 36, 28S–50S.

Dym, B. & Hutson, H.C. (2005). *Leadership in Nonprofit Organizations*. Thousand Oaks, CA: Sage Publications.

Einolf, C.J. (2009). Will the boomers volunteer during retirement? Comparing the baby boom, silent, and long civic cohorts. *Nonprofit and Voluntary Sector Quarterly*, 38, 181–199.

Evers, A. & Leville, J.-L. (2010). *The Third Sector in Europe*. Cheltenham, UK and Northampton, MA, USA: Edward Elgar.

Fischer, R.L. & Beimers, D. (2009). 'Put me in coach': a pilot evaluation of executive coaching in the nonprofit sector. *Nonprofit Management and Leadership*, 19, 507–522.

Fletcher, K.M. (2005). The impact of receiving a master's degree in nonprofit management on graduates' professional lives. *Nonprofit and Voluntary Sector Quarterly*, 34, 433–471.

Francis, S. & Kelleher, J. (2011). Time to raise bar for non-profits. *National Post*, March 22, FP12.

Gainer, B. & Padanyi, P. (2005). The relationship between market-oriented activities and market orient culture: Implications for the development of market orientate in nonprofit service organizations. *Journal of Business Research*, Special Section: The nonprofit marketing landscape, 58, 854–862.

Gibelman, M. (2000). The nonprofit sector and gender discrimination: a preliminary investigation into the glass ceiling. *Nonprofit Management and Leadership*, 10, 251–269.

Goldstein, H. (2003). Another blow for the public image of charities. *Chronicle of Philanthropy*, May 15, 15.

Green, J.C. & Griesinger, D.W. (1996). Board performance and organizational effectiveness in social service organizations. *Nonprofit Management and Leadership*, 8, 381–401.

Greenlee, J., Fischer, M., Gordon, T. & Keating, E. (2007). An investigation of fraud in nonprofit organizations. *Nonprofit and Voluntary Sector Quarterly*, 36, 676–694.

Hale, M. (2007). Superficial friends: a content analysis of nonprofit and philanthropy coverage in nine major newspapers. *Nonprofit and Voluntary Sector Quarterly*, 36, 465–486.

Haley-Lock, A. (2006) Variations in part-time job quality within the non-profit human service sector. *Nonprofit Management and Leadership*, 19, 421–442.

Handy, F. & Katz, E. (1998). The wage differential between nonprofit institutions and corporations: getting more by paying less. *Journal of Comparative Economics*, 26, 246–261.

Herman, R.D. & Associates (2005). *The Jossey-Bass handbook of nonprofit leadership and management*, 2nd edn. San Francisco: Jossey-Bass.

Herman, R.D. & Renz, D.O. (1997). Multiple constituencies and the social construction of nonprofit effectiveness. *Nonprofit and Voluntary Sector Quarterly*, 26, 185–206.

Herman, R.D. & Renz, D.O. (1998). Nonprofit organizational effectiveness: contrasts between especially effective and less effective organizations. *Nonprofit Management and Leadership*, 9, 23–38.

Herman, R.D. & Renz, D.O. (1999). Theses on nonprofit organizational effectiveness. *Nonprofit and voluntary Sector Quarterly*, 28, 107–126.

Herman, R.D. & Renz, D.O. (2008). Advancing nonprofit organizational effectiveness research and theory: nine theses. *Nonprofit Management and Leadership*, 18, 399–415.

Holtfreter, K. (2008). Determinants of fraud losses in nonprofit organizations. *Nonprofit Management and Leadership*, 19, 45–63.

Hon, L.C. & Grunig, J.E. (1999). *Guidelines for Measuring Relationships in Public Relations*. Gainesville, FL: Institute for Public Relations.

Hong, S.-J., Morrow-Howell, N., Tang, F. & Hinterlong, J. (2009). Engaging older adults in volunteering: conceptualizing and measuring institutional capacity. *Nonprofit and Voluntary Sector Quarterly*, 38, 200–219.

Hostetler, D.W. & Pynes, J.E. (2000a). Sexual orientation discrimination and its challenges for nonprofit managers. *Nonprofit Management and Leadership*, 11, 49–63.

Hostetler, D.W. & Pynes, J.E. (2000b). Don't ask, don't tell prevails in boy scouts. *Nonprofit Management and Leadership*, 11, 235–237.

Hudson, M. (2005). *Managing at the Leading Edge: New Challenges in Managing Nonprofit Organizations*. San Francisco, CA: Jossey-Bass.

Hurrell, S.A., Warharst, C. & Nickson, D. (2010). Giving Miss Marple a makeover: graduate recruitment, systems failure, and the Scottish voluntary sector. *Nonprofit and Voluntary Sector Quarterly*, 39, 1–20.

Jackson, T. (2009). A critical cross-cultural perspective for developing nonprofit international management capacity. *Nonprofit Management and Leadership*, 19, 443–466.

Jaskyte, K. (2004). Transformational leadership, organizational culture, and innovativeness in nonprofit organizations. *Nonprofit Management and Leadership*, 15, 153–168.

Jaskyte, K. & Fressler, W. (2005). Organizational culture and innovation in nonprofit human service organizations. *Administration in Social Work*, 29, 23–41.

Jegers, M. (2009). Corporate' governance in nonprofit organizations: a nontechnical review of the economic literature. *Nonprofit Management and Leadership*, 20, 143–164.

Johnson, J.L. (2007). The nonprofit leadership deficit: a case for more optimism. *Nonprofit Management and Leadership*, 19, 285–304.

Joslyn, H. (2002). Driven by mission: nonprofit employees trade high pay for job satisfaction. *Chronicle of Philanthropy*, October, 18–23.

Joslyn, H. (2003). Charity's glass ceiling. *Chronicle of Philanthropy*, 15, 47–50.
Judd, N. (2004). On branding: building and maintaining your organization's brand in an AMC. *Association Management*, 56, 17–19.
Katzenbach, J. (2000). *Peak Performance: Aligning the Hearts and Minds of Your Employees*. Boston, MA: Harvard Business School Press.
Keller, E.W., Data-on, M.C. & Shaw, D. (2009). NPO branding: preliminary lessons from major players. *International Journal of Nonprofit and voluntary Sector Marketing*, 15, 105–121.
Kellock Hay, G., Beattie, R., Livingstone, R.M. & Munro, P. (2007). Change, HRM and the voluntary sector. *Employee Relations*, 23, 240–255.
Kim, S.E. & Lee, J.W. (2007). Is mission attachment an effective management tool for employee retention? An empirical analysis of a nonprofit human services agency. *Review of Public Personnel Administration*, 27, 227–248.
Laidler-Kylander, N. & Simonin, B. (2009). How international nonprofits build brand equity. *International Journal of Nonprofit Voluntary Sector Marketing*, 14, 57–69.
Laidler-Kylander, N., Quelch, J.A. & Simonin, B. (2007). Building and valuing global brands in the nonprofit sector. *Nonprofit Management and Leadership*, 17, 253–277.
Lawler, E.E. (2003). *Treat people right*. San Francisco, CA: Jossey-Bass.
Lawler, E.E. & Worley, C.G. (2006). *Build to Change: How to Achieve Sustained Organizational Effectiveness*. San Francisco, CA: Jossey-Bass.
Leete, L. (2000). Wage equity and employee motivation in nonprofit and for-profit organizations. *Journal of Economic Behavior and Organization*, 43, 423–446.
Leete, L. (2001). Whither the nonprofit wage differential? Estimates from the 1990 Census. *Journal of Labor Economics*, 19, 136–170.
LeRoux, K. & Wright, N.S. (2010). Does performance measurement improve strategic decision making? Findings from a national survey of nonprofit social service agencies. *Nonprofit and Voluntary Sector Quarterly*, 39, 571–578.
Letts, C.W., Ryan, W.P. & Grossman, A. (1999). *High Performance Nonprofit Organizations: Managing Upstream for Greater Impact*. New York: John Wiley.
Levine, D. (1991). Cohesiveness, productivity, and wage dispersion. *Journal of Economic Behavior and Organization*, 15, 237–255.
Lewis, G.B. (2009). Why do so many lesbians and gay men work for nonprofit organizations? *Administration and Society*, 42, 720–768.
Lewis, N. (2002). Women and minorities slowly gain board seats, report says. *Chronicles of Philanthropy*, 14, 30–32.
Liao-Troth, M.A. (2005). Are they here for the long haul? The effects of functional motive and personality factors on the psychological contracts of volunteers. *Nonprofit and Voluntary Sector Quarterly*, 34, 510–530.
Light, P.C. (2002a). The content of their character: the state of the nonprofit workforce. *Nonprofit Quarterly*, 9, 6–16.
Light, P.C. (2002b). *Pathways to Nonprofit Excellence*. Washington, DC: Brookings Institution Press.
Martin, L. & Kettner, P. (2009). *Measuring the Performance of Human Service Professions*. Thousand Oaks, CA: Sage Publications.
McCurley, S. (2005) Keeping the community involved: recruiting and retaining volunteers. In R.D. Herman & Associates (eds), *The Jossey-Bass Handbook of*

Nonprofit Leadership and Management, 2nd edn. San Francisco, CA: Jossey-Bass, pp. 587–622.

McDonald, R.E. (2007). An investigation of innovation in nonprofit organizations: the role of organizational mission. *Nonprofit and Voluntary Sector Quarterly*, 36, 256–281.

McKee, M.C. & Driscoll, C. (2008). Creating stabilizers and safety nets for successor executives' high-wire act. *Nonprofit Management and Leadership*, 18, 341–357.

Mirabella, R.M. (2001). Filling the hollow state: capacity building within the nonprofit sector. *Public Performance and Management Review*, 25, 8–13.

Mirabella, R.M. (2007). University-based educational programs in nonprofit management and philanthropic studies: a 10-year review and projection of future trends. *Nonprofit and Voluntary Sector Quarterly*, 36, 11S–27S.

Mirabella, R.M. & Wish, N. (2000). The 'best place' debate: a comparison of graduate education programs for nonprofit managers. *Public Administration Review*, 60, 219–229.

Mirabella, R.M. & Wish, N.B. (2001) University-based educational programs in the management of nonprofit organizations: An updated census of US programs. *Public Performance and Management Review*, 25, 30–41.

Mirvis, P.H. (1992). The quality of employment in the nonprofit sector: An update on employee attitudes in nonprofits versus business and government. *Nonprofit Management and Leadership*, 3, 23–41.

Moore, G. & White, J.A. (2000). Gender and networks in a local voluntary sector elite. *Voluntas*, 11, 309–330.

Nanus, B. & Dobbs, S.M. (1999). *Leaders Who Make a Difference*. San Francisco, CA: Jossey-Bass.

Neville, L. & Murray, E.J. (2008). Succession, strategy, culture, and change at Santropol Roulant. *Nonprofit Management and Leadership*, 19, 107–121.

Nickson, D., Warhurst, C., Dutton, E. & Hurrell, S. (2008). A job to believe in: recruitment in the Scottish voluntary sector. *Human Resource Management Journal*, 18, 20–35.

Oldenhall, T. & O'Neill, M (1994). *Women and Power in the Nonprofit Sector*. San Francisco, CA: Jossey-Bass.

O'Neill, M. & Fletcher, K. (1998). *Nonprofit Management Education: US and World Perspectives*. Westport, CT: Praeger.

O'Neill, M. & Young, D.R. (1988). *Educating Managers of Nonprofit Organizations*. New York: Praeger.

Oster, S.M. (1995). *Strategic Management for Nonprofit Organizations*. New York: Oxford University Press.

Ostrower, F. (2007) Nonprofit governance in the United states: findings on performance and accountability from the first national representative study. Washington, DC: Urban Institute.

Ostrower, F. & Stone, M.M. (2010). Moving governance research forward: a contingency-based framework and data application. *Nonprofit and Voluntary Sector Quarterly*, 39, 921–924.

Packard, T. (2010). Staff perceptions of variables affecting performance in human service organizations. *Nonprofit and Voluntary Sector Quarterly*, 39, 971–990.

Parry, E., Kelliher, C., Mills, T. & Tyson, S. (2005). Comparing HRM in the voluntary and public sectors. *Personnel Review*, 34, 588–602.

Paton, R. & Cornforth, C. (1992). What's different about managing in voluntary and non-profit organizations? In Basleer, J., Cornforth, C. & Paton, R. (eds), *Issues in Voluntary and Nonprofit Management*. Reading, MA: Addison-Wesley, pp. 36–46.

Paton, R., Mardaunt, J. & Cornforth, C. (2007). Beyond nonprofit management education: leadership development in a time of blurred boundaries and distributed learning. *Nonprofit and Voluntary Sector Quarterly*, 34, 148S–162S.

Perkins, D.C. & Fields, D. (2010). Top management team diversity and performance of Christian churches. *Nonprofit and Voluntary Sector Quarterly*, 39, 825–843.

Pfeffer, J. (1998). *The Human Equation: Building Profits by Putting People First*. Boston, MA: Harvard Business School Press.

Pfeffer, J. & Sutton, R. (2000). *The Knowing–Doing Gap: How Smart Companies Turn Knowledge into Action*. Boston, MA: Harvard Business School Press.

Post, S. & Neimark, J. (2007). *Why Good Things Happen To Good People: The Exciting Research that Proves a Link between Doing Good and Living a Longer, Healthier, Happier Life*. New York: Broadway Books.

Preston, A.E. (1989). The nonprofit worker in a for-profit world. *Journal of Labor Economics*, 7, 438–463.

Preston, A.E. (1990). Women in the white-collar nonprofit sector: the best option or the only option? *Review of Economics and Statistics*, 72, 560–568.

Pynes, J.E. (2000). Are women underrepresented as leaders of nonprofit organizations? *Review of Public Personnel Administration*, 20, 35–48.

Pynes, J.E. (2008). *Human Resources Management for Public and Nonprofit Organizations: A Strategic Approach*, 3rd edn. San Francisco, CA: Jossey-Bass.

Quelch, J.A. & Laidler-Kylander, N. (2006). *Global brands: Managing nongovernment organizations in the 21st century*. Cincinnati, OH: Thompson South Western.

Ridder, H.-G. & McCandless, A. (2010). Influences on the architecture of human resource management in nonprofit organizations: An analytical framework. *Nonprofit and Voluntary Sector Quarterly*, 39, 124–141.

Ritchie, R.J.B., Swami, S. & Weinberg, C.B. (1999). A brand new world for nonprofits. *International Journal of Nonprofit and Voluntary Sector Marketing*, 4, 26–42.

Ritchie,W.J., Kolodinsky, R.W. & Eastwood, K. (2007). Does executive intuition matter: an empirical analysis of its relationship with nonprofit organization financial performance. *Nonprofit and Voluntary Sector Quarterly*, 36, 1140–155.

Ronquillo, J.C. (2010). Servant, transformational and transactional leadership. In Agard, K.A. (ed.), *Leadership in Nonprofit Organizations*. Thousand Oaks, CA: Sage, pp. 345–353.

Rothschild, J. & Milofsky, C. (2006). The centrality of values, passions, and ethics in the nonprofit sector. *Nonprofit Management and Leadership*, 17, 137–143.

Rothwell, W.J., Prescott, R.K. & Taylor, M.W. (2008). *Human Resource Transformation: Demonstrating Strategic Leadership in the Face of Future Trends*. Mountain View, CA: Davies-Black Publishing.

Rowold, J. & Rohmann, A. (2009a). Relationships between leadership styles and followers' emotional experience and effectiveness in the voluntary sector. *Non-profit and Voluntary Sector Quarterly*, 38, 270–286.

Rowold, J. & Rohmann, A. (2009b). Transformational and transactional leadership styles, followers' positive and negative emotions, and performance in German nonprofit orchestras. *Nonprofit Management and Leadership*, 20, 41–59.

Ruhm, C.J. & Borkoski, C. (2003). Compensation in the nonprofit sector. *Journal of Human Resources*, 38, 992–1021.

Salamon, L. & Gellar, S.L. (2007). *The Nonprofit Workforce Crisis: Real or Imagined.* Baltimore, MD: Johns Hopkins Center for Civil Society Studies.

Solomon, L. & Sandahl, Y. (2007). *Stepping Up or Stepping Out: A Report on the Readiness of Next Generation Nonprofit Leaders.* New York: Young Nonprofit Professionals Network.

Salterio, S. (2011). Accounting for non-profits. *National Post*, July 20, FP15.

Sampson, S.D. & Moore, L.L. (2008). Is there a glass ceiling for women in development? *Nonprofit Management and Leadership*, 18, 321–339.

Sherlock, J.J. & Nathan, M.L. (2007) Nonprofit association CEOs: how their context shapes what, how and why they learn. *Nonprofit Management and Leadership*, 18, 19–39.

Shilbury, D. & Moore, K.A. (2006). A study of organizational effectiveness for National Olympic sporting organizations. *Nonprofit and Voluntary Sector Quarterly*, 3, 5–38.

Sisodia, R., Wolfe, D.B. & Sheth, J. (2007). *Firms of Endearment: How World-Class Companies Profit from Passion and Purpose.* Upper Saddle River, NJ: Wharton School Publishing.

Sowa, J.E., Selden, S.C. & Sandfort, J.R. (2004). No longer unmeasureable? A multidimensional integrated model of nonprofit organizational effectiveness. *Nonprofit and Voluntary Sector Quarterly*, 33, 711–727.

Spurgeon, P.C., Burke, R.J. & Cooper, C.L. (2012). *The Innovation Imperative in Health Care Organizations: Critical Role of Human Resources Management in the Cost, Quality and Productivity Equation.* Cheltenham, UK and Northampton, MA, USA: Edward Elgar.

Suarez, D.P. (2010). Street credentials and management backgrounds: careers of nonprofit executives in an evolving sector. *Nonprofit and Voluntary Sector Quarterly*, 39, 695–716.

Sundeen, R.A., Raskoff, S.S. & Garcia, M.C. (2007). Differences in perceived barriers to volunteering to formal organizations: lack of time versus lack of interest. *Nonprofit Management and Leadership*, 17, 279–300.

Taniguchi, H. (2006). Men's and women's volunteering: gender differences in the effects of employment and family characteristics. *Nonprofit and Voluntary Sector Quarterly*, 35, 83–101.

Themudo, N.S. (2009). Gender and the nonprofit sector. *Nonprofit and Voluntary Sector Quarterly*, 38, 663–683.

Tierney, T. (2006). *The nonprofit sector's leadership deficit.* San Francisco, CA: Bridgespan Group.

Tschirhart, M.J., Reed, K.K., Freeman, S.J. & Anker, A.L. (2008). Is the grass greener? Sector shifting and choice of sector by PA and MBA graduates. *Nonprofit and Voluntary Sector Quarterly*, 37, 668–688.

Tschirhart, M., Reed, K.K., Freeman, S.J. & Anker, A.L. (2009). Who serves? Predicting placement of management graduates on nonprofit, government, and business boards. *Nonprofit and Voluntary Sector Quarterly*, 38, 1076–1085.

Ulrich, D. (1997). *Human Resource Champions: The Next Agenda for Adding Value and Delivering Results*. Boston, MA: Harvard Business School Press.

Ulrich, D. & Brookbank, W. (2005). *The HR Value Proposition*. Boston, MA: Harvard Business School Press.

Ulrich, D. & Smallwood, N. (2003). *Why the Bottom Line Isn't: How to Build Value through People and Organization*. New York: John Wiley.

US Census Bureau (1998). *Statistical Abstract of the United States 1998*. Washington, DC: US Census Bureau.

Vigoda, E. & Cohen, A. (2002). Work emergence and excellence in human resource management: empirical evidence from the Israeli nonprofit sector. *Review of Public Personnel Administration*, 25, 1–24.

Waters, R.D. (2007). Nonprofit organizations' use of the internet: a content analysis of communication trends on the internet sites of the Philanthropy 400. *Nonprofit Management and Leadership*, 18, 59–76.

Waters, R.D. & Bortree, D.S. (2010). Building a better workplace for teen volunteers through inclusive behaviors. *Nonprofit Management and Leadership*, 20, 337–355.

Waters, R.D. & Lord, M. (2009). Examining how advocacy groups build relationships on the internet. *International Journal of Nonprofit and Voluntary Sector Marketing*, 14, 231–241.

Webster, K. (2002). Branding the nonprofits. *Social Service Journal*, 5, 5–7.

Weisman, C. (2003). Building a board with a passion for the mission. *Nonprofit World*, 21, 27–29.

Wolverton, B. (2003a). Fighting charity fraud. *Chronicle of Philanthropy*, August 7, 15–20.

Wolverton, B. (2003b). Charity fraud exceeds $1 billion. *Chronicle of Philanthropy*, November 27, 16.

Yanay, G.V. & Yanay, N. (2008). The decline of motivation: from commitment to dropping out of volunteering. *Nonprofit Management and Leadership*, 19, 65–78.

Yoo, J. & Brooks, D. (2005). The role of organizational variables in predicting service effectiveness: an analysis of a multilevel model. *Research in Social Work Practice*, 14, 267–277.

Yoo, J., Brooks, D. & Patti, R. (2007). Organizational constructs as predictors of effectiveness in child welfare interventions. *Child Welfare*, 86, 53–72.

Zack, G.M. (2003). *Fraud and Abuse in Nonprofit Organizations: A Guide to Prevention and Detection*. Hoboken, NJ: John Wiley.

Zimmerman, J.A.M. & Stevens, B.W. (2008). Best practices in board governance: evidence from South Carolina. *Nonprofit Management and Leadership*, 19, 189–202.

2. HRM in the voluntary sector

Ian Cunningham

INTRODUCTION

The UK voluntary sector workforce has grown considerably as a direct consequence of the outsourcing of public services to non-profit organizations since the early 1990s. Human resource management (HRM) has become an increasing area of academic attention in recent years. Studies have focused on the impact of interorganizational relations on employment; the sustaining and management of employee commitment, pay and conditions, unionization and HR policies and procedures (Cunningham, 2008; Parry and Kelliher, 2009; Alatrista and Arrowsmith, 2004). More recently, the impact of self-directed care or personalization has been identified as having potentially profound implications for HR in non-profit organizations. In the latter case, this emerging interest is not only due to the implications personalization has for public service delivery, but it has wider resonance in debates concerning the impact of new actors (in this case service users) in shaping employment relationships in organizations beyond the traditional employer–employee dichotomy. Moreover, managing HR in the sector is facing considerable challenges in the current era of austerity as central and local government cut back on funding to public services. This chapter presents an overview of current research examining challenges to HR professionals in voluntary organizations in the era of outsourcing, public service austerity and the move to more personalized services.

The chapter is divided into six subsequent sections. The first provides a definition of the sector, and outlines the context under which it has operated in recent years. The second explores the impact of this environment on workforce size and HR policies and practices such as recruitment, performance management and training. The third explores the impact on pay and other working conditions. The fourth addresses issues of workforce commitment, particularly in the context of austerity and the challenges brought about by personalization, and further explores the challenge to line managers in sustaining this commitment. The fifth addresses industrial relations implications, and the final section provides discussion and conclusions.

THE VOLUNTARY SECTOR: DEFINITION AND HR CONTEXT

There is no internationally accepted definition of the voluntary sector (see Vincent and Harrow, 2005 for an overview of the debate), but this chapter adopts a narrow definition of the sector (Kendall and Almond, 1998), where voluntary organizations are defined as constitutionally independent and self-governing organizations that are non-profit-distributing and include a degree of voluntarism (Kendall and Knapp, 1996; Kendall and Almond, 1998). This definition covers a vast number of established charities, with huge budgets and paid professional staff, operating in areas such as the environment, education and training, religious activities, overseas aid, social services, health, advocacy, leisure activities and the protection of animals (Vincent and Harrow, 2005).

Early assessments of the management of HR in non-profit, voluntary organizations adopt a unitarist framework characterized by relatively harmonious and reciprocal management–employee relationships. Voluntary organizations had a distinctive culture of shared values between management and employees linked to the organization's cause or mission. Employees operated in participative workplaces where they were allowed input into the shaping of services, and were highly committed to their employer's cause, resulting, if necessary, in an acceptance of smaller pay packets and less personal advancement and job security (Paton and Cornforth, 1992). For management, high levels of commitment were used to encourage employees to work longer hours to address the needs of the most vulnerable in society, without adequate resources (Orlans, 1992). It was recognized, however, that the sector should not be overtly exploitative of the goodwill of its workforce. As a result, in return for high levels of commitment, the United Kingdom (UK) voluntary sector workforce previously benefited from having the determination of pay and conditions based on local authority scales (Ball, 1992).

There is no evidence of whether the above scenario was ever a reality. Recently, however, a body of work has emerged that recognizes that managing HR in voluntary organizations is now more complex than this unitary view. HR specialists in the sector have to introduce policies and practices that fit with the specific values and mission of voluntary organizations, but also coordinate these with organizational responses to diverse, contradictory and increasingly changing external funding and regulatory constraints (Ridder and McCandless, 2008).

Governments of all political persuasions outsource public services to the third sector (Evans, Richmond and Shields, 2005; Evans and Shields,

2002). This began in the UK with the Thatcher government accepting the 'New Right' critique that the welfare state was inefficient due to an absence of market incentives and pressures (Walsh, 1995; Osborne, 1997). Successive Conservative governments, therefore, sought to create a mixed economy of welfare under which local and health authorities changed from being monopoly providers of care to becoming enablers, contracting-out services to non-statutory providers in the private and voluntary sectors (Harris et al., 2001).

Public bodies increasingly regulated voluntary organizations through legalistic contracts rather than grants, bringing greater performance management and auditing. Commercial private sector practices emerged as the preferred approach to management for the sector, with voluntary organizations expected to demonstrate that they were 'business-like' (Perri and Kendall, 1997; Tonkiss and Passey, 1999; Harris et al., 2001). The origins of this greater scrutiny and managerialism came from the application of the principles of New Public Management (NPM), the underpinning philosophy of which was to encourage continuous increases in efficiency, professional management, and a labour force disciplined to productivity in the provision of public services (Pollit, 1995). This policy continued and increased during the period of office of the Labour governments of 1997–2010, which proclaimed that 'third sector' organizations possessed virtues or attributes that made it desirable to give them a greater role in public service delivery. These virtues included their greater closeness to service users, specialist skills, their expertise and capacity for innovation and reduced cost (Wistow et al., 1992; Davies, 2007).

Resource dependence on government funding increased. The National Council for Voluntary Organisations (NCVO) estimated that income from statutory sources in 2006/07 accounted for £12 billion or one-third of the sector's total (£33.2 billion). The highest proportion of income to the voluntary sector is received by social care organizations, totalling £4.2 billion in 2006/07, a direct consequence of outsourcing (Clark et al., 2009). Despite this increase in income, the voluntary sector continued to experience insecurity of funding throughout Labour's period in office (Davies, 2011; Cunningham, 2008).

Changes in government funding would considerably impact on the sustainability of the sector. The UK coalition government of Conservative and Liberal Democrat parties has announced massive reductions in public expenditure. In June 2010, the coalition announced £1.2 billion of cuts in local government grants. Reports from the voluntary sector indicate that pressure for related cuts from funders quickly emerged as a consequence of this reduction in central government support (NCVO, 2010). Another recent survey shows that 65 per cent of voluntary sector organizations anticipate their financial situation to worsen over the 12 months to June 2011; a higher level of concern than the 63 per cent expressed at the peak of uncertainty about spending cuts in the last quarter of 2010 (NCVO, 2011a). Voluntary organizations surviving the cuts will be operating in an environment characterized by increased pressure on commissioners to 'obtain more for less'. Clear tensions will occur between the emphasis on cost cutting, and the coalition government's goal of expanding the role of the voluntary sector in public service provision through, for example, the *Open Public Services White Paper 2011* (see Cabinet Office, 2011). The government has attempted to alleviate this pressure by establishing a 'Big Society Bank' but sector lead bodies argue that this fails to provide finance to the whole sector (NCVO, 2011a).

Such reforms take on a number of strands. The coalition advocates the development of the 'Big Society', encouraging greater participation and voice to civil society, and the growth of voluntary organizations in the provision of public services. The coalition shares New Labour's objective of using voluntary organizations to improve service quality, avoiding problems associated with the public sector through delivering services that are more in tune with local needs (Davies, 2011). Despite more demands on voluntary organizations, the public service expenditure cuts threaten to 'hollow out' the financial stability and service provision of many providers in the sector.

The implications from this changing financial environment on employment in the sector remain uncertain. HR policies will be to a significant degree determined by the interorganizational relationship that voluntary organizations have with their funders. The influence of other actors in the employment relationship beyond the strict employer–employee relationship (and their representatives) is a growing area of interest (see Marchington et al., 2005). Research reveals how, as in other supply chain relationships (see Hunter, Beaumont and Sinclair, 1996; Rubery, Earnshaw, Marchington, Cooke and Vincent, 2002; Truss, 2004), commissioning organizations intervene to shape employment policies of voluntary organizations with which they have contractual relations in the areas of pay and conditions, work organization, HR policies, training and industrial relations (Cunningham, 2008). Moreover, as with broader literature (Marchington et al., 2005; Scarborough, 2000; Bresnen, 1996) it is acknowledged that state–voluntary sector relations are characterized by complex contractual relationships with potential variable consequences for employment conditions that are shaped by management's ability to exercise levels of strategic choice in relations with external funders (Cunningham, 2008). These relationships can also shift according to changes in power relations between purchasers and providers through a 'renegotiation of order' between the parties (Truss, 2004). It is feared that the current era of austerity will tip the balance of that order towards the funder, rather than voluntary sector providers.

Another increasingly influential policy direction for the voluntary sector is the implications from the personalization of social services. The principles of service user choice lie at the heart of personalization and the future of social care. Within self-directed care individuals are empowered to make their own choices about when, how and from whom they receive care. Personalization of services has most often been implemented through people holding their own budgets for care, to spend them as they see fit. In the UK this has been done through the mechanisms of means tested 'Direct Payments' (where the service user pays the service provider direct for social care) or 'Individual Budgets' (where the service user directs a budget held by a third party) (Help the Aged, 2008). Central government has encouraged local authorities to extend this provision, and it is estimated that by April 2013 1 million people in England will be receiving a Direct Payment (DP) (SCIE, 2010).

Even under a programme of personalization, voluntary organizations are likely to remain key providers in social services as it has been found that people with DPs choose to have services delivered by agencies they are familiar with (Baxter et al., 2010). Personalization, therefore, has significant implications for providers of social care services and the management of staff as the thrust of government policies increasingly link the needs of the service user (customer) to workforce reform (Kessler and Bach, 2011; Rubery and Urwin, 2011). If this is to be the case, then a new actor (alongside employers, employees and their representatives and government agencies) will increasingly emerge within the sector to shape employment outcomes – the service user.

Provider organizations in the sector will also adapt to personalization at a different pace, depending on stages of organizational development and the nature of their client group. We can anticipate that types of providers may gradually emerge along a spectrum of outcomes. At one end of the spectrum would be services provided in the traditional care management format, while at the other the notion of the organization as 'broker' will emerge. In the latter case, this could involve organizations marketing themselves to people who use services as bodies that can provide them with a choice from a group of potential personal assistants (PAs), who they have provided with training and support. The PA is then directly employed and accountable to the person and their family. The organization provides a safety net to both people and their families and to PAs, through ongoing training, advice and monitoring the quality of support.

It is debatable to what extent many, if any, voluntary organizations will become full brokers. Many voluntary organizations will probably deliver a mix of traditional care management and personalized approaches to services depending on the needs of individual service users. This suggests different tiers of workforce emerging in forthcoming years.

IMPLICATIONS FOR THE MANAGEMENT OF HR IN THE VOLUNTARY SECTOR

The Voluntary Sector Workforce

In terms of numbers employed in the sector, HR practitioners have seen significant employment growth as funding from the state has increased. The UK voluntary sector workforce stood at 765 000 in 2010, an increase of 40 per cent since 2001, and compares with a headcount of 408 000 employees in 1995. Women account for over two-thirds of the workforce and in 2010 over half a million women (522 000) were employed in the voluntary sector (NCVO, 2011). Almost four out of ten workers (38 per cent) are part-timers (NCVO, 2011b). A higher proportion of voluntary sector employees are employed on temporary contracts (one in ten, compared to less than 10 per cent in the public and private sectors) (Wainwright et al., 2006; Wilding et al., 2004; Clark and Wilding, 2011). In focusing on social care, more than half (57 per cent) of the voluntary sector workforce were employed in health and social work, equating to 437 000 people (NCVO, 2011b). More recent figures show that between 1996 and 2008 there was a significant rise in the number of voluntary sector workers employed in social work activities, rising from 202 000 to 374 000 – an increase of 85 per cent (Clark and Wilding, 2011).

The current climate of uncertainty over funding raises questions regarding the extent to which voluntary organizations can continue to see growth in paid staff. The NCVO has reported how its most recent figures on long-term employment growth in the sector precede recently released figures showing indications of a downturn in voluntary sector employment during 2011. A survey conducted immediately after the UK coalition government's Emergency Budget found how 27 per cent of respondents had plans to decrease paid staff numbers over the next three months (NCVO, 2011b).

The sector is also unique in terms of its use of volunteers. The number of people participating in volunteering at least once a year from among the UK adult population is estimated to be 21.4 million, and 14.1 million formally volunteered at least once a month. It is estimated that 1.2 million full-time

UK workers would be needed to replace formal volunteers, well over twice the number of full-time equivalent paid employees. This would be at a cost of approximately £27.5 billion (based on the national average wage), demonstrating the continuing role of volunteering in underpinning the activities of the sector (NCVO, 2007). Within the debates regarding the 'Big Society' and the personalization of services there is speculation regarding the extent to which volunteers will be taking over tasks previously the responsibility of paid workers. Although there is insufficient space to discuss this issue fully here, it may be reasonable to suggest that the management of volunteers may become more pertinent to HR professionals in the sector in the future.

HR Policies and Practices

Our knowledge of how this changing context has shaped HR policies and practices has gradually increased in recent years. A study of Investors in People in the sector found a deep integration of the values of this quality award into the working practices and HR policies of voluntary organizations (Paton and Foot, 2000). Another study highlighted how external pressure led to policies such as discipline and grievance, health and safety, and equality policies within the voluntary sector being brought up to the standard of those common in public organizations (Cunningham, 2008).

However, it is also clear that we need to avoid an image of the sector as a passive recipient of such isomorphic pressure from the state. The degree of influence that state bodies have over management policies in the sector do depend on factors such as the degree of resource dependency and the level of strategic choice exercised by management in the non-profit sector (Leiter, 2005; Parry and Kelliher, 2009).

More recent evidence suggests that the impact of the tightening economic climate and subsequent public expenditure cuts have led to changes in the style of management in voluntary organizations. A recent study in Scotland found management in the sector adopting a stricter regime with regard to managing sickness absence, with 77 per cent reporting an increased use of return-to-work interviews; a third reducing the length of sick leave entitlement; and a fifth of organizations introducing waiting days for sick pay. Performance management was also receiving more attention, with 86 per cent reporting an increased focus on it. Interviews also revealed a link between performance management and absence, with organizations reporting how opportunities for promotion and career progression had recently been linked to absence records. Several organizations had also begun to dismiss employees for the first time on the grounds of lack of capability and absence (Cunningham, 2011).

It is also anticipated that management in the sector will introduce significant changes to HR policies and practices as a consequence of personalization of services. HR planning will become increasingly complex as workforce numbers will be partially determined by the preferences of DP and IB (Individual Budget) holders. Within this context, there remains scope for local authorities to assist in the transformation of voluntary sector providers if the former are strategic in their thinking. This can be achieved by capturing purchasing information among those that use DPs and IBs. In doing so, they could then inform voluntary sector providers about such demand to assist overall workforce planning (NMDF, 2010).

Recruitment and selection policies could also face considerable change. One study has found that changes to recruitment included selecting candidates that fit with the individual aspirations and service plans of the client groups. Selection events increasingly include participation by service users and their families, with workers chosen on the basis of sharing the interests of clients. Moreover, HR was increasingly using zero/variable hour's contracts to fit employee working time with the individual aspirations and needs of the service user: leading to further casualization of the voluntary sector workforce. Furthermore, workers could be recruited on contracts that have variable or fragmented hours on any given working day, depending on service user preferences (Cunningham and Nickson, 2010). Here, questions emerge regarding whether tensions will arise between the particular lifestyle preferences of people who use services, and employee work–life balance and provider equal opportunities policies. In the latter case, problems may arise regarding demand for greater unsocial hours working that may disproportionately exclude female workers with domestic responsibilities from applying for posts in the sector.

The same report also highlights considerable changes to performance management policies, as workers were becoming increasingly accountable for meeting service user needs and aspirations. Voluntary organizations reportedly are prepared to 'let go' employees who do not meet the new ways of working and performance requirements under personalization. This is despite the same research indicating how the degree to which a client achieves particular service outcomes and lifestyle changes depends on factors outside the employee's control, for example resource constraints and client health. The HR function in the voluntary sector will have to take such factors into account when designing new performance management policies (Cunningham and Nickson, 2010).

Workforce Skills and Training

The UK government has sought to extend workforce accreditation among the care workforce to ensure that they possess the skills outlined above. Increased state regulation through the introduction of new care standards and the requirements for workforce accreditation through NVQ/SVQ qualifications has been placed on all care providers by the Care Quality Commission (Cunningham, 2008).

Evidence suggests that financial problems means funders have, to a degree, failed to pass adequate resources to fund such training in the sector. The Scottish Social Services Council (SSSC) reports how voluntary sector providers are seen as having access to far lower sums of money for training than their local authority counterparts (SSSC, 2008). Another study has found that among major voluntary sector providers in Scotland, 64 per cent of the workforce are neither fully nor partially qualified to the standards required for registration by the SSSC (Community Care Providers Scotland, 2007).

These resource constraints on training are problematic. The NCVO has found that just under one-fifth (18 per cent) of voluntary sector employers report staff with skills gaps, with the same proportion reporting that they provide no training for their employees at all. The main impact of these skills gaps is an increase in the workload of other employees (NCVO, 2011b).

Personalization also has implications for workforce skills. Estimates of the range of skills for HR to develop as a consequence of personalization include employees at the level of Social Worker increasingly being seen as involved in roles that focus on prevention; dealing with a multitude of agencies; involve personal advocacy counselling and risk assessment; and navigating service users to the type of services they require (Leadbetter and Lownsbrough, 2005). Other studies highlight the need to develop multi-skilled workers at all levels involved in 'hybrid roles', doing tasks previously undertaken by other professions in health, housing, leisure and employment. Yet evidence from the aforementioned pilot study finds how resources for training and developing the workforce for personalization are limited, with evidence of employees having to fund their own NVQ/SVQ accreditation (Cunningham and Nickson, 2010).

In the current era of austerity, training and development in the sector is also vulnerable to public sector cuts. The aforementioned study into the impact on terms and conditions in voluntary organizations during economic recession found that 60 per cent of organizations had reduced their training budget over the previous three years. A quarter also indicated that they had reduced resources devoted to ensuring compliance with the SSSC workforce qualification targets. Finally, this squeeze on training resources was also potentially impacting on the capacity of organizations to deliver services, as 50 per cent of those reporting a reduction in their training budget also reported the existence of skill shortages among their staff (Cunningham, 2011).

PAY AND WORKING CONDITIONS

Prior to the development of the quasi-market, pay scales were in many cases aligned to local authority terms and conditions (Ball, 1992). However, exploratory studies focusing on the Conservative era of contracting revealed how terms and conditions of employment within voluntary organizations came under pressure from government calls for 'efficiency savings', and 'value for money' (Cunningham, 2001; Knapp et al., 2001).

Studies of the New Labour era highlight similar downward pressure on terms and conditions of employment in voluntary organizations (Barnard, Broach and Wakefield, 2004). Studies undertaken by the author confirms this downward spiral in pay and conditions. A qualitative study of 24 voluntary organizations revealed how many had moved away from public sector pay comparability, and among those that retained the link, pressure remained on this and other aspects of their reward package. To control costs further, management also reverted to intensifying work through altering skill mixes among lower-level front-line workers, while fewer higher-paid workers were recruited (Cunningham, 2008).

There is also strong evidence that since 2008 the current economic conditions and cuts to public expenditure are having further dramatic impact on pay and other terms and conditions of employment. Workers in the sector have experienced pay freezes and cuts to income (sometimes between 20 and 30 per cent); the removal of opportunities to receive final salary pensions; reductions in opportunities to earn additional income during unsocial hours; work intensification; changes to skill mix; and a reduction in opportunities for supervision. There was also evidence of the emergence of a two-tier workforce (three tiers with regard to pensions), with new entrants into the sector facing the severest cuts (Cunningham, 2011). As a consequence of the above pressures on pay, it is no surprise that gross weekly pay in the voluntary sector amounted to an average of £397.71 in 2010, lower than in both the private and public sectors (£452.60 and £466.53) respectively (NCVO, 2011b).

Personalization, again, may have profound implications for pay and conditions. Studies have revealed that there are concerns with the cost containment aspects to the programme, with estimates of savings of 30–40 per cent for local authorities allocating funds through DPs (Yeandle and Stiell, 2007; Carr and Dittrich, 2007; Help the Aged, 2008). The pay and conditions voluntary agencies can then offer their staff in these funding regimes will be constrained by what is affordable within the price set by public commissioners. This means voluntary agencies, again, could be under-resourced and perhaps will have look at drawing additional funds from organizational reserves. Alternatively, this could lead to further fragmentation of the workforce, as employees who are working with service users who favour DPs are employed on inferior terms and conditions compared to other workers.

The aforementioned exploratory study of personalization confirmed how employers feared that taking on services through DPs could lead to fragmentation and individualization of pay within the sector. Indeed one case study highlighted how pay rises were directly linked to the capacity of a service user's budget to meet pay increases, with the effect that workers undertaking similar tasks were in some cases operating on different pay rates, suggesting that if this phenomenon were repeated it would lead to multiple tiers of pay and conditions (Cunningham and Nickson, 2010). Finally, another study has found how personalization has been directly linked with public expenditure cuts. At least one local authority in Scotland has announced the use of DPs as the default mechanism to commission services, and that their value was approximately 20 per cent less than if they had been issued through normal block contracts. Moreover, the impact of this on voluntary sector providers has been profound, with one organization reporting how this has led to it having to implement pay cuts of approximately £700 for workers earning at most £18,500 (Cunningham, 2011).

SUSTAINING EMPLOYEE COMMITMENT: THE ONGOING CHALLENGE

These above pressures pose a challenge for HR professionals in terms of sustaining worker commitment in voluntary organizations. Employees in the sector do possess strong altruistic tendencies, but also more instrumental orientations based on career development, training, pay and conditions, and so on (Ford et al., 1998; Nickson et al., 2008; Cunningham, 2008).

The implication for HR practitioners in the sector is that cuts to terms and conditions of employment could lead to significant employee discontent. Evidence has been found in the USA, Canada and Australia where the introduction of tighter financial controls and performance indicators from state funding bodies on the sector have led to similar programmes of

NPM-inspired deterioration in terms and conditions of employment. As a consequence, the same studies have found how the previously strong commitment of employees in the respective non-profit sectors can be undermined, leading to disillusionment, burnout and quitting (Mirvis, 1992; Brown and Yoshioka, 2003; Onyx and Maclean, 1996; Saunders, 2004; Baines, 2004).

In the UK, voluntary sector workers are seen to have limits to the extent to which they can accept poor wages. Here, pressure on living standards because of poor wages, irrespective of their commitment to the organization and service user, leads to quitting. There is also evidence to suggest that work intensification, again brought about by cuts in funding, have led to significant reductions in employee morale as a consequence of working through unsocial hours, with clients with challenging behaviours leading to stress and burn-out (Cunningham, 2008; Ford et al., 1998). It is unsurprising, therefore, that analysis of turnover in the voluntary sector reveals figures averaging around 23 per cent, which are higher than for the public sector (12 per cent) (SCVO, 2004).

Personalization also brings potential tensions that could undermine employee morale. Management in voluntary organizations have raised concerns over the sustainability of employee commitment in an environment that demands increasing skills from workers, but a possibly diminishing standard of living because of pressure on pay. Moreover, there are concerns over the impact of personalization on employee morale and commitment, in the way it projects how previous ways of working with service users were inadequate (Cunningham and Nickson, 2010).

The Role of Line Managers in Sustaining Commitment

Sustaining employee commitment is dependent on the successful implementation of the HR policies and practices of voluntary organizations and good terms and conditions. With regard to the former, HRM literature argues that a central factor contributing to HR-inspired successful organizational outcomes includes positive social relations between different organizational actors including line managers (LMs) and subordinates (Purcell and Hutchinson, 2007; Sanders and Frenkel, 2011). The devolution of HR responsibilities to LMs (including recruitment, training, team building and appraisal) is said to involve the creation of management–employee relations that are underpinned by concepts of 'mutuality' which engender greater personal trust, flexibility and informal control; the ultimate aim being to create a climate of management–employee relations based on commitment, employee well-being, quality, flexibility and profitability (Storey, 1992; Guest and Conway, 2004). Stronger affective commitment among staff has been found where LMs positively engage in feedback and goal setting (Kidd and Smewing, 2001; Gilbert et al., 2011). Clear tensions have been found to exist, however, in private and public organizations between the LM role of ensuring that staff exhibit sufficient commitment to the organization, on the one hand, and operational pressures on the other (Brunetto et al., 2010; Ackroyd et al., 2007).

The role of LMs in securing the commitment of employees is as significant a focus for concern in the voluntary sector as in the public and private sectors, as they represent the focus of distributed and interactive leadership required by voluntary organizations delivering public services. Workers will exhibit elements of continuance and affective commitment to varying degrees, as employees will require stable pay and benefits, and have expectations of supportive, long-term, reciprocal relations, training and development, a participative work environment and career progression in return for their attachment to the organization. LMs will also have to manage a continuing desire among voluntary sector workers to serve a cause or a particular social group. For LMs the task is to create workplace environments that sustain these dimensions of employee commitment.

Yet the underlying forces driven by outsourcing and NPM shape the sector's employment relationships and make it difficult to sustain or control these aspects of commitment. Workers can become disenchanted if they experience personal instrumental losses in terms of pay and conditions or a lack of training opportunities, and/or a reduction in their capacity to be involved in decision-making because of the standardization of work. Moreover, any perception among staff that the organization is failing to serve the needs of a client group can affect commitment. Securing continued employee commitment in the sector also has to be seen in the context of the difficult working environment for LMs themselves. Much of the monitoring and responding to requests for statistics and target setting in the sector falls on LMs (Cunningham, 2008) increasing their workload (Cunningham, 2011). This raises questions regarding whether LMs can effectively sustain employee commitment in voluntary organizations.

One option is for voluntary organizations to invest in LM leadership behaviour skills that will sustain these different aspects of commitment. Research highlights the importance of encouraging five leadership behaviours among LMs that influence employees' affective commitment – specifically relations-orientated leadership behaviours (Yukl et al., 2002; Gilbert et al., 2011) – which are:

- supporting staff when undertaking difficult and stressful tasks;
- helping staff to improve their skills through offering coaching and development opportunities;

- recognizing, promoting and praising effective performance;
- consulting staff over issues that affect them and taking on their ideas and suggestions; and
- empowering and allowing additional discretion and responsibility among staff (Yukl et al., 2002).

There is also a need to establish and invest in leadership behaviours among LMs that sustain people's desire to care and 'make a difference'. These orientations have been found to lead to significant levels of self-sacrifice among workers with regard to workload and tolerance for poor terms and conditions (Evans, Richmond and Shields, 2005). While these orientations are thought to be fairly resilient, they are vulnerable if externally driven bureaucratic, auditing and financial requirements (such as those under NPM) interfere with the organization's mission in a way that makes front-line staff feel that they cannot 'make a difference' or where the values of the funder overwhelm that of the voluntary agency and lead to 'mission drift' (Thompson and Bunderson, 2003). In developing the LM role in sustaining such orientations, voluntary organizations will have to develop 'service-orientated leadership behaviours', including:

- 'leading by example' in difficult circumstances through the LM's own personal sacrifice to 'make a difference', for example in time spent working over without pay and other forms of unsocial hours working;
- building effective teams among workers with potentially different, variable and complex orientations (ideological, faith-based, activists and professionals);
- using their knowledge and experience of the sector, client group and job to create workplace cultures that minimize the threat of burnout among staff; and
- helping staff with strong mission values that are focused on the client group, and balance their notion of quality services and traditional ways of working with the sometimes contradictory bureaucratic, cost-cutting and target setting involved in working under government contracts.

At the same time, voluntary organizations face the vicious circle of demand for greater training and development in an era of cuts, which limits the potential for resourcing training for LMs. Personalization also raises the possibility of workplace regimes where employees are increasingly delivering services in communities, with little contact or potential use for LMs, leading to the possibility of job losses among this level of management.

INDUSTRIAL RELATIONS IMPLICATIONS

The Labour Force Survey revealed how during the 1990s, union membership failed to keep pace with the rise in the voluntary sector workforce, so maintaining low levels of union density (Passey, Hems and Jaz, 2000). Estimates of density place it at around 15–20 per cent (Unison, 2006). Legislative changes such as the Employment Relations Act 1999 (Amended by the Employment Act 2004) and the Information and Consultation Regulations, and the growth of outsourcing to the sector, has led to significant implications for the management of industrial relations by HR practitioners within the sector. This includes increased campaigns for recognition by trade unions in voluntary organizations leading to employers accepting unions within voluntary sector organizations for the first time (Cunningham, 2000, 2008).

Despite some of these agreements being established under the heading of 'partnership' arrangements, recognition of trade unions has not come without its inherent tensions for HR specialists. Union recognition drives have been accompanied by real employee concerns about cuts to pay and conditions, working unsocial hours, casualization, work intensification, lone working and violence against staff from vulnerable clients (Cunningham, 2000; Simms, 2003, 2007; Hemmings, 2011).

In addition, among employers with long-established recognition agreements the aforementioned studies have shown previously stable collective bargaining arrangements being undermined as employee terms and conditions have been threatened or cut. In some cases, this has led to the threat or actual incidence of industrial action, and increases in employee turnover and absence (Simms, 2003; Cunningham, 2008). The era of austerity is placing more strain on management union relations. Unison has embarked on industrial action ballots and at least one strike within a high-profile voluntary organization over cuts to terms and conditions as a result of funding cuts (Unison, 2011).

Despite the voluntary sector representing an opportunity to use new organizing techniques (Short, 2011), it is likely that unionization will remain low in the sector for the foreseeable future. The aforementioned studies highlight how unions have difficulties organizing the sector because of its diverse and geographically spread workforce (Simms, 2007). These problems are exacerbated by continued hostility and negative tactics among employers within the sector; difficulties organizing small workplaces; problems within the unions of recruiting sufficient activists to mobilize and represent the workforce; a lack of tradition among the paid voluntary sector workforce of unionization; contacting employees working unsociable hours; and competition for internal union resources to devote to organizing the sector (Cunningham and James, 2010; Short, 2011).

CONCLUSIONS

Our knowledge of HRM in the voluntary sector has increased in recent years. This chapter has revealed how the voluntary sector's relationship with the state is a key shaper of people management policies. The period of outsourcing from the Thatcher and New Labour eras has been characterized by a updating of HR policies and procedures, but also a persistent under-resourcing of the sector, leading to problems for HR specialists in meeting workforce accreditation targets, maintaining competitive pay levels and sustaining employee morale.

Two related contemporary developments are exacerbating these problems: personalization and the era of austerity in public services. Although on the one hand personalization brings with it the promise of more rewarding and involving work with the potential for more skills development and training, on the other it threatens to bring greater levels of vulnerability to parts of the voluntary sector workforce through greater casualization, exposure to performance management targets that are shaped by service users and their families, fragmentation of pay and conditions, and an undermining of previous approaches to caring for vulnerable people. The era of public service austerity is leading to job cuts, widespread deterioration in terms and conditions of employment, a tightening of absence and performance management standards, cuts in training budgets (including those apportioned to train employees in the skills of personalization) and increasing tensions with unions.

This leads to an increasingly complex and challenging environment for HR professionals to construct a HR climate which contributes to fulfilling voluntary sector missions and delivering on public service commitments. These financial pressures will also persist, if not intensify, given that the 2001 Autumn Budget Statement (*Guardian*, 2011) anticipates that cuts to public services will persist beyond the next Parliament. This chapter raises fears that personalization, and further outsourcing to the sector under the banner of the 'Big Society', are merely covering a deeper agenda of widespread cuts in welfare provision for vulnerable people. Moreover, as the financial and human capacity of the voluntary sector is 'hollowed out', fears are raised regarding whether non-profit organizations can continue to deliver quality public services for the vulnerable in a way that meets the aspirations of projects such as personalization.

REFERENCES

Ackroyd, S., Kirkpatrick, I. & Walker, R. (2007). Public management reform in the UK and its consequences for professional organization: a comparative analysis. *Public Administration*, 85(1), 9–26.

Alatristra, J. & Arrowsmith, J. (2004). Managing employee commitment in the not-for-profit sector. *Personnel Management*, 33(5), 536–548.

Baines, D. (2004). Caring for nothing: work organisation and unwaged labour in social services. *Work, Employment and Society*, 18(2), 267–295.

Ball, C. (1992). Remuneration policies and employment practices: some dilemmas in the voluntary sector. In Batsleer, J., Cornforth, C. and Paton, R. (eds), *Issues in Voluntary and Non-profit Management*. Wokingham: Addison-Wesley, pp. 112–134.

Barnard, J., Broach, S. & Wakefield, V. (2004). Social care: the growing crisis. Report on Recruitment and Retention Issues in the Voluntary Sector by the Social Care Employers Consortium, London.

Baxter, K., Wilberforce, M. & Glendenning, C. (2010). personal budgets and the workforce implications for social care providers: expectations and early experiences. *Social Policy and Society*, 10(1), 55.

Bresnen, M. (1996). An organisational perspective on changing buyer–supplier relations: a critical review of the evidence. *Organisation*, 3(1), 121–146.

Brown, W.A & Yoshioka, C.F. (2003). Mission attachment and satisfaction as factors in employee retention. *Non-Profit Management and Leadership*, 14(1), 1–14.

Brunetto, Y., Farr-Wharton, R. & Shacklock, K. (2010). The impact of supervisor–subordinate relationships on morale: implications for public and private sector nurses' commitment. *Human Resource Management Journal*, 20(2), 206–225.

Cabinet Office (2011). *Open Public Services White Paper*, at http://www.cabinetoffice.gov.uk/resource-library/open-public-services-white-paper, accessed 16 December 2011.

Carr, S. & Dittrich, R. (2007). Issues in the development of direct payments scheme for older people in England. In Ungerson, C. and Yeandle, S. (eds), *Cash for Care in Developed Welfare States*. Basingstoke: Palgrave, pp. 15–35.

Clark, J., Dobbs, J., Kane, D. and Wilding, K. (2009). *The State and the Voluntary Sector: Recent Trends in Government Funding and Public Service Delivery*, London: NCVO.

Clark, J. and Wilding, K. (2011). Trends in voluntary sector employment. *Voluntary Organisations and Public Service Delivery*, London: Routledge.

Community Care Providers Scotland (2007), Qualification rates and training costs for voluntary sector care providers. Edinburgh: CCPS, June.

Cunningham, I. (2000). Prospects for union growth in the UK voluntary sector: the impact of the Employment Relations Act, 1999. *Industrial Relations Journal*, 31(3), 192–206.

Cunningham, I. (2001). Sweet Charity! Managing employee commitment in the UK voluntary sector. *Employee Relations Journal*, 23(3), 226–240.

Cunningham, I. (2008). *Employment Relations in the Voluntary Sector*, London: Routledge.

Cunningham, I. (2011), *Employment Conditions in the Scottish Social Care Voluntary Sector: Impact of Public Funding Constraints in the Context of Economic Recession*, A report for Voluntary Sector Social Services Workforce Unit, Edinburgh.

Cunningham, I. & James, P. (2010). Strategies for union renewal in the context of public sector outsourcing. *Economic and Industrial Democracy*, 31(1), 34–61.

Cunningham, I. and Nickson, D. (2010). Personalisation and its implications for work and employment in the voluntary sector. Voluntary Sector Social Services Workforce Unit.

Davies, S. (2007). Third sector provision of local government and health services. Unison, May.

Davies, S. (2011), Outsourcing and the voluntary sector: a review of the evolving policy landscape. *Voluntary Organisations and Public Service Delivery*, London: Routledge.

Evans, B., Richmond, T. & Shields, J. (2005). Structuring neoliberal governance: the nonprofit sector, emerging new modes of control and the marketisation of service delivery. *Policy and Society*, 24(1), 73–97.

Evans, B. & Shields, J. (2002). The third sector: neo-liberal restructuring, governance and the rethinking of state–civil society relationship. In Dunn, Christopher (ed.), *The Handbook of Canadian Public Administration*. Don Mills, Canada: Oxford University Press, pp. 139–158.

Ford, J., Quiglars, D. & Rugg, J. (1998). *Creating Jobs: The Employment Potential of Domiciliary Care*, Joseph Rowntree Foundation, Community Care into Practice Series. Bristol: Policy Press.

Gilbert, C., De Winnea, S. & Selsa, L. (2011). The influence of line managers and HR department on employees' affective commitment. *International Journal of Human Resource Management*, 22(8), 1618–1637.

Guardian (2011). The autumn statement: cuts as far as the eye can see. http://www.guardian.co.uk/commentisfree/2011/nov/29/autumn-statement-george-osborne-editorial, accessed 5.12.2011.

Guest, D. & Conway, N. (2004). Employee well-being and the psychological contract: a report for the CIPD. London: CIPD.

Harris, M., Rochester, C. & Halfpenny, P. (2001). Voluntary organisations and social policy: twenty years of change. In Harris, M. and Rochester, C. (eds), *Voluntary Organisations and Social Policy in Britain: Perspectives on Change and Choice*. Basingstoke: Palgrave, pp. 1–20.

Help the Aged (2008). Personalisation in social care: progress in the UK and abroad. London: Help the Aged.

Hemmings, M. (2011). 'What problems you got?'Managerialisation and union organising in the voluntary sector. *Industrial Relations Journal*, 42(5), 473–485.

Hunter, L., Beaumont, P. & Sinclair, D. (1996). A partnership route to HRM. *Journal of Management Studies*, 33(2), 235–257.

Kendall, J. & Almond, S. (1998). The UK voluntary (third) sector in comparative perspective: exceptional growth and transformation. Unpublished paper, University of Kent, Canterbury.

Kendall, J. & Knapp, M. (1996). *The Voluntary Sector in the UK*, Johns Hopkins Nonprofit Sector Series. Manchester: Manchester University Press.

Kessler, I. & Bach, S. (2011). The citizen-consumer as industrial relations actor: new ways of working and the end-user in social care. *British Journal of Industrial Relations*, 49(1), 80–102.

Kidd, J. & Smewing, C. (2001). The role of supervisor in career and organizational commitment. *European Journal of Work and Organizational Psychology*, 10(1), 25–40.

Knapp, M., Hardy, B. & Forder, J. (2001). Commissioning for quality: ten years of social care markets in England. *Journal of Social Policy*, 30(2), 283–306.

Leadbetter, C. & Lownsbrough, H. (2005), *Personalisation and Participation: The Future of Social Care in Scotland*. London: Demos.

Leiter, J. (2005). Structural isomorphism in Australian nonprofit organisations. *Voluntas: International Journal of Voluntary and Nonprofit Organisations*, 16(1), 1–31.

Marchington, M., Grimshaw, D., Rubery, J. & Wilmott, H. (2005). *Fragmenting Work: Blurring Organisational Boundaries and Disordering Hierarchies*. Oxford: Oxford University Press.

Mirvis, P. (1992). The quality of employment in the nonprofit sector: an update on employee attitudes in nonprofits versus business and government. *Nonprofit Management and Leadership*, 3(1), 23–41.

National Council for Voluntary Organisations (NCVO) (2007). Almanac 2007 – Volunteering – formal volunteering is slowly increasing. http://www.ncvo-vol.org.uk/node/2958, accessed 17th November 2009.

National Council for Voluntary Organizations (NCVO) (2010). *The UK Civil Society Almanac 2010*. London: NVCO.

NCVO (2011a). Charity Forecast 2011. NCVO, http://www.ncvo-vol.org.uk/news/civil-society/our-latest-charity-forecast-survey-shows-charities-are-fearing-their-future, London, accessed 16th December 2011.

NCVO (2011b). *The Voluntary Sector Almanac, 2011*. London: NCVO.

National Market Development Forum (NMDF) (2010). National Market Development Forum Papers. London.

Nickson, D., Warhurst, C., Dutton, E. and Hurrell, S. (2008). A job to believe in: recruitment in the Scottish voluntary sector. *Human Resource Management Journal* 18(1), 20–35.

Onyx, J. & Maclean, M. (1996). Careers in the third sector. *Nonprofit Management and Leadership*, 6(4), 331–345.

Orlans, V. (1992). Stress in voluntary and non-profit organisations. In Batsleer, J., Cornforth, C. and Paton, R. (eds), *Issues in Voluntary and Non-profit Management*. Wokingham: Addison-Wesley, pp. 36–46.

Osborne, S.P. (1997). Managing the coordination of social services in the mixed economy of welfare: competition, cooperation or common cause? *British Journal of Management*, 8, 317–328.

Parry, E. & Kelliher, C. (2009). Voluntary sector responses to increased resourcing challenges. *Employee Relations*, 31(1), 9–24.

Passey, A., Hems, L. & Jaz, P. (2000). *The UK Voluntary Sector Almanac*, London: NCVO.

Paton, R. & Cornforth, C. (1992). What's different about managing in voluntary and non-profit organisations. In Batsleer, J., Cornforth, C. & Paton, R. (eds), *Issues in Voluntary and Non-Profit Management.* Wokingham: Addison Wesley, pp. 36–46.

Paton, R & Foot, J. (2000). Nonprofits' use of awards to improve and demonstrate performance: valuable discipline or burdensome formalities? *Voluntas*, 11(4), 329–353.

Perri 6 & Kendall, J. (1997). Introduction. in Perri 6 and Kendall, J. (eds), *The Contract Culture in Public Services.* Aldershot: Arena, Ashgate, pp. 1–15.

Pollit, C. (1995), *Managerialism and Public Services.* Oxford: Blackwell.

Purcell, J. and Hutchinson, S. (2007). Front-line managers as agents in the HRM performance causal chain: theory, analysis and evidence. *Human Resource Management Journal*, 17(1), 3–20.

Ridder, H.G. & McCandless, A. (2008). Influences on the architecture of human resource management in nonprofit organisations: an analytical framework. *Nonprofit and Voluntary Sector Quarterly*, 20(10), 1–18.

Rubery, J., Earnshaw, J., Marchington, M., Cooke, F.L. & Vincent, S. (2002). Changing organisational forms and the employment relationship. *Journal of Management Studies*, 39(5), 645–672.

Rubery, J. & Urwin, P. (2011). Bringing the employer back in: why social care needs a standard employment relationship. *Human Resource Management Journal*, 21(2), 122–137.

Sanders, K. and Frenkel, S. (2011). HR–line management relations: characteristics and effects. *International Journal of Human Resource Management*, 22(8), 1611–1617.

Saunders, R. (2004). Passion and commitment under stress: human resource issues in Canada's non-profit sector – a synthesis report. Canadian Policy Research Networks Series on Human Resources in the Non-Profit Sector, No.5, January.

Scarborough, H. (2000). The HR implications of supply chain relationships. *Human Resource Management Journal*, 10(1), 5–17.

Scottish Council for Voluntary Organisations (SCVO) (2004). Voluntary Sector Scottish Sector Profile, 2004. SCVO.

Scottish Social Services Council (SSSC) (2007). Fit for the future: maximising the potential of the social services workforce. Dundee.

Short, M. (2011). Trade union organising in the voluntary sector. In Cunningham, I. & James, P. (eds), *Voluntary Organisations and Public Service Delivery.* London: Routledge, pp. 54–73.

Simms, M. (2003). Union organizing in a not-for-profit organisation. In G. Gall (ed.), *Union Organizing: Campaigning for Trade Union Recognition.* London: Routledge, pp. 97–113.

Simms, M. (2007). Managed activism: two union organising campaigns in the not-for-profit sector. *Industrial Relations Journal*, 38(2), 119–135.

Social Care Institute for Excellence (SCIE) (2010). Personalisation, productivity and efficiency. London: SCIE.

Storey, J. (1992). *Developments in the Management of Human Resources.* Oxford: Blackwell.

Thompson, J.A. & Bunderson, P. (2003). Violation of principle: ideological currency in the psychological contract. *Academy of Management Review*, 28(4), 571–586.

Tonkiss, F. & Passey, A. (1999). Trust, confidence and voluntary organisations: between values and institutions. *Sociology*, 33(2), 257–274.

Truss, C. (2004). Whose in the driving seat managing human resources in a franchise firm. *Human Resource Management Journal*, 11(4), 3–21.

Unison (2006). www.unison.org.uk/voluntaryindex, accessed 19.5.06.

Unison (2011). Community and voluntary sector. http://www.unison.org.uk/community/, accessed 5.12.2011.

Vincent, J. & Harrow, J. (2005). Comparing thistles and roses: the application of governmental–voluntary sector relations theory to Scotland and England. *Voluntas*, 16(4), 375–395.

Wainwright, S., Clark, J., Griffith, M., Jochum, V. & Wilding, K. (2006). *The UK Voluntary Sector Almanac 2006*, London: NCVO Publications.

Walsh, K. (1995). *Public Services and Market Mechanisms*. Basingstoke: Macmillan.

Wilding, K., Collins, G., Jochum, V. & Wainright, S. (2004). *The UK Voluntary Sector Almanac 2004*. London: NCVO Publications.

Wistow, G., Knapp, M., Hardy, B. & Allen, C. (1992). From providing to enabling: local authorities and the mixed economy of social care. *Public Administration*, 70(1), 25–45.

Yeandle, S. & Stiell, B. (2007). Issues in the development of the direct payments scheme for older people in England. In Ungerson, C. & Yeandle, S. (eds), *Cash for Care in Developed Welfare States*. Basingstoke: Palgrave.

Yukl, G., Gordon, A. & Taber, T. (2002). A hierarchical taxonomy of leadership behavior: integrating a half century of behavior research. *Journal of Leadership and Organizational Studies*, 9, 15–32.

3. The roles nonprofit organizations play in society in the United States

Susan M. Chandler and Morgen Johansen

INTRODUCTION

The purpose of this chapter is to describe and analyze the changing roles that nonprofit organizations and the nonprofit sector play in the United States (US). We start by briefly defining the current nonprofit sector before discussing the role of nonprofit organizations in civil society. We then explore the evolving role of nonprofit organizations in American history. Finally, we discuss the changing landscape of the nonprofit community and analyze what these changes may mean for the roles of nonprofit providers, for their volunteers and for the citizens they serve, followed by concluding thoughts.

WHAT IS THE NONPROFIT SECTOR? DEFINITION, SIZE AND SCOPE

Before we discuss the role of nonprofit organizations in society, it is important to understand what the sector looks like in the US (also hereafter, America). The term 'nonprofit organization' and the nonprofit sector are relatively new in our vocabulary. The sector has always been difficult to define and this may be why it has so many names: the voluntary sector, the charitable sector, the civil society sector, the third sector, the non-governmental sector, the independent sector and the tax-exempt sector. One definition of a nonprofit organization is an organization that 'is precluded, by external regulation or its own governance structure, from distributing its financial surplus to those who control the use of organizational assets' (Powell and Steinberg, 2006, p. 1). In other words, a nonprofit organization is one that does not exist to make money for its owners or investors. Rather, the organization is driven by and dedicated to a specific mission or cause (Board Source, 2011).

However, as the lines between what nonprofit organizations and their for-profit and governmental colleagues do become less clear, the common defining characteristic of a nonprofit organization today is if it has a charitable, educational or community-based mission and receives some type of a special property or income tax status (Worth, 2009). Thus, the term 'nonprofit' is used most commonly to describe charitable and voluntary organizations that fall into specific tax policy and regulatory schemes that govern the manner in which they may operate. These may be trusts, foundations, organizations formed for charitable and civic purposes, or health, educational and religious organizations.

These organizations are usually governed so they will be exempt from property or proceeds taxation and their donors may make tax-exempt contributions to these organizations (Hall, 2006). However, there are many voluntary associations, organizations and not-for-profit organizations that may or may not be tax-exempt, may not pay property taxes and may not permit donors to receive deductions from their income taxes when they give cash donations. Nonetheless, we will use the term 'nonprofit' to cover all of these types of organizations that do not make profits and are organized to serve a broad civic or community purpose.

Size and Scope

The current 1.4 million nonprofit organizations in the United States today include hospitals, museums, schools and universities, orchestras, public television and radio, soup kitchens, professional associations, social welfare groups, political and community advocacy organizations, civic organizations, culture and the arts, humane societies, daycare organizations, religious organizations, environmental groups and hundreds of other types of organizations formed to benefit the broad public interest. There are an additional 137 000 nonprofit advocacy organizations ranging from the National Rifle Association to the Sierra Club (Independent Sector Newsletter, 2011).

The variety of the organizations in the nonprofit sector in America is so broad that it is likely that every person in the United States is or will be touched in some way by a nonprofit organization in their lifetime. The vast network of nonprofit organizations falls into eight major categories (Independent Sector Newsletter, 2011):

1. Arts, culture, and humanities, such as museums, symphonies and orchestras, and community theatres.
2. Education and research, such as private colleges and universities,

independent elementary and secondary schools, and non-commercial research institutions.
3. Environment and animals, such as zoos, bird sanctuaries, wildlife organizations and land protection groups.
4. Health services, such as hospitals, public clinics and nursing facilities.
5. Human services, such as housing and shelter, organizers of sport and recreation programs, and youth programs.
6. International and foreign affairs, such as overseas relief and development assistance.
7. Public and societal benefit, such as private and community foundations, civil rights organizations, civic, social and fraternal organizations.
8. Religion, such as houses of worship and their related auxiliary services.

Nonprofit organizations in the United States employ over 13.5 million people (approximately 10 percent of the country's workforce) and account for 9 percent of all wages and salaries paid (BEA, 2010). The nonprofit share of the American gross domestic product (GDP) was 5.5 percent in 2009, which is $751 billion of output (BEA, 2010). Public charities reported $2.56 trillion in total assets, over $1.41 trillion in total revenues and $1.40 trillion in total expenses (NCCS, 2009). Of the revenue, 22 percent comes from contributions, gifts and government grants. Seventy-six percent comes from program service revenues, which include government fees and contracts, and 11 percent comes from 'other' sources including dues, rental income, special event income, and gains or losses from goods sold (NCCS, 2009). Volunteer activity in 2009 totaled 8.1 billion hours of service, which produced an estimated value of $169 billion (Corporation for National and Community Service, 2010). Clearly, the nonprofit sector plays an extremely diverse and important role in American society.

THE ROLE OF NONPROFITS IN SHAPING CIVIL SOCIETY

Armed with an image of the nonprofit sector in America, we can now explore the ways in which the sector enhances civil society. Civil society is an autonomous sphere of society that is voluntary, self-generating and self-supporting in which 'we answer together the most important questions: what is our purpose, what is the right way to act, and what is the common good' (Elshtain, 1999, p. 21, cited in Eikenberry and Kluver, 2004, p. 132).

The terms 'voluntary sector' and 'civil society' are often used interchangeably because they both 'mobilize private initiative for the common good' and they both occupy the sphere between the market and government. Salamon (2002) suggests that civil society is composed and expressed through charitable, voluntary, civic and social organizations that form the basis of a well-functioning society. Civil sector organizations include all kinds of organizations, clubs, associations, religious bodies, cultural groups, trade unions and interest groups that are not a part of any government, the public sector or the commercial markets.

There are four ways that voluntary organizations and associations enhance civil society: service provision, advocacy, building social capital and value guardianship (Salamon, 2002).

Service Provision

The predominant way that nonprofit organizations contribute to civil society is by providing services to improve the quality of life for citizens or to prevent it from becoming worse (Ott and Dicke, 2012). Salamon (2002) defines service provision as providing direct services to individuals or groups in need such as offering free or low-cost health care, domestic abuse and homeless shelters, soup kitchens, or youth after-school programs.

An additional aspect of service provision is that nonprofit organizations offer program or service innovations that have been partially tested in a community. Smith (2012) calls this the social risk capital of human society. Nonprofit organizations often experiment with and test new ideas for addressing social problems that may then, if successful and efficient, be adopted more generally by society. Indeed, Smith contends that 'nearly every function currently performed by government at various levels was once a new social idea and the experiment of some voluntary group' (Smith, 2012, p. 72). Nonprofit organizations have pioneered many programs and services that are commonplace today: for example, assistance to AIDS victims, hospice care, food pantries for the hungry and drug abuse treatment services (Salamon, 2002, p. 10).

In addition to experimenting with the best way to provide social services, nonprofit service provision often lowers the cost of public services (Smith, 2010b). One reason that nonprofit organizations have been charged with carrying out the functions of government usually reserved for the public sector (such as health care, social services, low-income housing, employment and training, community development and education) is because nonprofits are expected to provide those services at a lower cost and with higher quality than if the government was providing them (Frumkin, 2005; Salamon, 2002). Indeed, many federal, state and local agencies rely almost entirely on nonprofit organizations to provide services as a way to save money and improve the effectiveness of services (Smith, 2010a, p. 132). This shifting of responsibility from government to nonprofit organizations is why the nonprofit sector is often referred to as the third sector, behind the government and business sectors.

More broadly, nonprofit organizations enhance civil society because they mobilize collective action to help and support one another for a common good. Thus, service provision is not only about providing food to the hungry, shelter to the homeless or medicine to the sick; it is about offering opportunities for fulfilling and creative work through volunteerism, to help one's community or neighbor, to see the world in a different way, to fight for what one believes in, and to help current and future generations. Service provision encompasses those services that support the community, the individual and the soul.

Advocacy

The second way that nonprofits enhance civil society is through policy or community advocacy (Balassiano and Chandler, 2009). Nonprofits provide services as well as seek to address the problem and attack the root causes behind the need. In other words, 'they serve as safety nets and are also expected to solve the problems that require the need for a safety net' (Ott and Dicke, 2012, p. 51). Thus, nonprofits not only provide services that the public sector and the government cannot or will not; they also identify problems that are unaddressed or new and get them onto the policy agenda (Salamon, 2002). Nonprofits build representational capacity; they are the means by which the interests of citizens are represented to the state (Warren, 2003; Guo, 2007). Nonprofit organizations put pressure on government and advocate for action on a wide variety of social issues (Child and Gronbjerg, 2007; Mosley, 2010; LeRoux, 2007; Suarez, 2009).

Nonprofit organizations enhance civil society because they encourage citizens to participate more actively in their own communities. Nonprofits allow citizens to get involved and more easily organize and exercise influence about issues important to them; they serve as pathways to participation. Instead of just participating in democracy and the civil society by being involved in political parties, voting and paying taxes, nonprofit organizations provide a pathway and support for citizens to join groups and take a more active role in policy issues affecting their community.

Building Social Capital

Thirdly, nonprofit organizations enhance civil society by building social capital (Salamon, 2002; Putnam, 2000; Marwell, 2007). Building social capital is accomplished by activities such as neighbors helping each other by babysitting one another's children, fixing a roof, watching out for criminals, bringing food over to a family during an illness or death, or helping each other clean up debris after a natural disaster. Nonprofit organizations enhance social capital by creating local social networks that make it easy and comfortable for individuals to connect with each other. Moreover, nonprofits contribute to personal capital – the ability to sustain positive, nurturing and helpful relationships with family, friends, neighbors and a community – by providing individuals with positive examples of civic engagement and the opportunity to create meaningful bonds with others (Van Til, 2005, p. 46).

These social and personal connections are critical for the community to solve problems, support individuals, and mobilize residents for collaborative action (Backman and Smith, 2000, p. 356). Social capital comprises those bonds of trust and reciprocity that are crucial for democracy and economic growth (Salamon, 2002; Anheier, 2009). By building social capital in their communities, nonprofits are better able to address serious social problems such as poverty and economic decline (Smith, 2010a; Kretzmann and McKnight, 1993; Putnam, 1993).

Value Guardianship

The fourth way nonprofit organizations enhance civil society is by instilling in the country two crucial national values: individualism and solidarity. Salamon (2002) calls this 'value guardianship'. Together these two values comprise the definition of civil society: private initiative for the common good (Salamon, 2002). Value guardianship perpetuates the values of volunteerism, charity and philanthropy.

The nonprofit sector builds cultural capital, which contributes to producing effective persons in society (Van Til, 2005, p. 46). Cultural capital is the ability to appreciate the role and importance of a shared cultural life in society. Culture may include art, values, faith, beliefs and norms. Nonprofit organizations may build cultural capacity in a variety of ways. They encourage people to find outlets for their creativity; they support people who wish to express their values, commitments and faith (Frumkin, 2005). They also may help to preserve and pass down old ideas or beliefs to others (Smith, 2012) and they help socialize new groups, such as when new immigrants move into the community or new workers join a specialized profession. Cultural capital fosters the community members' ability to appreciate the arts, to have faith, to come together around common beliefs, values and norms that strengthen people's connections to each other, their community and society as well.

The United States has had a plethora of voluntary and charitable organizations that have contributed to civil society for over 300 years. Looking back, we see that many of these nonprofit organizations were playing roles that we still see today.

THE EVOLVING ROLES OF VOLUNTARY ORGANIZATIONS IN EARLY AMERICAN SOCIETY

In addition to contributing to civil society, voluntary associations, charities and religious organizations have always played an important and unique role in the United States. This is because, philosophically, most Americans do not expect or want their government to be too deeply involved in their lives or in their communities. The deep-seated American value of self-reliance means that individuals and families are expected to be and should be primarily responsible for themselves. Individuals and families are expected to provide voluntary, mutual assistance, cultural activities, and the support and social services necessary to meet the needs of their own communities.

According to de Toqueville (1945), America's zeal for voluntary, self-help organizations is the quintessential American contribution to its unique form of democracy. These voluntary organizations played a distinctive role in the community and many still do. Citizens would join groups, successfully organize, make suggestions and sometimes demands, and were effective in solving most of the problems and challenges in their communities. They were often quite successful in influencing the public sector and bringing about changes in laws or policies.

Early Voluntary Associations

A civil society was created early in America's history. Religious organizations became extremely active in seventeenth-century America and many saw their role as crucial in helping families settle into their new communities and to insure and transfer the church's teachings and religious values to the newcomers (Queen and Harper, 1894). Voluntary organizations played key roles in the American Revolution in 1776 and influenced the governing structures of the early colonial communities. Many voluntary associations were formed to provide help, support and sustenance to members and others in the community during wartime, and were a major method for sharing news and information.

The role of these voluntary associations in early American society was to address social needs at a time when the public sector was weak and many local governmental structures barely existed, or if they did, they chose not to provide many services. Citizens formed mutual associations where they assisted with various 'public' tasks such as building and maintaining roads and buildings, fire fighting, and protecting their towns and villages. These voluntary associations, loosely defined, were self-governed and provided the community with essential non-governmental services. As the United States grew, these voluntary and civic organizations also grew, diversified and continued to play an important role in society, primarily because of citizens' mistrust and fear of both government and corporations, as well as their preference for non-governmental responses.

NEW TYPES AND NEW ROLES OF VOLUNTARY ASSOCIATIONS

Post-Civil War America experienced huge changes in society with an influx of immigrants from across Europe, and rapid industrialization and urban development in the north. In response to these social changes, in many communities a new type of voluntary organization emerged, made up of disenfranchised groups such as African-Americans, women, veterans, the poor and the newly arriving immigrants. People formed and joined voluntary associations out of a sense of necessity (Kaufman, 2002).

Many of these organizations were structured to help others but many were organized primarily to provide direct help and support to their own members. These types of associations and organizations gave members a sense of community and solidarity and worked to address a variety of societal problems through an emerging style of group advocacy (Hall, 2005). As communities began to struggle with increasingly serious and complex problems, more types of charitable and voluntary organizations emerged. New associations developed new roles with a stronger advocacy focus and were formed to tackle such issues as slavery, drunkenness, child welfare and violence.

American civil society was enhanced as new types of voluntary associations with new roles grew and changed again in the late nineteenth century. They are difficult to categorize or classify due to their diversity; some were ad-hoc, small community-based groups that met intermittently with a single focus, while others were extremely wealthy, formalized trusts donating millions to different causes across the nation. Membership organizations, such as labor unions, professional trade associations, recreational clubs, welfare councils, and political parties flourished to help their members (Tschirhart, 2006). During this time of increased urbanization, the nation saw the rise of new worker associations and guilds designed to protect working people, craftspeople, and professionals. A stock market crash in the early 1870s created an economic depression that lasted for several years and this gave rise to the growth of labor unions.

The Rise of Labor Unions

New organizations of workers in trade and industrial unions and worker federations significantly changed the lives of working people. Through these new associations, members worked through collective action, strikes and advocacy for new laws that improved the pay and working conditions for working people. As the labor union movement grew, it began to exert significant political influence and to weaken the power of businesses and corporations in American society. These new organizations, through collectively bargaining for their members, obtained new protections and benefits for their workers.

They also began to use their growing number of members to become influential in the political arena and they used their organization to elect labor-friendly politicians. Labor unions, such as the United Mine Workers of America, not only successfully formed worker associations that became quite powerful and exerted a strong influence on worker rights, but they also were successful in influencing politicians to begin to rein in corporate abuses. Professional groups of lawyers, engineers and doctors also began to form professional associations designed to set practice standards, licensure and certification requirements as well as to function as mutual support groups and educational guilds (for example the American Medical Association and the American Bar Association).

Other types of community-based organizations were also forming and becoming engaged in political mobilization. Veterans formed associations to advocate for veterans' rights and benefits, and other reform-oriented, social movements developed around issues such as women's suffrage, prohibition, eliminating child labor, combating racial and ethnic discrimination, and reducing poverty.

With these new roles and new types of nonprofit organizations, concerns about the role and place of these non-governmental, private organizations in society were raised and debated (Hall, 1992). One perspective suggests it is inherent in the American form of democracy that governmental intervention and the public sector should remain as minimal as possible in the lives of citizens, and thus there is a need for a broad swath of volunteer-led, community-based organizations to support what the public sector and the market cannot or will not do. The other perspective, however, is that this large and influential non-governmental sector in America is due to the abrogation of what essentially should be a public responsibility, particularly in such major areas as health, education and social welfare, and perhaps even in the areas of cultural activities and the arts. This debate about the role of the non-governmental sector and the building of civil society continues today.

THE BEGINNINGS OF THE MODERN NONPROFIT SECTOR

As previously outlined, the modern nonprofit sector grew naturally out of America's early history with voluntary organizations and associations. The more recent nonprofit sector has grown and changed as it attempts to solve public problems on a national scale; collective action to solve public problems expanded to the national sphere. Organizations such as the American Red Cross, the YMCA and the Salvation Army are good examples. Another thrust may be seen through philanthropists such as John Rockefeller and Andrew Carnegie, who had amassed great personal wealth, and granted large endowments to many institutions dedicated to providing public services such as libraries, hospitals and universities across the country.

Tax-Exempt Status

Wealthy Americans not only wanted to do good, they also wanted to find new tax-avoidance mechanisms both to park their funds and to exert their influence over community development activities. Thus, they founded large, largely tax-free foundations. The immense wealth of these foundations made them extremely influential in American society. The US Congress's first attempt to regulate the influence of these wealthy donors was the passage of the Revenue Act of 1909. This act designated a tax-exempt status only to an organization that was operating exclusively for religious, charitable or educational purposes and stated that no part of the net income could benefit any private stockholder or individual. This subsequently became the requirement for a tax-exempt organization: it must operate for charitable purposes (Arnsberger et al., 2008).

A New Form of Charitable Giving Changes the Role of Nonprofits

At the local level, the Cleveland, Ohio, Chamber of Commerce invented a new type of charitable donor structure called 'The Community Chest'. This fund-raising scheme encouraged both businesses and individual citizens to give cash donations to charitable organizations. It not only encouraged donations, but it also began to stress the importance of giving only to the most efficient and effective of the nonprofit organizations in that community. The Chamber developed a list of recommendations and selected the charitable organizations that were 'deserving' of its support. The genius of this idea was that the Community Chest was a fund-raising scheme that flattened out the donor pool by reaching out and soliciting charitable donations from middle- and working-class Americans (Tuennerman-Kaplan, 2001).

The Community Chest, a precursor of the United Way (now the largest coalition of charitable organizations in America), significantly changed the role of nonprofit organizations by developing the concept that nonprofit, charitable organizations should be held to high standards of accountability and efficiency in order to become an approved 'member' of the Community Chest or join the United Way 'family'. This preferred list of agencies designated by business leaders in many communities helped small, individual donors learn more about the business practices of the charities to which they were donating money; however, it also maintained business's role in directing and influencing how money should go to charitable organizations. Business leaders liked the idea of their colleagues researching and approving which organizations should be supported and which ones should not. This coalition of nonprofit organizations also agreed, as a requirement of being selected as a member, jointly to solicit funds for all members of the group and only solicit individual donations and contributions during a specific, limited time frame.

Another aspect of this collective approach was that community-based campaigns encouraged residents to become more civically engaged in the life of their community by not only donating cash, but also volunteering in these charitable organizations (Brilliant, 1990). This new strategy resulted in business leaders and their employees becoming actively engaged in organizing and collecting donations from a broad-based community of donors. Citizens also became more involved in how donations from individual and corporate donors would be distributed to the 'preferred' charitable organizations.

Nonprofit organizations not selected for these coalitions now had to develop more aggressive donor campaigns and needed to begin to make public more information about their fund-raising activities, how their money was being spent, and with what effect or impact. In response to a perceived 'Protestant preference' of the United Way and other Community Chests, new religiously based charitable groups such as Catholic Charities and the United Jewish Appeal formed to develop their own benevolent institutions aimed at organizing and receiving donations for their own causes.

The growing size and increasing numbers of foundations, the rise in American philanthropy, and the subsequent creation of tax-exempt status set the stage for the current roles that nonprofit organizations play in their communities. The next section of this chapter describes how they have become enmeshed, and essential to the functioning of the public sector.

NONGOVERNMENTAL ORGANIZATIONS AS CRUCIAL GOVERNMENTAL PARTNERS

The role of the nonprofit sector as more than just civil society started with President Herbert Hoover, who served from 1929 to 1933. Under Hoover, nonprofit organizations became crucial government partners. He believed the solution to the nation's complex problems could not be found by extending the government into the community's economic or social life (Hoover, 1921). He supported the development of public–private partnerships, which meant that the government would (and should) only be involved in helping to coordinate and assist businesses and corporations in doing their work. Hoover envisioned a society with hundreds of businesses and private organizations and associations working in partnership with governmental agencies. His vision included for-profit organizations, businesses and corporations all joining the public service enterprise. Hoover's administration influenced the growth and influence of nonprofit, voluntary associations, many of which functioned as small businesses and saw the potential of becoming partners with government.

In the 1930s, as the US experienced its worst economic depression, economic disparities, poverty and unemployment soared. It became clear that the business sector was floundering and the voluntary associations, charities and religious groups that existed in the community did not have the capacity to help the huge and growing number of homeless, hungry and unemployed. The government needed to step up and step in.

Thus, even though Americans have never been comfortable with the role of a big government, the way out of the depression seemed to be to have many new governmental services and programs funded by the public sector. This provided new opportunities for nonprofit organizations, since the services and programs would be federally funded but delivered through private and/or non-governmental entities. This was an acceptable arrangement because of the popular belief that the nonprofit sector is efficient, effective and necessary for a strong civil society. This view remains deeply engrained in America's values and philosophy and has contributed heavily to the expansion of the nonprofit sector that now provides the majority of government funded services (O'Neill, 2009).

THE NEW DEAL AND NEW ROLES FOR THE NONPROFIT SECTOR

The Great Depression saw a large increase in the scope and size of government as well as the growth of civil sector organizations. New governmental programs were created to hire millions of out-of-work Americans. Many were hired to work on construction projects like the interstate highway system and the building of dams, bridges and parks, and the federal government provided new subsidies to encourage private sector growth and charitable giving (Hall, 2005). President Roosevelt's New Deal was carried out by non-governmental institutions, yet funded by government contracts, user fees, and tax exemptions and deductions.

Many of the New Deal Public Works Projects indirectly supported the development of the nonprofit sector. For example, public projects funded civic centers and municipal auditoriums in small towns across the country; hundreds of libraries were constructed, as well as new classrooms and additional support for the civil society (Adams and Goldbard, 1995). This shift in the relationship between the public sector and the nonprofit sector fostered the growth of a new type of public–private partnership. This partnership has continued to develop so that today the majority of governmental programs and services funded by the public sector are implemented through nonprofit organizations that are privately contracted for their service delivery.

Nonprofit organizations are now playing a significantly different role from those earlier charitable associations: previously 'outsiders', these new nonprofit partners are playing increasingly important roles as influential 'insiders' and collaborators with government – if not almost extensions of government (Hall, 2006). Today, the interdependence between the public and nonprofit sectors in America is clearly acknowledged; whether this extent of privatization of public sector functions is at an appropriate level, is still being debated.

BIGGER AND MORE DIVERSE ROLES FOR THE NONPROFIT SECTOR

Nonprofit organizations took on a multitude of new roles and responsibilities in civil society as they began providing a wide array of programs and services for the public welfare during the 1960s and 1970s. With President Johnson's Great Society, hundreds of new governmental programs were designed to help the poor and vulnerable and to attack a wide array of social problems. Nonprofit organizations became significant players in their communities as new governmental contracts were awarded to fund specific programs and services. Nonprofits became more deeply enmeshed and ingrained in the fabric of American government.

President Nixon in the early 1970s strongly relied on the privatization of health and human services and his administration established a clear and strong preference to contract almost all governmental products and services out to private, nonprofit organizations (Tannebaum and Reisch, 2001). This era gave rise to the term 'third party government', where although government programs and spending grow, the size of the federal government (staffing, agencies, and so on) does not. This is achieved through the awarding of government contracts, grants and vouchers to nonprofit agencies to provide the majority of social services, housing and other support to communities.

This trend continued under President Reagan (1981–89), who also favored small government and the extensive involvement of the private sector in public service delivery. The role of nonprofit organizations continued to expand and broaden as his philosophy of 'Reaganomics' strived to cut taxes and reduce governmental services and spending in the hope that private sector initiatives would grow and replace the need for big government. Reagan's huge cuts in federal spending stimulated a large growth of nonprofits (the sector grew 30 percent between Reagan's first and last years in office) and set off another expansion of the nonprofit sector.

President George H.W. Bush, following Reagan's thrust to decrease the size of government and increase the voluntary sector, coined the phrase 'a thousand points of light' to describe his vision for dismantling the government-run health and social welfare sector and replacing it almost totally with nonprofit, community-based alternatives. Nonprofits were now the major provider of services for residential and rehabilitation services, outpatient clinics and hospitals, and most services for elderly and other needy people.

Under President Clinton, nonprofit organizations began to enter into the new field of welfare reform and became active in providing job training programs, childcare services and a variety of support services in response to changes to the welfare programs. Nonprofit organizations also began to infiltrate public sector organizations by obtaining contracts to redesign the public sector's eligibility, administrative, management and informational systems. Nonprofit organizations were now providing executive 'coaching' services for governmental agency directors and staff. The public sector was becoming quite dependent on the skills of the nonprofit sector.

The current American Welfare State is now one in which nonprofit entities provide for the general welfare of citizens (Salamon, 2002). Non-profits provide the majority of health, education and social services in society. The rise of third-party government means that the responsibility for providing federal services has shifted first to the states and localities, and then to private, nonprofit entities. In 2009, there were nearly 33 000 human service providers with almost 200 000 government contracts (Boris et al., 2010).

NEW ROLES, CHALLENGES AND THE CHANGING LANDSCAPE OF THE NONPROFIT SECTOR

Competitive Challenges

This huge expansion of the nonprofit sector has created competition among nonprofit organizations, which has implications for the nature and future of the sector and civil society. They must now compete with each other as well as with for-profit entities for funding and for clients. While the public sector has become quite dependent on the nonprofit sector to provide its services, nonprofit organizations have also become more dependent on state and local contracts and grants for funding and their very survival. Competition for charitable donations is keen and donors and volunteers have many more nonprofit organizations to choose from to give their dollars and volunteer hours. With the devolution of funds from the federal government to state and local entities, the increasing privatization of public services, and an increase in the number of for-profit organizations entering the competition for governmental contracts and funds, the role of the nonprofit sector in society has become less clear and the boundaries between nonprofit and for-profit organizations is eroding.

Other recent changes in the roles of the nonprofit sector may be related to several factors. Firstly, there has been a huge increase in the demand for social welfare services over the last decade or so, particularly in field of community-based services, health care, housing, welfare and substance abuse services (Smith, 2010a). Secondly, perhaps aligned with the huge increase in demand is the significant decrease in the capacity of government actually to deliver direct services. As the number of public sector employees has been cut back in all levels of government, there has been a decrease in the government's capacity and ability to contract, monitor and evaluate the privatized services it is contracting for. This has led to a consolidation of some nonprofit organizations as governments choose to award fewer contracts (often called a master contract) with one large nonprofit organization in order to streamline the transaction costs and monitoring obligations of the public agency (Allard, 2009).

Thirdly, Kettl (2005) contends that the influence of the new public management movement in the public sector, which is demanding increased efficiency, effectiveness and accountability, is also requiring changes in the nonprofit sector. Performance-based contracting, demands for more transparency, as well as requirements for data to document successful outcomes are now common elements in government contracts with nonprofit providers. Many public sector contracts will only pay nonprofit organizations for documented client improvement, not just a documented count of the number of clients served or the number of activities outlined in the contract.

Government at all levels is searching for more efficient ways to deliver and/or provide services and is increasing its demands on contractors. The contracting-out system permits the government to retain the legal authority and 'ownership' of a project or program, while utilizing the services of a nonprofit company that will do the tasks presumably more efficiently and at less cost (Salamon, 2002). This action relieves the government of the burden of directly providing services, so that the government can spend more time and effort on improving the coordination of services. Nonprofit organizations presumably can be more flexible and innovative in the design and delivery of its services.

Implications of Contracting

However, the public sector's dependence on contracting with the nonprofit sector and the reduced size of the public sector workforce may have resulted in less governmental oversight and an inability to know, with certainty, how well the nonprofit sector is doing the work it is contracted to do. This is problematic because the public sector can never really give up its statutorily mandated responsibilities. So, even while a governmental agency can contract out and privatize almost any service it chooses, it can never give up its overall responsibility and duty to the public and the taxpayer (Chandler and Pratt, 2011). Taxpayers will always hold the public sector responsible and liable for any problem that may occur, even if the public agency has completely privatized an activity to a nonprofit (or for-profit) organization.

If the nonprofit organization fails to deliver on the expected outcomes, whatever the reason (poor staffing, fraud or ineptitude), it is still the government's failure, since it was the public entity that contracted for the services. The public sector now has become quite dependent on the nonprofit sector for its work. If the nonprofit organization leaves town, fails or flounders, the government is in a difficult position because it does not have the trained or available workforce to pick up the work needed; it must seek and find another nonprofit organization.

A Loss of Mission?

On the other hand, as nonprofit organizations struggle for resources and are forced to work in more competitive environments, they must become more entrepreneurial in order to survive (Salamon, 2002). External environmental pressures, decreases in charitable giving, as well as reductions in more recent governmental funding have forced many nonprofits to generate more of their own commercial revenue. New strategies such as charging fees for services previously provided for free, selling products to raise capital, or incorporating for-profit ventures along with the nonprofit organizational structure, are becoming more common in the nonprofit sector. Some nonprofits are subcontracting with for-profit organizations to help them raise or earn money. Fund development experts are now almost a requirement for staffing most nonprofits today.

As the public sector moves to adopting more market-based values and business practices, the emphasis on entrepreneurialism and profit may be viewed as incompatible with the values of democracy, and particularly the values of fairness and justice. This 'marketization' is also impacting the role of the nonprofit sector, perhaps with equally dire consequences, and may be a serious threat to the major purpose of the nonprofit sector. These changes may be viewed as a threat to the nonprofit's basic identity – its core mission (Eikenberry and Kluver, 2004).

The newly competitive environment challenges the nonprofit organization's ability to manage the activities devoted to its core mission. Smaller nonprofits are also being threatened with takeovers by larger, better-financed nonprofits. For-profit companies are also becoming serious competitors and are engaging in providing many services that were traditionally the purview of the nonprofit sector, as they are vying quite successfully for governmental contracts. Salamon (2002) notes that these risks also pose a threat to the public trust and confidence upon which the sector is dependent.

A Diminishing Civil Society?

Eikenberry and Kluver (2004, p. 132) cite several examples in which nonprofit organizations are modeling for-profit business plans and becoming entrepreneurial at the possible expense of their role as 'value guardians'. Some see these for-profit-like business strategies as violating the very essence of the nonprofit sector's service and advocacy role, and as builders of social capital and a strong civil society. For example, the Boys and Girls Club of America negotiated a deal for $60 million with the Coca-Cola Company to market its drinks exclusively in their clubs (Reis and Clohesy, 1999). This raises questions about this huge youth organization's mission and role in civil society. For example, would it simultaneously be able to launch a health-oriented campaign against drinking sugary drinks, which is possibly a major cause of youth obesity, while under an exclusive contract with Coca-Cola?

This example demonstrates a new and worrisome strategy for generating revenues among nonprofit organizations. Rather than receiving direct donations from corporations, some nonprofits are now negotiating 'deals' for marketing or advertising certain products in return for contributions. Another example is the American Cancer Society endorsement of one brand of a nicotine patch in return for a large grant from the maker of that patch. It also teamed up with a sunscreen manufacturer for a portion of its proceeds. Of course, more market-oriented business models may make the sector and nonprofit organizations more efficient, more innovative and more accountable, but does this threaten their independent role in civil society? Can they still be independent and advocate for their causes?

Becoming overly dependent on governmental contracts for its major source of funds challenges the sector's independence and role as advocate. As they are required to spend more of their time and money on generating resources, will nonprofit organizations move away from their goals and mission-driven strategies? Will the values of helping the needy be replaced when a more competitive business model emerges and organizations must charge fees for services or get reimbursements for the services they want to provide? Will the new nonprofits only serve those who can pay for their services?

A Money Chase?

Seeking or chasing money and donors may change or compromise the core mission of the nonprofit sector. For example, decisions about whether to go into a new, perhaps less profitable line of 'business' could influence a nonprofit organization's mission-related activities and result in the elimination or reduction in the type and array of services that were traditionally provided. For example, if there is only one nonprofit organization providing a needed service in a community, but it moves to a wealthier geographical community (or elects to change its service and introduce a fee structure) this could have devastating consequences for those in need and dependent on this nonprofit.

Another risk could be that an organization, in response to competition, may recruit new board members primarily because they can raise money for the organization or because they have important professional and powerful political networks. This is a critical departure from the traditional role of board members, who are selected to reflect the community in which the organization serves and who are presumably knowledgeable about the needs and the services being provided.

In addition to a threat to mission, the governance of these organizations may affect the advocacy role of nonprofit organizations. The traditional role of community-based policy advocacy may disappear, based on the desires of the funding sources' interests or the new board's concern about providing 'unprofitable' activities. As the nonprofit sector struggles with more competition, and is pushed into new forms of partnerships and collaborations, the sector may become less responsive to its original purpose. As government contracts become more constraining and funders push the small organizations to follow more stringent business models, the nonprofit sector's role may become more like that of the for-profit sector.

CONCLUDING THOUGHTS

Nonprofit organizations represent the most widespread organized expression of America's dedication to the common good (Panel on the Nonprofit Sector, 2007). The public has extremely high expectations for the ethical standards and impact of this sector on the nation. The credibility of the entire sector is tested whenever wrongdoing among non-governmental organizations is reported in the media, such as corruption, theft, abuses and scandals, including misappropriation of funds and embezzlement. Although Gibelman and Gelman (2004) find that any such wrongdoings are rare and that the crux of the problem lies in the governance of these organizations, this kind of problem can shake the public's faith in the nonprofit sector and tarnish its image, impacting the sector's ability to raise funds and conduct good works, as well as bringing unwanted calls for more governmental regulation.

New state and national associations of nonprofit organizations have come together to resist government attempts to regulate further nonprofits' board activities, reporting requirements, transparency and governance. These associations believe that strengthening the accountability and transparency of the sector is the responsibility of the sector itself and that it can and will develop ethical standards and practices to preserve the public confidence. This role of preserving and protecting the credibility of the nonprofit sector may be its new and most interesting future obligation.

Although it faces many challenges and threats, the nonprofit sector is founded first and foremost on its commitment to benefit the common good. The ways in which nonprofit organizations pursue their missions may change, and some may even lose their way, but the nonprofit sector as a whole is likely to continue to play an integral role in American civil society. This role will, of course, evolve and change just as it has over America's history, but nonprofit organizations will continue to exist in the United States because their role is essential to the future of democracy.

REFERENCES

Adams, D. & Goldbard, A. (1995). New Deal Cultural Programs: Experiments in Cultural Democracy. Talmage, CA: The Institute for Cultural Democracy. www.wwcd.org/policy/US/newdeal.html. Retrieved, November 26, 2011.

Allard, S.W. (2009). *Out of Reach: Place, Poverty, and the New American Welfare State*. New Haven: Yale University Press.

Anheier, H.K. (2009). What kind of nonprofit sector, what kind of society? Comparative Reflections. *American Behavioral Scientist*, 52, 1082–1094.

Arnsberger, P., Ludlum, M., Riley, M. & Stanton, M. (2008). Statistics of income bulletin. The Internal Revenue Service, Winter.

Backman, E. & Smith, S.R. (2000). Health organizations, unhealthy communitites? *Nonprofit Management and Leadership*, 10(4), 355–373.

Balassiano, K. & Chandler, S.M. (2009). The emerging role of nonprofit associations in advocacy and public policy: trends, issues, and prospects. *Nonprofit and Voluntary Sector Quarterly*, 39, 946–955.

BEA (2010). Bureau of Economic Analysis, U.S. Department of Commerce. 2010 Release.

Board Source (2011). What is the nonprofit sector? In J. Steven Ott and Lisa A. Dicke (eds), *The Nature of the Nonprofit Sector*, 2nd edn. Boulder, CO: Westview Press, pp. 10–11.

Boris, E.T., de Leon, I., Roeger, K.L. & Nikolova, M. (2010). National Study of Nonprofit-Government Contracting: State Profiles. Washington, DC: Urban Institute.

Brilliant, E.L. (1990). *The United Way: Dilemmas of Organized Charity*. New York: Columbia University Press.

Chandler, S.M. & Pratt, R.C. (2011). *Backstage in a Bureaucracy: Politics and Pubic Service*. Honolulu, HI: University of Hawaii Press.

Child, C.D. & Gronbjerg, K.A. (2007). Nonprofit advocacy organizations: Their characteristics and activities. *Social Science Quarterly*, 88(1), 259–281.

Corporation for National and Community Service (2010). Volunteering in America 2010: National, State and City Information. http://www.volunteering in america.gov/assets/resources/IssueBriefFINALJune15.Pdf]Source: NCCS Business Master File 08/2011).

de Tocquille, A. (1945). *Democracy in America, 1935–1840*. Translated by Henry Reeve. NY: Alfred A. Knopf.

Eikenberry, A. & Kluver, J.D. (2004). The marketization of the nonprofit sector: Civil society at risk. *Public Administration Review*, 64(2), 132–140.

Frumkin, P. (2005). *On Being Nonprofit: A Conceptual and Policy Primer.* Cambridge, MA: Harvard University Press.

Guo, C. (2007). When government becomes the principal philanthropist: the effects of public funding on patterns of nonprofit governance. *Public Administration Review*, 67(3), 458–473.

Gibelman, M. & Gelman S.R. (2004). A loss of credibility: patterns of wrongdoing among nongovernmental organizations. *Voluntas: International Journal of Voluntary and Nonprofit Organizations*, 15, 335–381.

Hall, P.D. (1992). *Inventing the Nonprofit Sector and Other Essays on Philanthropy, Voluntarism, and Nonprofit Organizations*. Baltimore: Johns Hopkins University Press.

Hall, P.D. (2005). 'Historical Perspectives on Nonprofit Organizations in the United States.' In Robert D. Herman (ed.) *The Jossey-Bass Handbook of Nonprofit Leadership and Management*, 2nd edn. San Francisco, CA: Jossey-Bass. pp. 3–38.

Hall, P.D. (2006). *A Historical Overview of Philanthropy, Voluntary Association, and Nonprofit organizations in the United States, 1600-2000*. In W. W. Powell & R. Steinberg (eds) *The Nonprofit Sector: A Research Handbook* (2nd edn). New Haven, CT: Yale University Press, pp. 32–66.

Hoover, H. (1921). *American Individualism*. Garden City, NJ: The Country Life Press.

Independent Sector Newsletter (2011, September). *IS Connects*. Retrieved September, 2011 from *www.independentsector.org*.

Kaufman, J. (2002). *For the Common Good? American Civil Life and the Golden Age of Fraternity*. New York: Oxford Press.

Kettl, D. (2005). *The Global Public Management Revolution*, 2nd edn. Washington, D.C. Brookings Institution Press.

Kretzmann, J. and McKnight, J. (1993). *Building Communities from the Inside Out: A Path Toward Finding and Mobilizing A Community's Assets*. Chicago, IL: ACTA Publications.

LeRoux, K. (2007). Nonprofits as civic intermediaries: the role of community-based organizations in promoting political participation. *Urban Affairs Review*, 42(3), 410–422.

Marwell, N.P. (2007). *Bargaining for Brooklyn: Community Organizations in the Entrepreneurial City*. Chicago: University of Chicago Press.

Mosley, J.E. (2010). Organizational resources and environmental incentives: understanding the policy advocacy involvement of human service nonprofits. *Social Service Review*, March, 57–76.

National Center for Charitable Statistics (NCCS) (2009). Quick facts about nonprofits. Retrieved November 5, 2011 from http://urban.org.statistics.quickfacts.dfm.

O'Neill, M. (2009). Public Confidence in Charitable Nonprofits. *Nonprofit and Voluntary Sector Quarterly*, 38(2), 237–269. *The Independent Sector newsletter www.independentsector.org*. Retrieved September 25, 2011.

Ott, J.S. & Dicke, L.A. (eds) (2012). *The Nature of the Nonprofit Sector*, 2nd edn. Boulder, CO: Westview Press.

Panel on the Nonprofit Sector (October 2007). Principles for Good Governance and Ethical Practice. A Guide for Charities and Foundations Convened by Independent Sector, Washington, D.C.

Powell, W.W. and Steinberg, R. (eds) (2006). *The Nonprofit Sector: A Research Handbook*. 2nd edn. New Haven, CT: Yale University Press.

Putnam, R.D. (1993). *Making Democracy Work*. Princeton: Princeton University Press.

Putnam, R.D. (2000). *Bowling Alone: The Collapse and Renewal of American Community*. New York: Simon and Schuster.

Reis, T. & Clohesy, S. (1999). Unleashing New Resources and Entrepreneurship for the Common Good: A Scan, Synthesis, and Scenario for Action. Battle Creek, MI: W.K. Kellogg Foundation. http://www.wkkf.org/Pubs/PhilVol/ Pub592.pdf.

Salamon, L.M. (2002). *The State of Nonprofit America*. Washington, DC: Brookings Institution Press.

Smith, S.R. (2010a). Nonprofits and Public Administration: Reconciling Performance Management and Citizen Engagement. *American Review of Public Administration*, 40(2), 129–152.

Smith, S.R. (2010b). Nonprofit organizations and government: Implications for policy and practice. *Journal of Policy Analysis and Management*, 29(3), 621–644.

Smith, D.H. (2012). The impact of the voluntary sector on society. In Ott and Dicke, 2012. *The Nature of the Nonprofit Sector*, 2nd edn. Originally published in *Voluntary Action Research*. Lexington, MA: Lexington Books.

Suarez, D.F. (2009). Nonprofit advocacy and civic engagement on the internet. *Administration & Society*, 41(3), 267–289.

Tannebaum, N. & Reisch, M. (2001). From Charitable Volunteers to Architects of Social Welfare: A Brief History of Social Welfare. *Ongoing Magazine*, University of Michigan School of Social Work, Chapter 15.

Tschirhart, M. (2006). Nonprofit Membership Association. In W. W. Powell & R. Steinberg (eds) *The Nonprofit Sector: A Research Handbook*, 2nd edn. New Haven, CT: Yale University Press, pp. 523–541.

Tuennerman-Kaplan, L. (2001). *Helping Others, Helping Ourselves: Power, Giving and Community Identity in Cleveland, Ohio, 1880–1930*. Kent, OH: The Kent State University Press.

Van Til, J. (2005). Nonprofit organizations and social institutions. In R.D. Herman (ed.) *The Jossey-Bass Handbook of Nonprofit Leadership and Management*, 2nd edn. San Francisco, CA: Jossey-Bass, pp. 39–62.

Warner, A. G., Queen, S. A. & Harper, E. B. (1894). *American Charities and Social Work*. New York: J.J. Little and Ives, Company.

Warren, M.E. (2003). The political role of nonprofits in a democracy. *Society*, 45–51.

Worth, M. J. (2009). *Nonprofit Management. Principles and Practice*. Thousand Oaks, CA: Sage Press.

PART II

Human resource management and nonprofit effectiveness

4. Reviewing the literature on leadership in nonprofit organizations

John C. Ronquillo, Whitney E. Hein and Heather L. Carpenter

INTRODUCTION

An acute focus on the leadership of nonprofit organizations (NPOs) is unquestionably merited under the constant change that these organizations are subject to. The success or failure of the start-up, maintenance, operations and sustainability of NPOs is largely correlated to the leadership core – executives and boards of directors – and their ability or inability to execute their responsibilities in a way that gives their respective organizations the stability they need to serve those who benefit from their services (Golensky, 2011; see also Heimovics et al., 1995; Young et al., 1993). In the wake of global recession, the paucity of resources available to nonprofits has logically forced leaders to exercise the most creative and innovative of their abilities to procure the funding necessary to recruit and retain talented employees and to serve their clientele.

The scope of this chapter is to review the literature on leadership in nonprofit organizations, the bulk of which will focus largely on select literature that has been produced over the past two decades. Literature has been drawn from various sources, including popular press publications as well as scholarly articles that span various disciplines. Though the scope of the chapter is simple, a challenge is clearly present in that the concept of leadership is very subjective and its literature voluminous, such that the profusion of nonprofit leadership literature is impossible to cover in a single chapter. For example, a search of the term 'leadership' in top nonprofit journals *Nonprofit and Voluntary Sector Quarterly* and *Nonprofit Management and Leadership* yields over 800 publications (including book reviews) in each journal, with *Voluntas* yielding approximately 200 publications addressing some element of leadership. Though the nonprofit leadership literature expands well beyond the pages of these journals, it is observably apparent that the topic is not unfamiliar among practitioners and academicians. It is, in essence, one of the most critical elements of the nonprofit sector as a whole.

The chapter proceeds as follows. We provide an introduction to nonprofit leadership through three interdisciplinary streams. Sections on various themes are then presented as emerging areas of nonprofit leadership as they relate to research. First, a section on the highly debated leadership deficit in nonprofit organizations is presented, followed by a section on educational approaches to nonprofit leadership. Next, a section on the reciprocity of leadership tactics between business and nonprofit organizations is presented, followed by a section on leading boards and volunteers. The chapter concludes with a brief summary of other volumes with significant treatment of issues in nonprofit leadership that can serve as additional resources to the reader.

INTERDISCIPLINARY VIEWS APPLIED TO LEADERSHIP IN THE NONPROFIT SECTOR

Perceptions of the Nonprofit Sector

Is leadership in the nonprofit sector so different from leadership in commercial firms and government organizations that it needs a distinction? Rost (1991) describes leadership studies as being interdisciplinary in nature, but he discredits leadership scholars who study one discipline. He states, 'These one-discipline scholars are easily recognized because they almost always put an adjective in front of the word leadership' (p. 19). There is intellectual merit behind this argument; however, various interdisciplinary views of leadership can be utilized for researching leadership in the nonprofit sector. Frumkin (2002) highlighted three important differences between nonprofit organizations and their public and private counterparts: '1) they do not coerce participation; 2) they operate without distributing profits to stakeholders; and 3) they exist without simple and clear lines of ownership and accountability … these structural features give these entities a set of unique advantages that position them to perform important societal functions neither government nor the market is able to match' (p. 3). These points underline that there are both potentially significant as well as nuanced differences in leadership traits among leaders in these three sectors. There are common stereotypes of the nonprofit sector that can also affect researchers' and practitioners' perceptions of leadership in the nonprofit sector. Many observers perceive nonprofits to generate little revenue, and to operate with only a volunteer staff (Carson, 2002). Additionally, donors have created the perception that effective nonprofits must have very small administrative overhead costs, despite research conducted by the Urban Institute's Nonprofit Overhead Cost Project (Hagar et al., 2004) finding otherwise, as 'inadequate infrastructure compromises organizational effectiveness' (p. 1). Nonprofits are also constantly scrutinized in the media, and in many instances for negative reasons including scandal, unresolved donor promises or poor leadership (Carson, 2002).

A Historical Perspective

Many of the early leadership scholars came to view leadership by studying historical and political leaders. For example, one of the earliest scholars in the leadership studies field, James McGregor Burns (1978), a political scientist, started out as a presidential biographer and eventually became one of the first social scientists to develop the distinguishing characteristics of the widely studied topics of transformational and transactional leadership (Sorenson, 2000; Ronquillo, 2011). Over time, as the field of leadership studies evolved, scholars created other new definitions of leadership and focused more on the leadership process. Scholars began using scientific methods of observing, testing and experimenting for their leadership theories (Antonakis et al., 2004).

Leadership was first studied by observing the personal traits and qualities of actual leaders. This technique is often associated with the Great Man Theory popularized by Scottish writer Thomas Carlyle, wherein individuals used their personal charisma, intelligence, wisdom or power in a way that had a significant historical impact (Antonakis et al., 2004). As an example, Dym and Hutson (2005) suggest Ghandi, Martin Luther King, Jr., Winston Churchill and Franklin D. Roosevelt to be transformative and visionary leaders whose leadership 'was based on ethical and national ideals and communicated in brilliant rhetoric and through acts of individual courage' (p. 42). These leaders, the authors claim, embodied their message in ways that magnified their credibility and attractiveness. 'What is more, they had an intuitive grasp of what their followers would and could do, a strategic empathy, if you will' (Dym and Hutson, 2005, p. 42).

Scholars have focused on reporting key qualities and traits of nonprofit leaders. For example, being an 'inspiring' leader is a very common trait among nonprofit founders and leaders (Nanus and Dobbs, 1999). Some of the earliest nonprofits in the United States (US) were churches and universities, predominantly run by men. For example, Harvard University is listed as one of the first nonprofit organizations in the US (Salamon, 1998). Trade publications such as the *Nonprofit Times* releases a list of the top 50 leaders in the nonprofit sector each year (see The NPT 2007 Power and Influence

Top 50, 2007). Each of these leaders are nominated and voted on by committees of other well-known leaders in the nonprofit sector. Consequently, 20 out of the 50 chosen leaders are women, and all of the leaders come from well-known large institutions. In 2007, a former chief executive officer (CEO) of the American Red Cross was chosen for the list, but was subsequently removed from his post in the organization after engaging in a personal relationship with a married subordinate employee (Williams, 2007). He was a widely respected leader in the nonprofit sector and his removal further amplified the public's negative perception of the nonprofit sector as a whole.

In contrast, nonprofit scholars have done little to be specific about the process in which they study leadership in the nonprofit sector. Herman and Renz (1998), for example, study nonprofit effectiveness, but do so from an organizational perspective and do not explicitly study leadership. Little has been done to highlight the processes or scientific nature of leadership studies in the nonprofit sector. As an example, in addressing the topics of servant, transformational and transactional leadership, Ronquillo (2011) notes that there has been little research – empirical or otherwise – on transformational leadership in nonprofit organizations. He cites Riggio, Bass and Orr (2004) who highlight this particularly in contrast to the significant research that has investigated transformational leadership in for-profit companies, government, military and educational institutions (Bass, 1998). Increased interest in nonprofit organizations as a field of research, however, will more than likely provide ample opportunities for this to change.

A Socio-cultural Perspective

In the socio-cultural view of leadership, theories are constructed by studying cultures. Schein (2004) believes managers maintain the culture of an organization while leaders change culture, thus noting also that leaders and managers are not necessarily synonymous. He also believes that leaders create and change culture based on their own assumptions and beliefs, and therefore, leadership and culture are intertwined. Additionally, Geertz (1973) believes that researchers' own interpretation of the world has an impact on how they study leadership. Taking Geertz's view into consideration, all individuals view leadership differently.

Looking back at the common perceptions of the nonprofit sector, nonprofit scholars study leadership through a unique lens. In utilizing the socio-cultural view of leadership, scholars argue that leadership in the nonprofit sector is different due to the cultural differences in nonprofits versus for-profits. Nanus and Dobbs (1999) state, 'The success of a nonprofit organization is measured not in profits or fulfillment of legislative intent but in terms of social good' (p. 5). They then go on to explain how many complexities to exercising nonprofit leadership exist due to diverse funding sources, constituencies and values-driven organizations. Specifically, they cite four suggestions nonprofit leaders need to focus on:

> 1) Inside the organization, where the leader interacts with the board, staff, and volunteers to inspire, encourage, enthuse, and empower them;
> 2) Outside the organization, where the leader seeks assistance or support from donors, grantmakers, potential allies, the media or other leaders in the business or public sectors;
> 3) On present operations, where the leader is concerned about the quality of services to clients and the community and also organizational structures, information systems, and other aspects of organizational effectiveness.
> 4) On future possibilities, where the leader anticipates trends and developments that are likely to have important impactions for the future direction of the organization. (Nanus and Dobbs, 1999, p. 17)

King (2004) argues that nonprofit leaders must also exercise social capital as a 'set of social resources, which encompasses relationships, trust, norms, and values' in order to be successful at carrying out the functions in a nonprofit organization (p. 471). This idea relates well to Schein's (2004) interdisciplinary view of leadership and culture. Though this may be the case, Carson (2002) feels that many of the perceptions of the nonprofit sector are misconstrued, which has an effect on how leadership research is conducted in the field. Carson states:

> The nonprofit sector is at a critical crossroads. It has an image problem that masks an even larger problem of purpose and meaning. Others are inaccurately defining the nonprofit sector, and if this is not corrected, it will continue to undermine the public's trust and confidence and, possibly, the participatory nature of our democracy. (p. 435)

A Political and Power-oriented Perspective

In the political and power-oriented view of leadership, researchers cannot help but to allow subjectivism – their personal bias, interests and privilege – when studying and evaluating leadership. Habermas (1968) frowns upon the socio-cultural and historical views of leadership because these views credit or discredit certain populations. He argues that researchers need to look at their own process of conducting research and studying leadership, and understand what motivates them to conduct this research.

The political and power-oriented view of leadership reveals implications for researching leadership in the nonprofit sector. This view of leadership brings up a many potential research questions and looks beyond the traditional method of studying leadership in the nonprofit sector. Firstly, to what degree is being 'inspiring' a trait that leaders must have in the nonprofit sector? Does inspiration promote overall effectiveness in the organization? Secondly, do lists like the *Nonprofit Times* Top 50 leaders promote the ideal of what a nonprofit leader should aspire to be? Thirdly, who are the scholars studying nonprofit leadership? Do they accurately represent the nonprofit sector, taking into consideration the diversity of all the types of organizations and leaders throughout the sector? Nonprofit scholars should make a significant effort to focus more on the process of researching leadership in the nonprofit sector and what implications their research has in shaping perceptions.

Stephenson (2007) explains how nonprofit leaders can use ethical imagination to 'identify permanent moral truths to guide their choice making' (p. 275). Although moral truths relate to the socio-cultural view of leadership, Stephenson further states that leaders should 'chart courses on the basis of something more than their tax status or operating environments' and leaders should lead 'on a conceptual basis other than simply adopting for-profit organization premises and practices' (p. 275). Stephenson advocates for leaders to challenge norms of the sector and do something different, beyond the status quo. Though researchers should look into emerging fields like leadership studies when studying leadership in the nonprofit sector, they should remain as objective as possible and not immediately accept the common perceptions, or misperceptions, of the nonprofit sector when conducting research.

EMERGING STREAMS OF LITERATURE ON NONPROFIT LEADERSHIP

A Leadership Deficit?

Beyond the element of resource scarcity, there exists also a debate among scholars and practitioners of a pending leadership deficit in the nonprofit sector. In a 2006 issue of the *Stanford Social Innovation Review*, Tom Tierney, chairman and co-founder of the Bridgespan Group, wrote that over the next decade the nonprofit sector must find 640 000 new executives to fill leadership positions left vacant by retiring baby boomers. He argued that in addition to the money NPOs need to survive, leadership is a second crucial component, and that there is a lack of qualified candidates. Tierney illustrated that the 'baby echo' population is not large enough to replace the baby boomers properly in the workplace due to the exponential growth of the nonprofit sector in general. His position is that society relies heavily on the nonprofit sector and large NPOs are growing at a faster rate than smaller NPOs, which in turn creates a problem because large NPOs have the greatest need for stronger leadership. Tierney states that if the nonprofit sector continues to grow, the number of executives needed could jump from 640 000 to 1 250 000. He suggests that time and money need to be invested in leadership programs, that leaders need to be generously compensated, and that NPOs should explore new talent pools for recruiting (Tierney, 2006).

Paul Light supports Tierney's argument in a back-and-forth opinion piece with his twin brother and nonprofit consultant, Mark Light, arguing the legitimacy of the supposed leadership deficit (Light and Light, 2006). Paul Light argues that the leadership deficit is a valid concern, while Mark Light argues that the potential of a future leadership deficit is not a problem that needs to be addressed now, but rather the focus should be placed on training and retaining current leaders. Only one in three executive directors plan on having the same job in the next five years, for reasons such as high rates of burnout in the workplace, poor executive–board relations, and the lure of better-paying jobs in other sectors with benefits (Bell et al., 2006). There is a clear need for an investment in building more effective organizations and a need for the next generation to be trained to affront the challenges of nonprofit work and to provide effective leadership (Light and Light, 2006).

Johnson (2009) also argues against the idea that the leadership deficit is an impending crisis. Although the lack of top executive leaders is a valid concern, she states that trends suggest that market and organizational adjustment will mitigate the overall deficit. She states:

> More expensive leadership may cause other organizations to merge in order to achieve greater economies of scale of leadership talent … Furthermore, with top leadership more expensive, funders will have greater incentives to pursue what has been termed venture or high-engagement philanthropy that ties management assistance to financial support. At the same time, on the supply side, nonprofit leaders will be lured to the market by rising wages, perhaps from other sectors, or perhaps by delaying retirement. (p. 290)

Other factors that will help to alleviate the loss of the baby boomer generation are an increased number of women with higher education degrees, young workers with formal education in nonprofit management, the ability to recruit from other sectors, and the fact that more retired baby boomers will lead to more potential volunteers.

An Educational Approach to Leadership

In addition to Johnson's (2009) assertion of an increased number of women with higher education degrees and more young workers with formal training in nonprofit management, the education element of leadership merits some examination. 'A question of leadership' by Altman et al. (2004) is a short piece that focuses on the question of whether for-profit and nonprofit investment in leadership development initiatives produce the desired outcomes of building leadership potential in individuals. A key challenge for organizations is to design evaluations that look at both short- and long-term effects of leadership development. The authors state that leaders need to identify desired outcomes and design leadership development initiatives to reach these outcomes. Leaders must not forget to factor in external forces, and they should model leadership development in a way that shows how these initiatives will contribute to specific organizational goals. The authors recommend that NPOs should take a field-wide approach to evaluating leadership development by learning through multiple programs.

Austin et al. (2011) focus on a model training program designed to build managerial leadership skills, and how this program was subsequently implemented. A group of directors from nonprofit human service organizations partnered with the University of California, Berkeley, to design and implement this program. The design and implementation of the training had four basic differences from alternative training methods, which were:

1. Program participants were involved in program designs.
2. Participants learned about agreed-upon agency issues that focused on management and leadership.
3. The training was participant-centered and used individual coaching.
4. The training was outcome-focused.

The training was based on two goals, which were:

1. To build individual capacities to enable managers to shift from a reactive management style to managerial leadership based on the vision of the organization.
2. To train managers to promote continuous improvement in their organizations.

The executive directors of the organization with involved participants were pleased with the outcome of the training. Program facilitators noted that the two most successful outcomes were that participants understood their management role and identity, and that participants shifted from a crisis management approach to a managerial leadership approach.

Paton, Mordaunt and Cornforth (2007) address the perceived problem that nonprofit management education is outdated and not keeping pace with changes in the nonprofit sector. The authors argue that these changes – strengthening relationships with government, cross-sector delivery of public services and shifts in funding sources – have many implications. There is a lack of quality leadership, there is more transfer between sectors, and more funding is coming from entrepreneurial sources rather than donations. These developments prompt the authors to propose a change in learning development in the nonprofit sector. There is a need for more staff training and development that is integrated across many programs and agencies, that is blended and includes the use of technology, and development programs should be structured, part-time and 'self-authoring' to be more geared towards the promotion of leadership in adults. This article examined other literature on the subject and drew on the authors' personal experience from working in nonprofit management and education programs in the United Kingdom.

Genis (2008) argues that many management support organizations (MSOs) and universities fall short when developing nonprofit leaders. Genis argues that most leadership programs are geared toward new executive directors and therefore focus more on the basic managerial concepts rather than leadership development. Two shifts are needed in order to rectify this: (1) more focus on building leadership competencies instead of managerial skills; and (2) best practices of adult learning should be used in leadership development. The author argues that all leadership programs should have a structure that allows time for self-reflection and self-awareness, individualized learning objectives and plans, and differentiating between good and great performance, and they should allow growth and development to occur on the job. In addition to these ideas, the author recommends several strategies for foundations that plan to fund leadership development programs in the nonprofit sector. These recommendations include to shift funding to new generations of leaders, to encourage boards to support leadership development, to support top performing leaders and to recognize potential executive coaching.

Business Perspectives of Nonprofit Leadership

Drucker (1989) put forth several lessons that business can learn from nonprofits. The fact that nonprofits are led by a mission and requirements to reach that mission puts the focus of the organization on action rather than a bottom line. This can also avoid the splintering effect that organizations without a clear mission sometimes face. Nonprofits usually start with the community to form their goals, while for-profits use their internal environment to set goals. Another lesson involves nonprofits' effective use of boards, where there is usually a high level of accountability between boards and CEOs since they can both review each other's performance. Another lesson that can be learned is nonprofits' use of volunteers. Volunteers are often professionals and function more as unpaid staff. Nonprofits who manage volunteers well give them clear objectives, high demands of accountability and place them in positions that suit them best. Drucker observed that it is important for people to 'know their purpose', and volunteering in the nonprofit sector feeds that need more so than working for a business trying to beat the bottom line. People thrive on responsibility and mission, and nonprofits tend to offer fulfilment in those areas more so than simply meeting the bottom line in the for-profit world.

Rierson and Miller (2006) state that the key difference in for-profits and nonprofits is that NPOs have people who work with them and not for them. A nonprofit organization's main objective is sustainability, not profit, and decisions are made with the idea of long-term capacity building. These key features of nonprofits naturally lead to the idea of focusing more on employees and volunteers. Miller recommends that if an agency relies heavily on volunteers, those people should be screened and selected with care. Volunteers should share the same vision and work ethic as the organization. Leaders of nonprofits should draw upon a range of experience and life skills to help manage and lead workers and volunteers in a nonprofit.

Suarez (2010) discusses the idea that the nonprofit sector is facing both a potential leadership deficit and increasing pressure to become more efficient and to act more businesslike. He focuses his article on research and interviews with 200 nonprofit executives in California. He discovered that many leaders advanced to their positions with only their management background, developed largely outside of the nonprofit sector. He also explores the question of how much nonprofit ethics and dedication to the nonprofit sector matter in leadership. He found that businesslike traits are good for the emerging culture of nonprofit management but have not yet taken the place of traditional leadership in nonprofits. From the institutional viewpoint of leadership, Suarez states that nonprofit executives must be credible with many groups of people including clientele, donors, staff and volunteers, among others. Most of this credibility has little to do with business skills. Leaders with strong business backgrounds also exaggerate isomorphism in the nonprofit sector.

The study also looked into the professional backgrounds and work experience of current nonprofit leaders. In general, more degree programs focus specifically on nonprofit managemt, but most current leaders have advanced degrees in something other than management. In fact, 56 percent of leaders had no management background at all. Suarez concludes that leadership in the nonprofit sector must require more than just management skills. He also found that although most leaders had experience in the nonprofit sector, more than half have experience in business and about half have experience in government. Sixty percent of leaders, however, were hired from within and nonprofit experience does matter in terms of having legitimacy and credibility in the sector. An overall takeaway is that having nonprofit experience is the main pathway to a leadership position in the field.

Suarez (2010) outlines four different kinds of nonprofit leaders and states that the shift towards more businesslike practices may begin to be reflected in the hiring process. The first kind of leader is the Nonprofit Lifer who is 'high nonprofit and low management'. This leader recognizes a social problem and is moved to fix it. 'Lifers' can't visualize answers to these social problems being fixed through any sector other than the nonprofit sector. The second kind of leader is the Substantive Expert who is 'low nonprofit and high management'. These leaders have training in specific areas such as social work or healthcare and fell into management roles in the nonprofit sector. There is no drive from nonprofit ethic, per se. The third kind of leader is the Social Entrepreneur, who is 'high nonprofit, high management'. This leader approaches nonprofit work with a focus on management and innovation, with an interest in cost and finance. They have vast substantive knowledge but are usually focused on business. They are dedicated to nonprofits but with a management orientation. The fourth kind of leader is the Professional Administrator who is 'low nonprofit, high management'. These leaders put business first and have the willingness to work in all sectors. They are similar to social entrepreneurs but generally lack the nonprofit focus.

The basic conclusion that Suarez comes to is that nonprofit leaders are skilled professionals but currently do not necessarily possess an appropriate background in management. The impending loss of the baby boomer generation and the evolving nonprofit sector leave room for more leaders with management skills in the future.

Boards and Volunteers

Employee Self-Leadership: Enhancing the Effectiveness of Nonprofits by Neck, Ashcraft and VanSandt (1998) discusses the idea that nonprofits often have a top-down approach to leadership that does not develop leadership capabilities in all levels of the organization. The authors present a counter-view that NPOs should focus more on developing self-leadership skills in both paid workers and volunteers. Self-leadership is closely tied to the concepts of self-regulation and self-management, and allows workers to participate more by influencing management decision-making. By drawing on arguments from several other scholars (Drucker, 1989, 1990; Powell, 1995; Young, 1993) the authors highlight three main aspects that are unique to NPOs and how self-leadership would lessen these challenges:

1. Nonprofits have a difficult task evaluating accomplishments compared to for-profits. Employees need to be self-motivated to monitor their own activities.
2. Nonprofits are both value-based and market-driven. Employees must have a strong sense of self within the organization to ensure it stays true to its mission and stays competitive in the market.
3. Nonprofits rely heavily on volunteers and employees have no real authority over them. To compound this issue, many executive directors of non-profits do not last more than a few years in an organization, so strong, self-motivated and self-leading staff and volunteers are crucial.

The authors argue that implementing self-leadership development in all levels of an NPO will result in a positive impact on both the behaviors and the cognition of workers and therefore will have a positive effect on the overall effectiveness of the organization.

Vandeventer (2011) argues that 'nonprofits must have influential board members who connect them to the community they serve' (p. 25). He uses the term 'civic reach' to signify that board members should be connected to the community and other organizations and should be tasked with linking nonprofits with for-profits that make an effort to participate in corporate social responsibility, hence linking nonprofits with donor funds. Vanderventer states that the social sector is the weakest of the three sectors with regard to power and money, and that a well-connected board can help compensate for that weakness. Vanderventer lists three basic factors that a board member with civic reach should have:

1. Personal and professional prestige.
2. Local knowledge.
3. Having or being able to form community or worldwide connections.

Other qualities that improve board member performance include having a good sense of the external environment, being able to advance or defend the

NPO's mission, having the ability to reach the broader public and having inside access to power. Vanderventer's main takeaway is that board members should have actual and real influence that can help the organization.

Smith and Shen (1996) conducted an empirical study of volunteer-managed NPOs and examined the factors that are related to the reputational effectiveness of volunteer managed NPOs. The study tested the following factors: (1) the nature of the group; (2) the governance within the NPO; and (3) the degree of formalization. In terms of having a reputation of effectiveness, the nature of the group was found to be significant, especially in terms of the size and age of the NPO, as well as focusing services on outside clients to increase visibility in the community. The governance of the organization affected reputation the most. Having officers, boards and committees were found to be significant, but having large boards and active committees with nominating committees and powerful committee chairs are even more important. Staff leadership was not found to be relevant. The third factor, the degree of formalization, was also found to be significant, especially when it came to mission statement, bylaws and member lists. The authors make a number of recommendations on how to increase reputational effectiveness in volunteer-managed NPOs, but only three that have to do with leadership. The recommendations include having more standard officers in the governance structure, having a developed board of directors and having a developed committee structure.

McClusky (2002) focuses on a framework that explores factors affecting the appropriate division of roles among boards, executives, staff and volunteers in nonprofit organizations. He presents a counterpoint to the idea that there can be a 'one-size' governance model for all NPOs. Unlike the well-known framework conceptualized by Houle (1960, 1989) and formalized by the National Center for Nonprofit Boards, McClusky believes that very few responsibilities can be universally assigned to one section of the NPO, the exception being that governance should always be the responsibility of the volunteer board of directors. The author outlines seven key factors that affect the division of roles in an NPO:

1. The size of the NPO budget, staff, and board.
2. The number of active volunteers and, more importantly, the range of roles that these volunteers perform.
3. The stage of the NPO's life cycle.
4. The level of trust between the executive director and the board, which McClusky argues is complex and fluid.
5. Executive transition (similar to the previous factor).
6. The pressure of organizational crisis, which may require an NPO to reconfigure internally more than once.

7. Environmental factors such as change in funding and pressure towards merger or collaboration.

One of the most important ideas highlighted in McClusky's analysis is that policy setting and boundary setting between the board and the staff are crucial. McClusky also stresses that his model is fluid and complex and should be explored more thoroughly.

Eisner et al. (2009) explore the idea of the importance of utilizing volunteers adequately in the nonprofit sector. The authors argue that most CEOs do not lead volunteers well, and state that one-third of the people who volunteer do not return to the same organization two years in a row. In a time when money is tight and the supposed leadership crisis is looming with more baby boomers retiring, managers must do a better job at leading volunteers. Many volunteers offer expertise, time, passion, the ability to get people to donate and the willingness to give personal donations. The reasons that the authors give as to why they are not returning are: skills are not matched with assignments, failure to recognize volunteer contributions, not measuring the value of volunteers, failing to train and invest in volunteers and staff, and failing to provide strong leadership. The suggestions given to remedy these problems are to rethink volunteer roles, assign appropriate tasks, create bonding experiences, support training of volunteers, incorporate the use of new technologies for matching volunteers to organizations, and to develop strategic plans to include volunteers. The authors argue that NPOs that do not utilize the wealth that exists in volunteers and lead them well will be at a disadvantage compared to other NPOs who lead volunteers successfully.

Perkins and Poole (1996) focus on a case study of an all-volunteer fire department, pseudonymously called the Village Volunteer Fire Department (VVFD), and explore the idea that the concept of oligarchy is useful in understanding leadership, membership participation and change in all volunteer-managed NPOS. The authors' method for this study combines participant analysis at the VVFD and draws from other literature (Michels, 1959; Pearce, 1980). Michels (1959) argues that oligarchies emerged to make democracies able to work efficiently without the presence of observable rewards. Pearce (1980) argues that without employee leaders there is no coercive power and therefore no real rewards. After lengthy analysis of the VVFD and a review of the literature, Perkins and Poole make two conclusions. Firstly, they determine that rewards do not need to be obvious before leadership emerges, and that sometimes power is reward enough. Leadership can be spontaneous and later become structural. Secondly, they find 'rewards' to be a problematic term and they do not agree with Pearce that an employed leader is needed to offer rewards that can be created or discovered by non-employed leaders. Examples of these rewards are social status and power: power to affect the culture of the organization and the ability to affect who participates.

Additional Resources

In addition to the select pieces reviewed here, there are a number of edited volumes that may also prove useful in finding more literature on nonprofit leadership. Agard's (2011) recent two-volume reference *Leadership in Nonprofit Organizations* includes 96 chapters over eight sections on various issues and elements of leadership. The volume starts with an overview of the nonprofit and philanthropic sector and progresses to sections on the history of the nonprofit and philanthropic sector, common interest areas of nonprofits and foundations, and nonprofit organizations and historically disenfranchised groups, before sections on leading nonprofit organization and grant-making foundations, leadership of nonprofits and the individual, and ethics and social responsibility in the nonprofit world are presented. Chapters include topics such as basic skills of nonprofit leadership (Hoefer, 2011), roles responsibilities and characteristics of nonprofit leadership (Carlson and Schneiter, 2011), leading volunteers in nonprofit organizations (Rehnborg et al., 2011) and human resource leadership and management (Word, 2011). Additionally, there are chapters on financial issues for leaders (Couturier, 2011), leading nonprofit partnerships with government (Ramanath, 2011) and the role of nonprofit leaders in setting values, vision and the mission for the organizations (Alaimo, 2011).

Herman & Associates' (2005) volume *The Jossey-Bass Handbook of Nonprofit Leadership and Management* also provides a section on key leadership issues, with chapters on board leadership and development (Axelrod, 2005), executive leadership (Herman and Heimovics, 2005), strategic planning approaches for nonprofits (Bryson, 2005), ethical nonprofit management (Jeavons, 2005), nonprofit lobbying (Smucker, 2005), and strategic alliances (Yankey and Willen, 2005).

Carver's (2006) *Boards that Make a Difference*, as the title indicates, focuses on board governance and leadership of nonprofit organizations. Carver details the various types of boards along with their 'predicted difficulties' and the need for more precise principles of governance. Additionally, he examines board policy, organizational results, administrative and programmatic issues, relationships between boards and staff, discipline issues and mission orientation. McNamara's (2008) *Field Guide to Leadership and Supervision for Nonprofit Staff* also serves as a useful, practical guide to leading nonprofit organizations. The topics covered include the basic elements of what nonprofits are and how they work; the roles of the board, CEO and staff; and how to lead and manage oneself, employees, volunteers, teams and organizations as a whole. Perhaps most germane to the topic presented in this chapter is McNamara's bibliography of scholarly articles, trade publications and professional reports on boards of directors, capacity building, consulting, financial management, fundraising, marketing, program evaluation, strategic planning and, of course, leadership.

CONCLUSION

This chapter details only a mere sampling of the profusion of nonprofit leadership literature that has been produced over the past several decades. A mission orientation versus a profit orientation within organizations provides significant and unique challenges that have rendered the topic of nonprofit leadership to be one of considerably increasing importance. Theories and perceptions are often divergent, but this variation on viewpoints only provides additional intellectual fodder for research in this area to continue. No single chapter can adequately cover the extant literature on nonprofit leadership, and certainly, no attempt is made here. The research that is covered, however, is timely, relevant and illustrates some of the more critical topics in the field. Our work here, if anything, is a foundation to build upon.

REFERENCES

Agard, K.A. (ed.) (2011). *Leadership in Nonprofit Organizations: A Reference Handbook*. Thousand Oaks, CA: Sage.

Alaimo, S.P. (2011). Role of nonprofit leaders in setting the values, vision, and mission of the organization. In Agard, K.A. (ed.), *Leadership in Nonprofit Organizations, Vol. 2*. Thousand Oaks, CA: Sage, 595–602.

Altman, D., Kelly-Radford, L., Reinelt, C. & Meehan, D. (2004). A question of leadership: what are the key challenges that for-profit and nonprofit organizations face in evaluating leadership development? *Leadership in Action*, 23(6), 13–14.

Antonakis, J., Cianciolo, A.T. & Sternberg, R.J. (2004). *The Nature of Leadership*. Thousand Oaks, CA: Sage.

Austin, M.J., Regan, K., Samples, M.W., Schwartz, S.L. & Carnochan, S. (2011). Building managerial and organizational capacity in nonprofit human service organizations through a leadership development program. *Administration in Social Work*, 35(3), 258–281.

Axelrod, N.R. (2005). Board Leadership and Development. In Herman, R.D. & Associates. *The Jossey-Bass Handbook of Nonprofit Leadership and Management*, 2nd edn. San Francisco, CA: Jossey-Bass, pp. 131–152.

Bass, B.M. (1998). *Transformational Leadership: Industrial, Military, and Educational Impact.* Mahwah, NJ: Erlbaum.

Bell, J., Moyers, R., Wolfred, T., & D'Silva, N. (2006). Daring to lead 2006: a national study of nonprofit executive leadership. http://www.compasspoint.org/assets/194_daringtolead06final.pdf, accessed December 15, 2007.

Bryson, J.M. (2005). The strategy change cycle: an effective strategic planning approach for nonprofit organizations. In Herman, R.D. & Associates. *The Jossey-Bass Handbook of Nonprofit Leadership and Management*, 2nd edn. San Francisco, CA: Jossey-Bass, pp. 171–203.

Burns, J.M. (1978). *Leadership.* New York: HarperCollins.

Carlson, K.A. & Schneiter, S. (2011). Roles, responsibilities, and characteristics of nonprofit leadership. In Agard, K.A. (ed.), *Leadership in Nonprofit Organizations, Vol. 1.* Thousand Oaks, CA: Sage, pp. 329–336.

Carson, E.D. (2002). Public expectations and nonprofit sector realities: a growing divide with disastrous consequences. *Nonprofit and Voluntary Sector Quarterly*, 31, 429–436.

Carver, J. (2006). *Boards That Make a Difference: A New Design for Leadership in Nonprofit and Public Organizations*, 3rd edn. San Francisco, CA: Jossey-Bass.

Couturier, J. (2011). Financial Issues for Leaders. In Agard, K.A. (ed.), *Leadership in Nonprofit Organizations, Vol. 1.* Thousand Oaks, CA: Sage, pp. 412–421.

Drucker, P.F. (1989). What business can learn from nonprofits. *Harvard Business Review*, July–August, 88–93.

Drucker, P.F. (1990). *Managing the Nonprofit Organization: Principles and Practices.* New York: HarperCollins.

Dym, B. & Hutson, H. (2005). *Leadership in Nonprofit Organizations.* Thousand Oaks, CA: Sage.

Eisner, D., Grimm Jr, R.T., Maynard, S. & Washburn, S. (2009). The new volunteer workforce. *Stanford Social Innovation Review*, 7(1), 32–37.

Frumkin, P. (2002). *On Being Nonprofit.* Cambridge, MA: Harvard University Press.

Geertz, C. (1973). *The Interpretation of Cultures.* New York, NY: Basic Books.

Genis, M. (2008). So many leadership programs, so little change: why many leadership development efforts fall short. *Journal for Nonprofit Management*, 12(1), 32–40.

Golensky, M. (2011). *Strategic Leadership and Management in Nonprofit Organizations.* Chicago, IL: Lyceum Books.

Habermas, J. (1968). *Knowledge and Human Interests.* Boston, MA: Beacon Press.

Hagar, M., Pollack, T., Wing, K. & Roney, P.M. (2004). Getting what we pay for. August, http://www.urban.org/uploadedpdf/311044_NOCP_3.pdf, accessed November 15, 2011.

Heimovics, R.D., Herman, R.D. & Jurkiewicz, C.L. (1995). The political dimension of effective nonprofit executive leadership. *Nonprofit Management and Leadership*, 5(3), 233–248.

Herman, R.D. & Renz, D.O. (1998). Nonprofit organizational effectiveness: contrasts between especially effective and less effective organizations. *Nonprofit and Voluntary Sector Quarterly*, 9(1), 23–38.

Herman, R.D. & Associates (2005). *The Jossey-Bass Handbook of Nonprofit Leadership and Management*, 2nd edn. San Francisco, CA: Jossey-Bass.

Herman, R.D. & Heimovics, R.D. (2005). Executive leadership. In Herman, R.D. & Associates (ed.), *The Jossey-Bass Handbook of Nonprofit Leadership and Management*, 2nd edn. San Francisco, CA: Jossey-Bass, pp. 153–170.

Hoefer, R. (2011). Basic skills of nonprofit leadership. In Agard, K.A. (ed.), *Leadership in Nonprofit Organizations, Vol. 1.* Thousand Oaks, CA: Sage, pp. 321–328.

Houle, C.O. (1960). *The Effective Board.* New York: New York Association Press.

Houle, C.O. (1989). *Governing Boards: Their Nature and Nurture.* San Francisco, CA: Jossey-Bass.

Jeavons, T.H. (2005). Ethical nonprofit management. In Herman, R.D. & Associates (ed.), *The Jossey-Bass Handbook of Nonprofit Leadership and Management*, 2nd edn. San Francisco, CA: Jossey-Bass, 204–229.

Johnson, J.L. (2009). The nonprofit leadership deficit: a case for more optimism. *Nonprofit Management and Leadership*, 19(3), 285–304.

King, N.K. (2004). Social capital and nonprofit leaders. *Nonprofit Management and Leadership*, 14, 471–483.

Light, M. & Light, P. (2006). Which light is right? The impending leadership deficit crisis. *Nonprofit Quarterly*, Fall, 70–73.

McClusky, J.E. (2002). Re-thinking nonprofit organization governance: implications for management and leadership. *International Journal of Public Administration*, 25(4), 539–559.

McNamara, C. (2008). *Field Guide to Leadership and Supervision for Nonprofit Staff.* Minneapolis, MN: Authenticity Consulting, LLC.

Michels, R. (1959). *Political Parties.* New York: Dover.

Nanus, B. & Dobbs, S.M. (1999). *Leaders Who Make a Difference.* San Francisco, CA: Jossey-Bass.

Neck, C.P., Ashcraft, R.F. & VanSandt, C.V. (1998). Employee self-leadership: enhancing the effectiveness of nonprofits. *International Journal of Organization Theory & Behavior*, 1(4), 521–551.

Nonprofit Times (2007). The NPT 2007 Power & Influence Top 50. August. http://www.nptimes.com/07Aug/070801Special%20Report.pdf, accessed November 15, 2011.

Paton, R., Mordaunt, J. & Cornforth, C. (2007). Beyond nonprofit management education: leadership development in a time of blurred boundaries and distributed learning. *Nonprofit and Voluntary Sector Quarterly*, Supplement, 36(4), 148S–162S.

Pearce, J.L. (1980). Apathy or self-interest? The volunteer's avoidance of leadership roles. *Nonprofit and Voluntary Sector Quarterly*, 9(1), 85–94.

Perkins, K.B. & Poole, D.G. (1996). Oligarchy and adaptation to mass society in an all-volunteer organization: implications for understanding leadership, participation, and change. *Nonprofit and Voluntary Sector Quarterly*, 25(1), 73–88.

Powell, J.L. (1995). *Pathways to Leadership.* San Francisco, CA: Jossey-Bass.

Ramanath, R. (2011). Leading nonprofit partnerships with government. In Agard, K.A. (ed.), *Leadership in Nonprofit Organizations, Vol. 2.* Thousand Oaks, CA: Sage, pp. 530–539.

Rehnborg, S.J., Poole, D.L. & Roemer, M.K. (2011). Leading Volunteers in Nonprofit Organziations. In Agard, K.A. (ed.), *Leadership in Nonprofit Organizations, Vol. 1*. Thousand Oaks, CA: Sage, pp. 354–366.

Rierson, B. & Miller, P. (2006). A question of leadership: what lessons can the corporate sector learn from the nonprofit sector about relational leadership – being in touch with the inter- and intrarelationships that affect and influence an organization? *Leadership in Action*, 26(5), 12–13.

Riggio, R.E., Bass, B.M. & Orr, S.S. (2004). Transformational leadership in nonprofit organizations. In Riggio, R.E. & Orr, S.S. (eds), *Improving Leadership in Nonprofit Organizations*. San Francisco, CA: Jossey-Bass, pp. 49–62.

Ronquillo, J.C. (2011). Servant, Transformational and Transactional Leadership. In Agard, K.A. (ed.), *Leadership in Nonprofit Organizations, Vol. 1*. Thousand Oaks, CA: Sage, pp. 345–353.

Rost, J.C. (1991). *Leadership for the 21st Century*. New York: Praeger.

Schein, E. (2004). *Organizational Culture and Leadership*. San Francisco, CA: Jossey-Bass.

Salamon, L.M. (1998). Nonprofit organizations: America's invisible sector. *Issues of Democracy*. http://usinfo.state.gov/journals/itdhr/0198/ijde/salamon.htm, accessed November 15, 2011.

Smith, D.H. & Shen, C. (1996). Factors characterizing the most effective nonprofits managed by volunteers. *Nonprofit Management and Leadership*, 6(3), 271–289.

Smucker, B. (2005). Nonprofit Lobbying. In Herman, R.D. & Associates (ed.), *The Jossey-Bass Handbook of Nonprofit Leadership and Management*, 2nd edn. San Francisco, CA: Jossey-Bass, pp. 230–253.

Sorenson, G. (2000). An intellectual history of leadership studies: the role of James McGregor Burns. http://www.academy.umd.edu/publications.asp, accessed November 15, 201.

Stephenson, M. (2007) The 'permanent things' and the role of the moral imagination in organizational life: revisiting the foundations of public and nonprofit leadership. *Administrative Theory & Praxis*, 29, 260–277.

Suarez, D.F. (2010). Street credentials and management backgrounds: careers of nonprofit executives in an evolving sector. *Nonprofit and Voluntary Sector Quarterly*, 39(4), 696–716.

Tierney, T.J. (2006). The leadership deficit. *Stanford Social Innovation Review*, 4(2), 26–35.

Vandeventer, P. (2011). Increasing civic reach. *Stanford Social Innovation Review*, 9(2), 25–26.

Williams, G. (2007). Red Cross CEO resigns under pressure. November 27. http://www.philanthropy.com/news/updates/index.php?id=3523, accessed November 15, 2011.

Word, J. (2011). Human resource leadership and management. In Agard, K.A. (ed.), *Leadership in Nonprofit Organizations, Vol. 1*. Thousand Oaks, CA: Sage, pp. 395–401.

Yankey, J.A. & Willen, C.K. (2005). Strategic alliances. In Herman, R.D. & Associates (ed.). *The Jossey-Bass Handbook of Nonprofit Leadership and Management*, 2nd edn. San Francisco, CA: Jossey-Bass, pp. 254–274.

Young, D.R. (1993). Introduction: emerging themes in nonprofit leadership and management. In Young, D.R., Hollister, R.M. & Hodgkinson, V.A. (eds), *Governing, Leading, and Managing Nonprofit Organizations.* San Francisco, CA: Jossey-Bass, pp. 1–14.

Young, D.R., Hollister, R.M. & Hodgkinson, V.A. (eds) (1993). *Governing, Leading, and Managing Nonprofit Organizations.* San Francisco, CA: Jossey-Bass.

5. Nine empirical guidelines for top leadership teams in nonprofit organizations

Chris W. Coultas, Breanne Kindel, Stephanie Zajac and Eduardo Salas

NINE EMPIRICAL GUIDELINES FOR TOP LEADERSHIP TEAMS IN NONPROFIT ORGANIZATIONS

Organizations, nonprofit and for-profit alike, are increasingly relying on teams to achieve their various goals (Salas, Stagl & Burke, 2004). An increasing reliance on leadership teams is similarly evident in research and practice (Hambrick, 2007; Morgeson, DeRue & Karam, 2010). And while team and top management team (TMT) research has blossomed in the past 30 years (Carpenter, Geletkanycz & Sanders, 2004; Hambrick, 2007), research on leadership teams in nonprofit organizations (NPOs) is sorely needed (Courtney, Marnoch & Williamson, 2006). It has been argued that the complexity of NPOs in comparison to for-profits (a function of the existence of multiple stakeholders, missions, donors, classes of workers and the saliency of the dual governance system) necessitates even more effective approaches to leadership (Anheier, 2005; Finkelstein, 1992; Jager & Beyes, 2010), and by extension, a more nuanced understanding of the construction and functioning of top leadership teams. NPOs are an increasingly important part of modern society (Anheier, 2005; Ferris, 1998), yet the majority of research focus is placed on for-profit organizations. Concepts and theories from the for-profit world are applicable to NPOs to a certain extent, though research tends to overlook the complexities of the nonprofit world when applying these constructs (Jager & Beyes, 2010). TMTs and corporate boards represent the core leadership teams in NPOs; to understand and facilitate effective leadership in NPOs, it is imperative that we understand the conditions, characteristics and processes that contribute to leadership effectiveness in these teams. Process-based models of teams have guided research and practice in other settings (e.g., Ilgen, Hollenbeck, Johnson & Jundt, 2005; Rosen et al., 2008; Salas, Bowers & Cannon-Bowers, 1995). To this end, we review relevant literature on top leadership teams (i.e., corporate boards and TMTs) in not-for-profit and for-profit organizations, in order to address qualitatively two key questions:

1. What are the key team mechanisms (i.e., processes and emergent states) that drive top leadership team performance in NPOs?
2. What are the boundary conditions (i.e., internal attributes and external conditions) that contribute (directly or indirectly) to top leadership team performance in NPOs?

What Are, and Why Consider, Top Leadership Teams?

As previously noted, leadership teams in NPOs (i.e., as opposed to for-profits) may have a greater hand in determining the fate of their organizations, largely due to the uncertainty implicit in the existence of any NPO (Anheier, 2005; Finkelstein, 1992; Heimovics, Herman & Jurkiewicz-Coughlin, 1993). Accordingly, it is imperative that we understand how to create and maintain effective top leadership teams that will be the drivers of organizational performance. In this chapter, we consider top leadership teams to consist of TMTs as well as corporate boards. While these are certainly two distinct types of teams, there is meaningful overlap of their functions (Anheier, 2005; Hambrick & Mason, 1984). We consider them in conjunction, not only to increase the generalizability of our guidelines, but also because while there is a wealth of literature on corporate boards in NPOs, much of the TMT research currently is in the context of for-profits. Jager and Beyes (2010) note that much of the literature does not consider the distinguishing characteristics of NPOs when applying research from for-profit contexts to leadership teams in NPOs. We now consider some of these factors that must be taken into consideration as we extract guidelines for facilitating effectiveness in NPO top leadership teams.

What Is Different About Top Leadership In Non-Profits?

Nonprofit organizations present a unique set of conditions that may necessitate different (or more contextualized) forms of organizational structure, strategy and leadership than those found in for-profits. Some characteristics of NPOs that make the findings of for-profit organizational research not entirely applicable are: lack of a clear 'bottom line', being mission-driven (as opposed to profit-driven), having a greater quantity and diversity of stakeholders, and the increased relevance of the dual governance structure

(Anheier, 2005). According to Gomez and Zimmerman (1993; as cited in Anheier, 2005), management in NPOs must incorporate four truths about nonprofits into their management approaches: holism, norms, strategy and development, and operations. 'Holism' refers to the fact that NPOs exist in highly complex environments that entail multiple stakeholders as well as multiple end goals. 'Norms' in NPOs have the potential for being much more salient than in for-profits, as they are mission- and values-driven. 'Strategy and development' acknowledges that NPOs are constantly evolving, both internally and in response to frequent external shifts. Finally, 'operations' refers to the fact that management in NPOs, as in for-profits, are responsible for ensuring that the operational mission and goals of the organization are accomplished. Top leadership teams must be able to integrate these four elements of NPOs into their leadership approach if they are to be effective. From these four components, it is clear that NPOs find their greatest departures from for-profits in terms of the saliency of organizational norms as well as the complexity of the operational environment. Accordingly, a process-based look at TMTs in NPOs that will serve to shed light into the 'black box' of top management in NPOs must also take these distinctives into account (Jager & Beyes, 2010). As we extract process-based guidelines from a broad literature base, we consistently refer back to the impact that organizational values and complexity has on what drives and defines top leadership team 'effectiveness' in NPOs.

MODELING TOP LEADERSHIP TEAM FUNCTIONING IN NPOS

For the past thirty years, the input–process–output (IPO) model of team functioning has been the standard model with which to assess, describe and research teams (Marks, Mathieu & Zaccaro, 2001). A variation of this model, the input–mediator–outcome (IMO) model, acknowledges the effects of processes (e.g., information sharing, conflict management) as well as emergent states (e.g., trust, cohesion) in mediating the inputs to outcomes relationships (Mathieu, Maynard, Rapp & Gilson, 2008). Yet despite the ubiquity of the IPO–IMO approach in other teams research, and calls for a research paradigm shift, team demography comprises the bulk of the research on TMTs (Edmondson, Roberto & Watkins, 2003). We apply the IMO model of team functioning to describe the functioning of top leadership teams in NPOs. And while there are key differences between NPOs and for-profits, much of the research that has been done on TMTs is in the context of for-profits, so we pull from TMT research in both NPOs and for-profits. However, in accordance with Jager and Beyes (2010), we are careful to point out characteristics of NPOs that may affect the theoretical and practical implications of findings from the for-profit world. In reviewing the literature and identifying propositions for designing and maintaining effective top leadership teams, we take a criterion-centric approach, first identifying the outcomes expected of top leadership teams, then the mediating mechanisms through which this effectiveness is achieved, and finally delineating the characteristics and conditions that indirectly (i.e., through the mediating mechanisms) and directly influence leadership outcomes.

Top Leadership Team Outcomes

In the traditional IPO model of teams, 'outcomes' refer to 'such criteria as performance quality and quantity, as well as members' reactions' (Marks et al., 2001, p. 356). In the context of top-level organizational leadership teams, outcomes consist of the fulfilment of their various responsibilities (i.e., proximal outcomes), as well as organization-level (i.e., distal) outcomes and results such as firm financial performance (Mathieu et al., 2008). Indeed, research on TMTs typically considers objective, organization-level outcomes (e.g., return on equity, return on assets) as the measures of effectiveness for TMTs; however, the relationships between team inputs and mediators to proximal outcomes are much stronger and less confounded than more distal relationships (cf. Bunderson & Sutcliffe, 2003). Accordingly, we subsequently identify the proximal and distal outcomes typical of highly functioning top leadership teams.

Proximal outcomes

Functional team leadership is doing what is necessary to ensure team performance (McGrath, 1962; Morgeson et al., 2010). By extension, the effective performance of top leadership teams can be considered to be the degree to which they perform the functions necessary to ensure organizational performance. Thus, at its most basic level, the responsibility of top leadership teams is to create, enact, implement and maintain the vision and mission of the NPO, with boards typically crafting and protecting the vision, and TMTs strategically and operationally implementing the vision (Anheier, 2005; Bradshaw, 2002).

Boards craft and protect the mission and vision of the organization through strategic planning as well as selecting and monitoring members of the TMT (Hillman & Dalziel, 2003; Miller, 2002; Stephens, Dawley & Stephens, 2004). Part of developing the mission is making sure that this mission is clear to all stakeholders, so as to ensure stakeholder confidence, unity and support of the organization (Prybil & Levey, 2010). Boards are responsible for financially supporting and strategically guiding the mission of the NPO (Bateman, 1991; Inglis, Alexander & Weaver, 1999; McNally, 2003), as well as assessing and monitoring the TMT (Anheier, 2005; Inglis et al., 1999; Hillman & Dalziel, 2003). Because of NPO complexity, ambiguous ownership and multiple stakeholders, NPO boards tend to monitor more idiosyncratically than boards in for-profits (Miller, 2002), but nonetheless, this is a key function of boards. Finally, the board is largely responsible for ensuring community needs are met and that the organization maintains a good public reputation among its stakeholders (Anheier, 2005; Inglis et al., 1999).

TMTs are responsible (to varying degrees) for planning and strategy, controlling organizational resources, monitoring employee performance, supervising and advising, coordinating efforts with other leaders, marketing and networking, developing and maintaining stakeholder relations, and consulting with other peers and professionals (Anheier, 2005). For example, a major responsibility of the TMT is to enact strategic organizational change (Boeker, 1997; Finkelstein & Hambrick, 1990; Kim, 2005; Ling et al., 2008). Enacting strategic organizational changes in NPOs may be more complex than in for-profits, due to the voluntary nature of many NPOs. Accordingly, getting buy-in for strategic change may be even more important than in for-profits – this is accomplished when the TMT is able to legitimize strategic changes to those in their organization (Jager & Kreutzer, 2011).

Distal outcomes

While for most lower-level teams judging effectiveness as a function of organizational performance is inappropriate and unfair, at the top levels of leadership teams, organizational level outcomes (e.g., financial performance, organizational culture) are meaningful metrics of team performance (Mathieu et al., 2008). Accordingly, research on TMT effectiveness has looked at such organization-level outcomes as firm financial performance (Eisenhardt, Kahwajy & Bourgeois, 1997; Simons et al., 1999), organizational culture (Moynihan & Pandey, 2006; Ling et al., 2008) and, specifically in NPOs, community impact (Callahan & Kloby, 2009). In NPOs, a large percentage of financial performance may be dependent on the ability of the organization to receive various governmental grants. Accordingly, in some NPO research this has served as a metric of TMT performance (Lewis, French & Steane, 1997). The effectiveness of an NPO board has also often been judged on the financial performance and sustainability of the organization (Bateman, 1991; Green & Griesiner, 1996; Inglis et al., 1999; Miller, 2002).

Top-level leadership has been shown to have significant effects on organizational culture. Accordingly, some research has considered the distal effects of top leadership team performance as the fostering of desirable organizational cultural characteristics. Boschee (2001) found that boards could have a significant, positive effect on the 'social entrepreneurship' of the organization (i.e., the degree to which the NPO creatively expanded its services) by fostering a culture of risk-taking and creativity. Ling et al. (2008) showed that TMTs in for-profits could have an impact on the degree of entrepreneurship their organization exhibited. Moynihan and Pandey (2006) found that TMTs in NPOs were essential in fostering results-focused, managerial-driven organizational cultures – an important finding as governmental stakeholders push NPOs to shift towards a more profit-driven model, one that requires a close focus on results and tangible outcomes. Due to this increasing emphasis on results, NPOs are more and more assessing their community impact, such as reductions in illiteracy, poverty or hunger; and the degree to which an NPO meets its community impact goals can also be considered a referendum on TMT performance (Callahan & Kloby, 2009). Finally, because NPOs are highly values- and mission-driven, and because they are often powered to a great extent by volunteer work, issues of value alignment and motivation are especially salient. TMTs in NPOs have been positively linked with employee motivation (Kim, 2005) and value alignment (Kim, 2005; McMurray et al., 2010); effective nonprofit TMTs must be able to align the values of their strategies and policies with the values of the organization and its employees at large, and must use this alignment to leverage and increase employee motivation.

Top Leadership Team Mediators

Team processes are foundationally defined as the 'members' interdependent acts that convert inputs to outcomes through cognitive, verbal and behavioral activities directed toward organizing taskwork to achieve collective goals' (Marks et al., 2001, p. 357). Team mediators also include the emergent cognitive, affective and motivational states of groups such as shared mental models and collective efficacy (Mathieu et al., 2008). Behavioral integration (Simsek, Veiga, Lubatkin & Dino, 2005) is a metaconstruct that refers to the degree to which there is social collaboration (e.g., social interaction, liking of members), information exchange (i.e., quality and quantity of shared information) and joint decision-making in a TMT. These processes describe the typical functioning of teams, and are what convert the surface-level characteristics of teams into outputs and outcomes. Cohesion (i.e., attraction to the members, task and prestige of a group) is a mediating condition of teams that has consistently been shown to be linked to team performance (Beal, Cohen, Burke & McLendon, 2003). Social integration (of which cohesion is a key component) has been shown to be significantly related to firm-level financial outcomes (Lin & Shih, 2008; Smith et al., 1994). Michalisin, Karau and Tangpong (2004) showed that the performance of simulated TMTs was partially explained by TMT cohesion. TMTs requiring high task integration and coordination were found to perform better (both proximally and distally) when there were high levels of team cohesion (Barrick, Bradley, Kristof-Brown & Colbert, 2007). Boards that are highly cohesive have been shown to have higher levels of satisfaction, commitment and per capita effort contributions, while at the same time decreasing excessive board member turnover; furthermore, cohesive teams are better able to coordinate each board member's specific skills and expertise and apply them to the tasks at hand (Forbes & Milliken, 1999). Cohesion is particularly relevant to the leadership of NPOs. Although it is a powerful motivational force for driving organizational performance (Beal et al., 2003), as the nonprofit sector becomes increasingly professional, NPO leadership teams are less and less able to rely on the shared interests and values of its members to foster organization-level cohesion (Anheier, 2005). Accordingly, nonprofit leadership must model group cohesion as a way to foster employee motivation and commitment on an intraorganizational social level, beyond that of the externally focused, mission-driven commitment typical of NPO employees and volunteers. Social cohesion is typically facilitated by familiarity and similarity (Friedkin, 2004), so top leadership teams should intentionally and consistently meet (ideally face to face), and emphasize shared goals focusing on the mission.

Guideline 1: Top leadership teams in nonprofits must possess high group cohesion, both to facilitate team-level performance as well as to model and foster cohesion among employees at multiple organizational levels. This can be facilitated through consistent, intentional, mission-focused interactions.

Part of cohesion and social integration is the degree to which there is healthy conflict and conflict management within top leadership teams. There is a delicate balance between social cohesion and conflict management that must be maintained within the group – too much cohesion can lead to groupthink and decreased quality of decision-making, but too much negative conflict can stop group productivity altogether (Forbes & Milliken, 1999). Task conflict is beneficial for highly cohesive teams and can help prevent the board from groupthink (Forbes & Milliken, 1999). Conflict management in TMTs is especially important, and has been linked to important organizational outcomes (Eisenhardt et al., 1997; Lewis et al., 1997; Finkelstein & Mooney, 2003). And especially in NPOs, where stakeholder confidence in the mission and long-term viability of the organization is essential for continued donations and revenue, unhealthy conflict within the TMT must not be allowed to seep into the organization at large and become a cultural norm (Lewis et al., 1997). Conflict is typically delineated into affective/relationship and cognitive/task conflict, where relationship conflict centers around interpersonal and task-irrelevant issues, and cognitive conflict focuses on disagreements with role assignments and goal completion (Ensley & Pearce, 2001). Relationship and task conflict can arise when there is diversity of organizationally relevant cognitive values or bases (Lankau et al., 2007). Ensley and Pearce (2001) found that cognitive conflict contributed to shared mental models of corporate strategy, which in turn contributed to higher organizational performance. Eisenhardt et al. (1997) showed how what separates some of the most effective TMTs from the less effective ones was the degree to which they had conflict of ideas within their teams. However, Ensley and Pearce (2001) also found that cognitive conflict was significantly linked to affective conflict, which was negatively related to organizational performance. It is essential that board leaders manage conflict effectively and understand which type(s) of conflict is beneficial and which type(s) is detrimental to board functioning (Kerwin, Doherty & Harman, 2011; Cornforth, 2001). Task conflict has been shown to improve the quality of ideas and lead to better-quality decisions while process and relationship conflicts can be damaging to board performance (Kerwin et al., 2011). Task conflict can even protect highly cohesive teams from succumbing to groupthink by creating an environment that focuses on the tasks at hand and encourages new ideas and opinions (Forbes & Milliken, 1999). These findings attest to the essential nature of proper conflict management within teams – top leadership teams must be able to leverage cognitive conflict to positive effect while avoiding the negative consequences of affective conflict (Amason, 1996). Conflict management for top leadership in NPOs is especially important, because dysfunctional leadership is indicative of the kind of instability that concerns political and financial supporters (Eadie, 1996; Lewis et al., 1997).

Guideline 2: Top leadership teams in nonprofits must engage in proper conflict management techniques to foster optimal task and cognitive conflict, minimize relationship and affective conflict, and present a united front to employees, volunteers and stakeholders.

Cognitive and informational processes such as debate and information exchange are key for ensuring high performance in almost any team.

However, due to its emphasis on strategic planning, as well as the complexity and financial uncertainty so typical of NPOs, decision comprehensiveness and strategic consensus are especially important for top leadership in NPOs. Simons et al. (1999) showed that increased debate within TMTs leads to more comprehensive and better decisions – a key finding, given the strategic importance of TMTs for firm performance. Similarly, in TMTs with high task interdependence, communication was found to be significantly related to firm performance (Barrick et al., 2007). In TMTs with more decentralized responsibilities (i.e., roles based on experience and skills as opposed to seniority or hierarchy), members are more motivated to apply their experience and skills to a variety of domains (Ling et al., 2008). Furthermore, decentralization of responsibilities within the TMT should encourage greater information exchange, as decision-making power is not isolated to the chief executive officer (CEO). TMTs that can engage in effective information exchange techniques should see improvements in firm performance across a variety of outcomes. Coordinating roles, tasks and information within the top leadership team also facilitates communication and decision-making ability. Role clarity has been shown to be one of the key processes related to board effectiveness (Cornforth, 2001). It is crucial that board members clearly understand their responsibilities to the board, the board's responsibilities to the organization, and the organization's responsibilities to the community. A key purpose of boards is to guide strategic planning (Green & Griesinger, 1996; Wilson, 1991); accordingly, formal meetings define much of the functional performance and behavioral expectations of boards. Issues of conflict (negatively) and agreement-seeking (positively) predicted the degree to which the TMT held similar views about the strategic direction of the firm (Knight et al., 1999). In a separate study, it was found that when TMTs shared similar perceptions of the firm's strategic direction, organizational performance was higher (Ensley & Pearce, 2001). Awareness of team tasks and goals (in this case, TMT strategy) should lead to more effective task coordination and ultimately, performance (Mohammed, Ferzandi & Hamilton, 2010). Integrating these findings, it is clear that information exchange is a key mediating mechanism in determining board effectiveness. Indeed, Jansen and Kilpatrick (2004) address this, noting that 'dynamic boards' must leverage effective communication and coordination strategies if they are to have useful board meetings. Simple techniques such as ensuring that meetings start and end on time, that all the predetermined organizational issues are addressed, and that board members have access to all necessary decision-making information, go a long way toward facilitating top leadership team effectiveness.

Guideline 3: Top leadership teams in nonprofits must engage in effective communication strategies (e.g., information sharing, healthy debate, meeting coordination) in order to improve decision comprehensiveness, strategic planning and consensus, and firm performance. This can be facilitated through effective communication patterns, and decentralized and clearly defined member roles and responsibilities.

Other emergent states of top leadership teams, such as risk-taking, learning orientation, and ethical and transformational leadership norms, have also been linked to organization-level outcomes. Risk-taking among the TMT has been linked to firm-level entrepreneurship (Ling et al., 2008). Similarly, team learning orientation, which refers to the team's tendency to emphasize skill development and exploration, has been linked to business-unit performance: while it was found to drive adaptive performance in response to prior poor performance, it also led to an overemphasis on exploratory team behaviors at the expense of performance after high-performance cycles (Bunderson & Sutcliffe, 2003). Extrapolating this to the organization level, TMTs that can manage their tendency toward either learning (exploration) or performance (exploitation), and adapt their strategic energies to the needs of the organization (e.g., by taking into account recent firm performance), should also be TMTs that lead their organizations to greater performance and effectiveness. Furthermore, ethical leadership behaviors within the TMT have been shown to trickle down to lower levels of management, creating organizational norms of ethicality (Mayer et al., 2009). Similarly, boards can facilitate internal motivation and effectiveness through transformational leadership techniques (i.e., individualized consideration; Bass, 1990); by intentionally pursuing a team climate in which board member needs are addressed (Oliver, 2010), board members will maintain motivation and commitment. Boards that espouse a mentality of constant improvement of services will also be more motivated, committed and (typically) successful (Holland & Jackson, 1998). The need for top leadership teams actively to manage their motivational and behavioral norms may be even greater in nonprofits, as the mission-driven nature of NPOs makes employee value alignment and motivation particularly salient (Kim, 2005; McMurray et al., 2010).

Guideline 4: Top leadership teams must identify, engage in and model desired behavioral norms (e.g., exploration/exploitation, ethicality, constant improvement) within their team. This not only will facilitate top leadership team motivation and commitment, but also will trickle down to lower levels, fostering desirable organizational characteristics such as commitment, ethicality and entrepreneurship.

Inputs to Top Leadership Team Functioning

Early research on TMTs typically considered objective characteristics of the team (Chaganti & Sambharya, 1987; Finkelstein & Hambrick, 1990; Hambrick & Mason, 1984; Wiersema & Bantel, 1992). However, in recent years these have been seen more as peripheral factors in predicting TMT effectiveness, taking into account environmental and market conditions as well as team process (cf., Eisenhardt et al., 1997; Haleblian & Finkelstein, 1993; Simons et al., 1999). Furthermore, other characteristics of TMTs, such as those relating to power structure (Ling et al., 2008) and psychological characteristics (Ritchie, Kolodinsky & Eastwood, 2007) of TMTs are now being taken into account when considering TMT effectiveness. In line with the IMO model of team functioning (Mathieu et al., 2008), we consider the role of three categories of TMT inputs – surface characteristics, external conditions and miscellaneous team traits – in driving TMT mediating mechanisms (e.g., communication, conflict management) as well as outcomes (e.g., organizational culture, firm performance).

Top Leadership Surface Characteristics

Much research on top-level leadership has focused on surface characteristics as a means to predict effectiveness; this was the premise of 'upper echelons theory' (Hambrick & Mason, 1984). Board diversity in NPOs has been shown to have positive effects. Demographic diversity has been shown to enhance the organization's reputation and influence with its stakeholders and constituents; stakeholders felt better represented by heterogeneous boards (Brown, 2002; Daley, 2002; Cornelius & Lew, 2009). Boards were viewed as more effective when their members' demographics matched those of their constituents (Daley, 2002). Functional and occupational diversity can be helpful in analyzing complex issues, generating ideas and adapting to changing external environments (Daley, 2002). Siciliano (1996) found positive relationships between occupational, gender and age diversity, and outcomes such as social performance and fundraising. TMT characteristics such as team size and diversity of age, gender, race and functional experiences have also been the subject of much research. On the whole, however, the relationship of demographic characteristics to team performance has been inconsistent (Cohen & Bailey, 1997; Pitcher & Smith, 2001), with the most robust demographic variable seeming to be team and organizational tenure (Cohen & Bailey, 1997). Smith et al. (1994) found that while heterogeneity of experience (i.e., in the industry and the firm) was negatively related to TMT process (communication) and performance, heterogeneity of education positively predicted performance. Boeker

(1997) found that the longer (on average) the members of TMTs had held executive positions, the less likely the team was to enact strategic change, but when these teams had diversity in their executive tenures, they were more likely to engage in strategic change. Furthermore, teams with higher TMT tenure typically exhibited changes that were more in line with industry standard strategies and practices. In a similar study, Liang and Picken (2010) found that the more distant a TMT member's management tenure was from the mean tenure of the TMT, the less frequently that manager would communicate with the rest of the team. However, in a series of case studies, Eisenhardt et al. (1997) found that the highest-performing TMTs (as measured by organizational performance) had heterogeneous teams; this provided multiple unique perspectives and fostered positive cognitive conflict. What these findings suggest is that while team heterogeneity may typically be disadvantageous to top leadership functioning, the most effective teams will be able to leverage this diversity to extract a wealth of unique perspectives and wisdom from all top leadership team members; this is done through the emphasizing of superordinate team and organizational goals (Jarzabkowski & Searle, 2004). While the bulk of this research was done in for-profits, this may be even truer in NPOs, where the foundational values and mission of the organization may provide a degree of commonality that transcends issues of diversity.

Guideline 5: Top leadership teams high in diversity may be prone to insufficient communication patterns and heightened conflict; effective nonprofit teams will leverage shared goals and utilize effective conflict management strategies to extract unique member perspectives from functional and experiential diversity, yielding heightened team creativity, innovation and performance.

Top Leadership Team External Conditions

Objective characteristics of top leadership teams can only predict so much, however. Indeed, the precursory line of thinking to upper echelons theory was that upper-level leadership has very little influence on the outcomes of organizations, and that it is largely uncontrollable external conditions that sweep organizations along (Hambrick & Mason, 1984). For example, environmental instability or turbulence has been shown to heighten the impact of TMTs on organizational outcomes (Haleblian & Finkelstein, 1993). Edmondson et al. (2003) argued that dynamic elements of the situation mitigate the relationship between TMT inputs and mediating mechanisms. Charismatic leadership styles were shown to be positively linked to organizational financial performance in times of organizational uncertainty (i.e., turbulent times), but not in times of certainty and stability (Waldman, Ramirez, House & Puranam, 2001). These findings extend to the nonprofit realm as well: issues of organizational crisis and stability affect what is expected and required of top-level leaders (Peterson & Van Fleet, 2008). For example, Peterson and Van Fleet (2008) found that among NPO leaders, while certain behaviors were always seen as vital (e.g., inspiration, team building), others were seen as vital only in times of organizational stability (e.g., consideration, praise and recognition), and still others were considered important primarily in times of crisis (e.g., problem-solving, obstacle elimination). The relationship between organizational uncertainty and leadership potency is especially salient in nonprofits, as NPOs are often highly subject to environmental instability, due to their reliance on a diverse array of donors and stakeholders (Anheier, 2005). Moynihan and Pandey (2006) found that the political and popular support for TMTs provided by various stakeholders of NPOs significantly predicted management's ability to enact strategic intraorganizational change. Extrapolating these findings to leadership in general, it is clear that leadership is more important in times of organizational uncertainty. Given that NPOs serve constituencies for whom remuneration for services is not always an option, financial uncertainty is a defining characteristic of NPOs (Anheier, 2005), making the leadership of TMTs and boards more impactful and more necessary. This is especially true for NPO boards, for whom procurement of financial resources and reduction of environmental and financial instability is a primary responsibility (Inglis et al., 1999; McNally, 2003).

Guideline 6: Top leadership teams are more potent in times of organizational turbulence than times of stability. NPO leadership must monitor the environment for uncertainty and adapt their leadership to the needs of the organization.

Issues of corporate governance represent some of the most important boundary conditions impacting the effectiveness of top leadership teams. TMTs may be afforded varying levels of authority in their management approaches, and boards may provide governance to the organization at various levels of involvement. Level of managerial discretion afforded to the TMT affects the importance of the TMT to organizational outcomes (Haleblian & Finkelstein, 1993; Hambrick, 2007). Issues of corporate governance, though not external to the organization, greatly impact the effectiveness of the TMT to the organization, especially in NPOs where the dual governance system is much more salient (Anheier, 2005). Corporate boards, CEO dominance and governmental micromanagement (Kim, 2005) are all issues that nonprofit TMTs must manage. Bureaucratic red tape is an issue especially relevant to NPOs, which typically rely heavily on assistance from governmental and various other organizations. Governmental bureaucracy and micromanagement will lead to managerial impetus and loss of organizational growth, unless TMTs foster a 'developmental' approach to leadership that emphasizes risk-taking, innovation and growth; this facilitates the organization in navigating the political channels effectively, without getting too bogged down in the red tape (Pandey, Coursey & Moynihan, 2007). Another element of the managerial discretion and organizational effectiveness relationship is the issue of the board–TMT interface. In NPOs, boards and TMTs must work together to provide and allocate resources and to develop and implement mission, among other things; this level of task integration necessitates a functional and coordinated relationship between these two leadership teams. Eadie (1996) and Koch (2003) lay out several guidelines for ensuring effective board–management relations, such as clearly laying out board–management role expectations, not micromanaging the TMT, and emphasizing the achievement of the mission and vision over their practical implementation. Issues of the dual governance interface are especially important in NPOs, where they may take a more active financial and strategic role than they would in other organizations (Anheier, 2005).

Guideline 7: Top leadership teams in NPOs must carefully navigate the dual governance structure by effectively coordinating roles and responsibilities between boards and TMTs.

Other TMT Characteristics

Despite the popularity of the upper echelons perspective, the link between objective TMT characteristics and outcomes and performance has been tenuous at times (Carpenter et al., 2004; Cohen & Bailey, 1997). Other factors have been shown to contribute to TMT processes and overall effectiveness as well. Existing research on TMTs has looked at both structural and psychological characteristics of TMTs. TMT size has been studied at some length. Haleblian and Finkelstein (1993) showed that larger teams performed better than smaller teams in 'turbulent environments' and when managerial discretion was high. More recent studies suggest that this may be due to the increased communication that uncertain environments elicit. Smith et al. (1994) found that TMT size was negatively related to within-team informal communication, yet this communication led to increased team performance. Similarly, boards are typically assumed to be more effective the smaller they are (e.g., less than 20), as they facilitate greater member contributions per capita (Stern, 2005), yet NPO boards are often quite large, and larger than for-profit boards (Forbes & Milliken, 1999). This is partially due to the financial uncertainty inherent in NPOs (as board members can provide a measure of stability), and partially due to the diversity of stakeholders that NPOs may serve – stakeholders prefer to see similar board members representing their interests at an organizational level (Brown, 2002; Cornelius & Lew, 2009). Team interdependence refers to the degree to which success requires team members to rely on one another to achieve team goals. Barrick et al. (2007) found that TMT interdependence predicts levels of team communication, and the interaction between interdependence and communication predicts firm performance, such that the relationship between communication and performance for highly interdependent TMTs was positive, but it was negative for teams with low interdependence. Taken together, these findings indicate that characteristics of the team, the task and the environment may partially define situationally appropriate communication patterns, which in turn predict top leadership team, and organizational, performance.

Guideline 8: Top leadership team size and interdependence necessitate heightened levels of communication; large, interdependent TMTs that have effective communication patterns will be characterized by high levels of performance.

Psychological characteristics of the TMT, such as personality and team decision-making orientation, have been linked to organizational-level outcomes. In fact, work by Harrison et al. (1998, 2002) has shown that over time (i.e., in 'real' teams), deep-level diversity (e.g., values, personality) has a greater effect on team process and performance than surface diversity (e.g., race, gender). Peterson, Smith, Martorana and Owens (2003), in a study of 17 TMTs, found that CEO personality significantly impacted TMT dynamics (e.g., neurotic CEOs led less cohesive and flexible TMTs; more agreeable CEOs led TMTs that were more cohesive and decentralized). Ritchie et al. (2007) found that nonprofits led by TMTs that utilized more intuitive decision-making styles (e.g., following hunches, 'gut instinct') tended to be more financially successful than other nonprofits with less intuitive TMTs. Pitcher and Smith (2001) showed that TMT personality heterogeneity positively contributed to organizational technical innovation (e.g., exploring new markets and products) as well as overall performance, even while leading to less administrative 'innovation' (e.g., instituting new bureaucratic policies). Heterogeneity in positive affect among TMT members has also been negatively linked to satisfaction with the team (i.e., cohesion) as well as firm-level financial performance (Barsade, Ward,

Turner & Sonnenfeld, 2000). Values play a major role in the functioning on NPOs, as they tend to be primarily mission-driven (Anheier, 2005). Accordingly, values dissimilarity within nonprofit TMTs should impact team process and performance; Lankau et al. (2007) found that value dissimilarity within the TMT was significantly related to relationship and task conflict. Research has also acknowledged the importance of value alignment for boards. Board members will be more engaged and willing to contribute if the interests of the organization and values entailed in its mission closely align with their own (Stern, 2005). This alignment leads to increased levels of commitment from the board members which is crucial for board effectiveness (Stephens et al., 2004; Prybil & Levey, 2010). Nonprofit TMTs must effectively manage this plethora of psychological differences in order to optimize team processes and performance.

Guideline 9: Deep-level diversity leads to heightened conflict and decreased cohesion and performance in teams; nonprofit top leadership teams should emphasize the superordinate goal of organizational values and mission achievement in order to foster cohesion and performance.

SUMMARY

Research on top leadership teams in nonprofits is scant in comparison to for-profit research, so the generalizability of these findings should be taken with a grain of salt (Jager & Beyes, 2010). However, most for-profit top leadership team research should be fairly applicable, provided researchers and practitioners take into account two key distinctives regarding NPOs: their mission-driven nature and the 'law of nonprofit complexity' (Anheier, 2005). As we are careful to highlight throughout this chapter, many of the findings from research on top leadership teams in for-profits is still meaningful in NPOs – in fact, they are likely to be more impactful, given that NPOs typically exist in a greater state of uncertainty than for-profits. Understanding these key components contextualizes much of the research on for-profit top leadership teams. In this chapter, we have conducted a high-level, qualitative review on the inputs, mediating mechanisms and outcomes of top leadership teams in both for-profits and nonprofits. And while our review is by no means comprehensive, we cover a wide array of the team inputs and mediating mechanisms, in the hope of developing a more complete understanding of how top leadership teams in nonprofits function. Process-based approaches have helped elucidate the inner workings of various types of teams; an overarching process-based model of top leadership teams in nonprofits will help us better understand these teams. In

Figure 5.1, we graphically represent a summary of the empirical relationships previously discussed, in a theoretical process-based model of top leadership teams in nonprofits. Furthermore, we have attempted to provide empirically grounded solutions, or best practices, regarding some of the issues TMTs face when leading non-profits. Future research should empirically test the degree to which findings from research on for-profit TMTs apply to nonprofit TMTs.

INPUTS →	MEDIATORS →	OUTCOMES
- Tenure diversity - Cognitive diversity - Demographic diversity - Values diversity - Personality - Team size - Environmental uncertainty - Political support - Managerial discretion - Prior performance - Prior organizational culture	- Behavioral integration - Social integration - Cohesion - Conflict management - Information exchange - Debate - Information processing - Propensity to take risks - Task coordination	- Firm financial performance - Community Impact - Organizational culture - Employee motivation - Strategic change - Quality/sustainability of services

Figure 5.1 Summary model of the relationships between inputs, mediators and outcomes for TMTs in nonprofit organizations

Practical Implications

In the previous sections, we have reviewed a glut of research on top leadership teams in both for-profit and nonprofit organizations. From this review, we extracted nine empirical guidelines. Given this wealth of empirical knowledge, we must now ask ourselves how we can practically apply these empirical guidelines to create, maintain and/or repair top leadership teams better in nonprofits. As Finkelstein and Mooney (2003) suggested in regards to forming effective corporate boards, it is the interpersonal and teamwork processes that will drive the effectiveness of top leadership teams, even over and above the characteristics of their component members. Accordingly, we suggest that while demographic characteristics can be a cue towards potential team creativity or conflict, special attention be paid to the processes and emergent states that we have identified, and that practitioners, such as executive coaches, human resource management (HRM) professionals, and members of TMTs themselves, intentionally engage in and foster these processes and emergent states. The review has been presented in the form of nine empirical guidelines, yet in actuality, these guidelines are manifestations of seven key constructs in team functioning:

cohesion (guideline 1; Ensley et al., 2003; Mathieu, Heffner, Goodwin, Salas & Cannon-Bowers, 2000), conflict management (guideline 2; Behfar, Peterson, Mannix & Trochim, 2008; De Dreu & Weingart, 2003), communication and debate (guidelines 3 and 5; Smith et al., 1994; Stewart & Barrick, 2000), consensus (guideline 3; Mathieu et al., 2000; Mohammed et al., 2010), coordination (guidelines 6 and 7; Entin & Serfaty, 1999; Stewart & Barrick, 2000), culture (guideline 4; Burke, Shuffler, Salas & Gelfand, 2010; Earley & Mosakowski, 2000), and composition (guidelines 8 and 9; Jackson, Joshi & Erhardt, 2003; Mohammed & Angell, 2004). We have reframed the findings mentioned above into a simple mnemonic device – the '7 C's of effective top leadership teams' – to reflect and consolidate these key constructs better, and to make them more conducive to practical application. These '7 C's' are indicative of the key constructs that form the basis for the nine guidelines presented and are presented as such for ease of utilization and application. See Table 5.1 for an explication of these constructs as well as relevant best practices from these constructs.

Our mediational emphasis is not coincidental, but is in line with Finkelstein and Mooney (2003), and follows from a glut of research that evinces the inconsistency of demographic input variables as predictors of TMT performance. Furthermore, a process-based approach is more practically helpful, because while top leadership team demographic or psychological composition may be difficult or impossible to change, awareness of the vital mediational mechanisms may help top leadership teams to engage in these intentionally, regardless of whether or not they have an ingrained propensity to engage in them.

Directions for Future Research

In this chapter, we have qualitatively integrated a wealth of empirical findings, from a variety of authors, using a variety of methodologies. In so doing, we set forth nine guidelines regarding the input variables that have been shown to impact top leadership team processes and emergent states, as well as the mediating mechanisms which serve to drive team and organizational performance. Future researchers would do well to explore how these guidelines function in conjunction with each other (i.e., looking at multiple processes and emergent states in the same sample). Additionally, future research could empirically examine the validity of these guidelines, which are largely based on research done in the for-profit world, to top leadership teams in real-world nonprofits. This is essential, because while we heed the warning of Jager and Beyes (2010) and take note of the differences between nonprofits and for-profits, we consistently take theoretical leaps in generalizing the findings of TMTs in the for-profit world to

Table 5.1 The 7 C's of effective top leadership teams in nonprofits

Construct	Impact	Best practices
Cohesion[1]	Helps minimize negative relationship conflict; improves commitment to the team and organization	Meet as frequently as necessary, face to face whenever possible, emphasize collective achievement of the organizational mission
Conflict management[2]	Minimizes relationship conflict in the team; encourages cognitive/task conflict and facilitates creativity; fosters public appearance of unity	Set mission-based, interdependent goals to facilitate task conflict and foster constructive controversy. Encourage high value consensus, trust and respect amongst team members
Communication & debate[3]	Yields more comprehensive/ better decisions (especially for highly interdependent teams)	Appeal to the expertise of team members and intentionally seek out significant input and contributions from diverse team members
Consensus[4]	Strategic consensus within top leadership teams guides the organization; helps coordinate mission implementation	Leverage effective communication techniques to achieve shared understanding of strategic plans
Coordination[5]	Shared understanding of team process and org. needs facilitates more effective communication and teamwork patterns	Establish clear patterns for communication and taskwork, clearly define member roles and responsibilities
Culture[6]	Internal behavioral norms of top leadership teams trickle down org. levels, impacting overall culture and employee motivation	Discuss and identify the necessary and desired cultural characteristics for the organization and apply them to team behavioral norms
Composition[7]	Occupational diversity may facilitate creativity; demographic diversity may foster conflict or improve reputation of the NPO	Ensure leadership team members have the requisite occupational diversity to meet org. needs and foster creativity

(Anheier, 2005; Forbes & Milliken, 1999; Friedkin, 2004; Lin & Shih, 2008)[1], (Amason, 1996; Eisenhardt et al., 1997; Lewis et al., 1997; Tjosvold, 1998; Jehn & Mannix, 2001)[2], (Barrick et al., 2007; Simons et al., 1999)[3], (Ensley & Pearce, 2001; Knight et al., 1999)[4], (Barrick et al., 2007; Mohammed et al., 2010)[5]; (Kim, 2005, Ling et al., 2008; Mayer et al., 2009)[6], (Brown, 2002; Cohen & Bailey, 1997; Daley, 2002; Wilson, 1991)[7]

TMTs in nonprofits. These theoretical leaps are justifiable, however, as the key differences between NPOs and for-profits tend to center around the mission-driven nature of NPOs, as well as the source of their environmental instability and complexity. We were able to acknowledge these differences and contextualize our propositions to the realm of NPOs; we primarily argued: (1) that the uncertainty of the nonprofit realm enhances the importance of top leadership teams over what is seen in the for-profit realm; and (2) that leveraging a common mission with the organization could aid top leadership teams in goal and value alignment, task coordination, strategic consensus and conflict management. Future research could look at the role of the changing emphases (i.e., mission-emphatic vs. profit-emphatic) within NPOs in impacting top leadership team processes and performance.

ACKNOWLEDGEMENT

This research was partially supported by the Office of Naval Research (ONR) Collaboration and Knowledge Interoperability Program and Office of Naval Research Multidisciplinary University Research Initiative (ONR MURI) Grant No. N000140610446. The research and development reported here was also partially funded by the National Science Foundation grant to Dr Matthew W. Ohland, Principal Investigator, Purdue University (0817403-DUE), subcontract to the University of Central Florida (UCF) (4101-25418). The views, opinions and findings contained in this article are the authors' and should not be construed as official or as reflecting the views of the University of Central Florida, the Department of Defense, or the authors' organizations with which they are affiliated or their sponsoring institutions or agencies.

REFERENCES

Amason, A.C. (1996). Distinguishing the effects of functional and dysfunctional conflict on strategic decision making: Resolving a paradox for top management teams. *Academy of Management Journal*, 39, 123–148.

Anheier, H.K. (2005). *Nonprofit Organizations: Theory, Management, Policy*. New York: Routledge.

Barrick, M.R., Bradley, B.H., Kristof-Brown, A.L. & Colbert, A.E. (2007). The moderating role of top management team interdependence: Implications for real teams and working groups. *Academy of Management Journal*, 50, 544–557.

Barsade, S.G., Ward, A.J., Turner, J.D.F. & Sonnenfeld, J.A. (2000). To your heart's content: A model of affective diversity in top management teams. *Administrative Science Quarterly*, 45, 802–836.

Bass, B.M. (1990). From transactional to transformational leadership: Learning to share the vision. *Organizational Dynamics*, 18, 19–31.

Bateman, C.L. (1991). The case of the captive board: How to regain control. *Nonprofit World*, 9(3), 13–15.

Beal, D.J., Cohen, R.R., Burke, M.J. & McLendon, C.L. (2003). Cohesion and performance in groups: A meta-analytic clarification of construct relations. *Journal of Applied Psychology*, 88, 989–1004.

Behfar, K.J., Peterson, R.S., Mannix, E.A. & Trochim, W.M.K. (2008). The critical role of conflict resolution in teams: A close look at the links between conflict type, conflict management strategies, and team outcomes. *Journal of Applied Psychology*, 93, 170–188.

Boeker, W. (1997). Strategic change: The influence of managerial characteristics and organizational growth. *Academy of Management Journal*, 40, 152–170.

Boschee, J. (2001). Eight basic principles for nonprofit entrepreneurs. *Nonprofit World*, 19(4), 15–18.

Bradshaw, P. (2002). Reframing board-staff relations: Exploring the governance function using a storytelling metaphor. *Nonprofit Management and Leadership*, 12, 471–484.

Brown, W.A. (2002). Inclusive governance practices in nonprofit organizations and implications of future practice. *Nonprofit Management and Leadership*, 12(4), 369–385.

Bunderson, J.S. & Sutcliff, K.M. (2003). Management team learning orientation and business unit performance. *Journal of Applied Psychology*, 88, 552–560.

Burke, C.S., Shuffler, M.L., Salas, E. & Gelfand, M. (2010). Multicultural teams: Critical team processes and guidelines. In K. Lundby (ed.) with J. Jolton, *Going global: Practical Application and Recommendations for HR and OD Professionals in the Global Workplace*. San Francisco, CA: Jossey-Bass, pp. 46–82.

Callahan, K. & Kloby, K. (2009). Moving toward outcome-oriented performance measurement systems. Managing for Performance and Results Series, IBM Center for the Business of Government.

Carpenter, M.A., Geletkanycz, M.A. & Sanders, G.W. (2004). Upper echelons research revisited: Antecedents, elements, and consequences of top management team composition. *Journal of Management*, 30, 749–778.

Chaganti, R. & Sambharya, R. (1987). Strategic orientation and characteristics of upper management. *Strategic Management Journal*, 8, 393–401.

Cohen, S.G. & Bailey, D.E. (1997). What makes teams work: Group effectiveness research from the shop floor to the executive suite. *Journal of Management*, 23(3), 239–290.

Cornelius, M. & Lew, S. (2009). What about the next generation of color? Advancing multicultural leadership. *Nonprofit World*, 27(4), 24–26.

Cornforth, C. (2001). What makes boards effective? An examination of the relationships between board inputs, structures, processes, and effectiveness in nonprofit organizations. *Corporate Governance: An International Review*, 9(3), 217–227.

Courtney, R., Marnoch, G. & Williamson, A. (2006). The adoption of strategic management by third sector organizations: Findings from a census of organizations in Northern Ireland. *Zeitschrift fur offentliche und gemeinwirtschaftliche Unternehmen*, 34, 8–21.

Daley, J.M. (2002). An action guide for nonprofit board diversity. *Journal of Community Practice*, 10(1), 33–54.

De Dreu, C.K.W. & Weingart, L.R. (2003). Task versus relationship conflict, team performance, and team member satisfaction: A meta-analysis. *Journal of Applied Psychology*, 88, 741–749.

Eadie, D.C. (1996). Boards can't go it alone: How to forge the board-executive partnership. *Nonprofit World*, 14(2), 16–19.

Earley, P.C. & Mosakowski, E. (2000). Creating hybrid team cultures: An empirical test of transnational team functioning. *Academy of Management Journal*, 43, 26–49.

Edmondson, A.C., Roberto, M.A. & Watkins, M.D. (2003). A dynamic model of top management team effectiveness: Managing unstructured task streams. *Leadership Quarterly*, 14, 297–325.

Eisenhardt, K.M., Kahwajy, J.L. & Bourgeois, L.J., III. (1997). Conflict and strategic choice: How top management teams disagree. *California Management Review*, 39, 42–62.

Ensley, M.D. & Pearce, C.L. (2001). Shared cognition in top management teams: Implications for new venture performance. *Journal of Organizational Behavior*, 22, 145–160.

Ensley, M.D., Pearson, A. & Pearce, C.L. (2003). Top management team process, shared leadership, and new venture performance: A theoretical model and research agenda. *Human Resource Management Review*, 13(2), 329–346.

Entin, E.E. & Serfaty, D. (1999). Adaptive team coordination. *Human Factors: The Journal of the Human Factors and Ergonomics Society*, 41, 312–325.

Ferris, J.M. (1998). The role of the nonprofit sector in a self-governing society: A view from the United States. *Voluntas: International Journal of Voluntary and Nonprofit Organizations*, 9, 137–151.

Finkelstein, S. (1992). Power in top management teams: Dimensions, measurement, and validation. *Academy of Management Journal*, 35, 505–538.

Finkelstein, S. & Hambrick, D.C. (1990). Top-management-team tenure and organizational outcomes: The moderating role of managerial discretion. *Administrative Science Quarterly*, 35, 484–503.

Finkelstein, S. & Mooney, A.C. (2003). Not the usual suspects: How to use board process to make boards better. *Academy of Management Executive*, 17, 101–113.

Forbes, D.P. & Milliken, F.J. (1999). Cognition and corporate governance: Understanding boards of directors as strategic decision-making groups. *Academy of Management Review*, 24(3), 489–505.

Friedkin, N.E. (2004). Social cohesion. *Annual Review of Sociology*, 30, 409–425.

Green, J.C. & Griesinger, D.W. (1996). Board performance and organizational effectiveness in nonprofit social services organizations. *Nonprofit Management and Leadership*, 6(4), 381–402.

Haleblian, J. & Finkelstein, S. (1993). Top management team size, CEO dominance, and firm performance: The moderating roles of environmental turbulence and discretion. *Academy of Management Journal*, 36, 844–863.

Hambrick, D.C. (2007). Upper echelons theory: An update. *Academy of Management Review*, 32, 334–343.

Hambrick, D.C. & Mason, P.A. (1984). Upper echelons: The organization as a reflection of its top managers. *Academy of Management*, 9(2), 193–206.

Harrison, D.A., Price, K.H. & Bell, M.P. (1998). Beyond relational demography: Time and the effects of surface- and deep-level diversity on work group cohesion. *Academy of Management Journal*, 41, 96–107.

Harrison, D.A., Price, K.H., Gavin, J.H. & Florey, A.T. (2002). Time, teams, and task performance: Changing effects of surface- and deep-level diversity on group functioning. *Academy of Management Journal*, 45, 1029–1045.

Hillman, A.J. & Dalziel, T. (2003). Boards of directors and firm performance: Intergrating agency and resource dependence perspectives. *Academy of Management Review*, 28(3), 383–396.

Holland, T.P. & Jackson, D.K. (1998). Strengthening board performance: Findings and lessons from demonstration projects. *Nonprofit Management and Leadership*, 9(2), 121–134.

Ilgen, D.R., Hollenbeck, J.R., Johnson, M. & Jundt, D. (2005). Teams in organizations: From input–process–output models to IMOI models. *Annual Review of Psychology,* 56, 517–543.

Inglis, S., Alexander, T. & Weaver, L. (1999). Roles and responsibilities of community nonprofit boards. *Nonprofit Management and Leadership*, 10(2), 153–167.

Jackson, S.E., Joshi, A. & Erhardt, N.L. (2003). Recent research on team and organizational diversity: SWOT analysis and implications. *Journal of Management*, 29, 801–830.

Jager, U. & Beyes, T. (2010). Strategizing in NPOs: A case study on the practice of organizational change between social mission and economic rationale. *Voluntas*, 21, 82–100.

Jager, U.P. & Kreutzer, K. (2011). Strategy's negotiability, reasonability, and comprehensibility: A case study of how central strategists legitimize and realize strategies without formal authority. *Nonprofit and Voluntary Sector Quarterly*, 40, 1020–1047.

Jansen, P.J. & Kilpatrick, A.R. (2004). The dynamic nonprofit board. *McKinsey Quarterly*, 2, 72–82.

Jarzabkowski, P. & Searle, R.H. (2004). Harnessing diversity and collective action in the top management team. *Long Range Planning*, 37, 399–419.

Jehn, K.A. & Mannix, E.A. (2001). The dynamic nature of conflict: A longitudinal study of intragroup conflict and group performance. *Academy of Management Journal*, 44(2), 238–251.

Kerwin, S., Doherty, A. & Harman, A. (2011). 'It's not conflict, it's differences of opinion': An in-depth examination of conflict in nonprofit boards. *Small Group Research*, 42(5), 562–594.

Kim, S.E. (2005). Three management challenges in performance improvement in human services agencies: A case study. *International Review of Public Administration*, 10, 83–93.

Knight, D., Pearce, C.L., Smith, K.G., Olian, J.D., Sims, H.P., Smith, K.A. & Flood, P. (1999). Top management team diversity, group process, and strategic consensus. *Strategic Management Journal*, 20, 445–465.

Koch, F. (2003). Building a strong board–exec relationship. *Nonprofit world*, 21(4), 11–13.

Lankau, M.J., Ward, A., Amason, A., Ng, T., Sonnefeld, J.A. & Agle, B.R. (2007). Examining the impact of organizational value dissimilarity in top management teams. *Journal of Managerial Issues*, 19, 11–34.

Lewis, D.S., French, E. & Steane, P. (1997). A culture of conflict. *Leadership & Organization Development Journal*, 18, 275–282.

Liang, X. & Picken, J. (2010). Relational demography, communication, and cognitive differences among top managers. *Leadership & Organization Development Journal*, 32, 689–714.

Lin, H.C. & Shih, C.T. (2008). How executive SHRM system links to firm performance: The perspectives of upper echelon and competitive dynamics? *Journal of Management*, 34, 853–881.

Ling, Y., Simsek, Z., Lubatkin, M.H. & Veiga, J.F. (2008). Transformational leadership's role in promoting corporate entrepreneurship: Examining the CEO–TMT interface. *Academy of Management Journal*, 51, 557–576.

Marks, M.A., Mathieu, J.E. & Zaccaro, S.J. (2001). A temporally based framework and taxonomy of team processes. *Academy of Management Review*, 26, 356–376.

Mathieu, J.E., Heffner, T.S., Goodwin, G.F., Salas, E. & Cannon-Bowers, J.A. (2000). The influence of shared mental models on team process and performance. *Journal of Applied Psychology*, 85, 273–283.

Mathieu, J., Maynard, M.T., Rapp, T. & Gilson, L. (2008). Team effectiveness 1997–2007: A review of recent advancements and a glimpse into the future. *Journal of Management*, 34, 410–476.

Mayer, D.M., Kuenzi, M., Greenbaum, R., Bardes, M. & Salvador, R.B. (2009). How low does ethical leadership flow? Test of a trickle-down model. *Organizational Behavior and Human Decision Processes*, 108, 1–13.

McGrath, J.E. (1962). *Leadership behavior: Some requirements for leadership training*. Washington, DC: US Civil Service Commission, Office of Career Development.

McMurray, A.J., Pirola-Merlo, A.P., Sarros, J.C. & Islam, M.M. (2010). Leadership, climate, psychological capital, commitment, and wellbeing in a non-profit organization, *Organization Development Journal*, 35, 436–457.

McNally, J.S. (2003). The board: The roles and responsibilities of nonprofit board membership. *Pennsylvania CPA Journal*, 73(4), 46–49.

Michalisin, M.D., Karau, S.J. & Tangpong, C. (2004). Top management team cohesion and superior industry returns: An empirical study of the resource-based view. *Group and Organization Management*, 29, 125–140.

Miller, J.L. (2002). The board as a monitor of organizational activity: The applicability of agency theory to nonprofit boards. *Nonprofit Management and Leadership*, 12(4), 429–450.

Mohammed, S. & Angell, L.C. (2004). Surface- and deep-level diversity in workgroups: Examining the moderating effects of team orientation and team process on relationship conflict. *Journal of Organizational Behavior*, 25, 1015–1039.

Mohammed, S., Ferzandi, L. & Hamilton, K. (2010). Metaphor no more: A 15-year review of the team mental model construct. *Journal of Management*, 36, 876–910.

Morgeson, F.P., DeRue, S. & Karam, E.P. (2010). Leadership in teams: A functional approach to understanding leadership structures and processes. *Journal of Management*, 36, 5–39.

Moynihan, D.P. & Pandey, S.K. (2006). Creating desirable organizational characteristics: How organizations create a focus on results and managerial authority. *Public Management Review*, 8, 119–140.

Oliver, E. (2010). What makes your board members tick? *Nonprofit World*, 28, 7.

Pandey, S.K., Coursey, D.H. & Moynihan, D.P. (2007). Organizational effectiveness and bureaucratic red tape: A multimethod study. *Public Performance and Management Review*, 30(3), 398–425.

Peterson, R.S., Smith, D.B., Martorana, P.V. & Owens, P.D. (2003). Impact of chief executive officer personality on top management team dynamics: One mechanism by which leadership affects organizational performance. *Journal of Applied Psychology*, 88, 795–808.

Peterson, T.O. & Van Fleet, D.D. (2008). A tale of two situations: An empirical study of behavior by not-for-profit managerial leaders. *Public Performance & Management Review*, 31(4), 503–516.

Pitcher, P. & Smith, A.D. (2001). Top management team heterogeneity: Personality, power, and proxies. *Organization Science*, 12, 1–18.

Prybil, L. & Levey, S. (2010). The right stuff: Key leadership factors for attaining a high level of operating performance. *Trustee*, 63(7), 20–22.

Ritchie, W.J., Kolodinsky, R.W. & Eastwood, K. (2007). Does executive intuition matter? An empirical analysis of its relationship with nonprofit organizational financial performance. *Nonprofit Voluntary Sector Quarterly*, 36, 140–155.

Rosen, M.A., Salas, E. Wilson, K.A., King, H.B., Salisbury, M., Augenstein, J.S., Robinson, D.W. & Birnbach, D.J. (2008). Measuring team performance in simulation-based training: Adopting best practices for healthcare. *Simulation in Healthcare*, 3, 33–41.

Salas, E., Bowers, C.A. & Cannon-Bowers, J.A. (1995). Military team research: 10 years of progress. *Military Psychology*, 7, 55–75.

Salas, E., Stagl, K. & Burke, C.S. (2004). 25 years of team effectiveness in organizations: Research themes and emerging needs. In C.L. Cooper & I.T. Robertson (eds), *International Review of Industrial and Organizational Psychology*. New York: Wiley, pp. 47–91.

Siciliano, J. (1996). The relationship of board member diversity to organizational performance. *Journal of Business Ethics*, 15(12), 1313–1320.

Simons, T., Pelled, L.H. & Smith, K.A. (1999). Making use of difference: Diversity, debate, and decision comprehensiveness in top management teams. *Academy of Management Journal*, 42, 662–673.

Simsek, Z., Veiga, J.F., Lubatkin, M.H. & Dino, R.H. (2005). Modeling the multilevel determinants of top management team behavioral integration. *Academy of Management Journal*, 48, 69–84.

Smith, K.G., Smith, K.A., Olian, J.D., Sims, H.P., Jr., O'Bannon, D.P. & Scully, J.A. (1994). Top management team demography and process: The role of social integration and communication. *Administrative Science Quarterly*, 39, 412–438.

Stephens, R.D., Dawley, D.D. & Stephens, D.B. (2004). Commitment of the board: A model of volunteer directors' level of organizational commitment and self-reported performance. *Journal of Management Issues*, 16(4), 483–504.

Stern, G. (2005). Mutual rewards: thoughts on serving as a board member for a nonprofit organization. *Community Dividend*, 4, 3.

Stewart, G.L. & Barrick, M.R. (2000). Team structure and performance: Assessing the mediating role of intrateam process and the moderating role of task type. *Academy of Management Journal*, 43, 135–148.

Tjosvold, D. (1998). Cooperative and competitive goal approach to conflict: Accomplishments and challenges. *Applied Psychology: An international Review*, 47(3), 285–342.

Waldman, D.A., Ramirez, G.G., House, R.J. & Puranam, P. (2001). Does leadership matter? CEO leadership attributes and profitability under conditions of perceived environmental uncertainty. *Academy of Management Journal*, 44, 134–143.

Wiersema, M.F. & Bantel, K.A. (1992). Top management team demography and corporate strategic change. *Academy of Management Journal*, 35, 91–121.

Wilson, L. (1991). How businesslike is your board? Test yourself. *Nonprofit World*, 9(5), 14–16.

6. The heart of the organization: developing the nonprofit brand

Stacy Landreth Grau and Susan Bardi Kleiser

In 2007, on its 25th birthday, Susan G. Komen for the Cure was rebranded with a new logo and new name (formerly the Susan G. Komen Breast Cancer Foundation). It also came with a new pledge: to raise and invest another $1 billion in the next decade for breast cancer research. Started by Nancy Brinker as a promise to her dying sister, Susan Komen, the organization was the first to recognize the impact of breast cancer on women of all races and ages and raise money for medical research to eradicate this type of deadly cancer. In the 1980s, the term 'breast cancer' was taboo in the United States (US) – indeed, it was not even allowed to be printed in newspapers. But all that changed with the first Race for the Cure held in Dallas, Texas (E. Callahan, personal communication, July 2009).

According to then Vice-President of Marketing, Emily Callahan, the rebranding discussion started many years prior to the launch as the organization wanted to move from being a well-respected breast cancer organization to being the icon in the fight against breast cancer. One of the primary problems with the original brand was the fragmented logos, names and programs from all of the local affiliates. Research showed that aided awareness was low. 'People did not understand if we were a race or a foundation or pink ribbons,' said Callahan. Add to that increased attention to pink ribbons and breast cancer by companies like Avon and others involved in cause-related marketing efforts (such as Yoplait), and the cause space had become crowded and confused. The goal was to connect a fragmented brand into an icon, while balancing the needs of more than 100 local affiliates. The new name – Susan G. Komen for the Cure – allowed the organization to explore more brand touch points (e.g. opportunities for stakeholders to interact with the brand). 'The effort for rebranding was led through public relations, and we examine share of voice quite a bit,' said Callahan. 'We feel that now there is an emotional connection and greater engagement with the Komen brand' (E. Callahan, personal communication, July 2009).

The brand is – or at least should be – the heart of the nonprofit organization. This chapter on the importance of nonprofit branding will: (1) define branding and emphasize the importance of developing a strong brand identity for nonprofit organizations; (2) present a brief discussion of the importance of brand image, especially in this crowded competitive space, as well as the importance of brand equity for nonprofits; (3) explore how to create a strong brand; and (4) examine the concept and models of brand equity for nonprofit organizations.

WHAT IS A BRAND?

Nothing can be more confusing in marketing than the concept of a brand. A brand has many different related terms and definitions. The American Marketing Association's definition of branding is a 'name, term, design, symbol, or any other feature that identifies one seller's good or service as distinct from those of other sellers' (www.marketingpower.com). According to Kevin Lane Keller, a leading brand authority in the US, branding reflects a unique social contribution; it comprises a promise to target audiences and stakeholders and reflects the mission and values of the organization (Keller, 2008). The purposes of brands are to inform stakeholders about what a company or organization has to offer; to reduce risk among the various options and competitors; and to create a positive image in the minds of stakeholders. Indeed, brand image includes each and every interaction between the company and, typically, the consumer. Almost all definitions have some elements in common; that is, a brand is an image that exists in the minds of your customers that is the result of all of the impressions (both good and bad) that exist anywhere. Scot Bedbury, one of the authors of *A New Brand World*, describes a brand as 'the sum of the good, the bad, the ugly and the off strategy … It is defined by the accomplishments of your best employee – the shining star of the company who can do no wrong – as well as by the mishaps of your worst hire ever' (Bedbury & Fenichell, 2002).

Strong brands are developed by marketers and yet a brand lives in the minds of people. Brands are influenced by all sorts of things, both rational and irrational. More recently, people have taken more control of defining brands – both good and bad – primarily due to their ability to communicate faster and more efficiently using social media. People make it what they believe it is and should be. Companies can try to influence these perceptions, but at the end of the day it is about the consumer's perceptions. The idea is that the organization's brand can create and deliver benefits to stakeholders. These benefits can be tangible or intangible, and once this value is delivered again and again, a bond between the stakeholder and the brand develops resulting in long-term commitment and loyalty. So brands are emotional bonds between the company and consumer based on a consistent delivery of quality and trust.

So just what is a nonprofit brand? Sargeant and Ford (2007) developed a branding framework to understand nonprofit brands. The core of the brand is the organization's vision including its mission, purposes, values, actions and principles. These are the foundation for what makes the organization valuable. But the brand needs to stand out and resonate with donors and volunteers. When you ask the typical nonprofit executive leader to describe their organization's brand personality, it is likely they will say 'caring', 'innovative', 'transformational', 'we are the only ones who do this', and so forth. While these are positive, the problem is that most nonprofits will say pretty much the same thing and therein lies the main problem: differentiation (or lack of it in this case).

It has been suggested that that brand orientation can help raise awareness, build loyalty with supporters (both donors and volunteers) and facilitate choice (Hankinson, 2000). Nonprofit brands, like other brands, have brand personalities and it is important to have one that is not only attractive, but also unique (Sargeant & Ford, 2007). Brand personality is a 'set of personality traits that reflects the vision, mission, unique selling proposition, values, actions and principles of the organization' (Sargeant & Ford, 2007, p. 43). Research shows that brand personality can enhance the image of the organization by harnessing the power of branding. Organizations can use brand personality to create a unique image by clearly communicating its personality dimensions (Venable et al., 2005). Sargeant and Ford's (2007) research found that several aspects of brand personality are shared among many nonprofit organizations. Indeed, the entire sector is endowed with benevolent traits like fairness, honesty and trustworthiness. While positive, these traits are neither earned, nor will they differentiate an organization. The second aspect is the cause dimension: organizations that share a common cause – like breast cancer or the arts – also share common personality traits. For example, arts organizations and education organizations are considered more elite; religious organizations also have traits such as spiritual, holy and devout. But even with these common attributes, many organizations find it difficult to stand out. Organizations can distinguish brands by focusing on the ways they are different from others. These include emotional stimulation, voice, service and tradition (Sargeant and Ford, 2007). Other research has examined the role of values within a nonprofit brand (Stride & Lee, 2007). De Chernatony and Dall'Olmo Riley

(1998, p. 427) argue that values are important to nonprofits and lie at the heart of the branding concept, and define it as 'a complex multidimensional construct whereby managers augment products and services with values and this facilitates the process by which consumers confidently recognize and appreciate these values'. Stride and Lee (2007) confirmed the importance of values in nonprofit brands, and the importance that these values be shared across the organization. While this conceptualization of brand is much more common in for-profit branding, it seems to be at the nascent stages for most nonprofits. After developing the core of the brand, the organization then turns its attention to the more tangible aspects of it – the look and feel of the brand.

Far more common in nonprofit branding is the more visual aspect of a brand. The visual expression of the brand includes things like the logo, color palette, typography, design elements, and photography and illustrations (Sargeant & Ford, 2007). The logo or symbol of the organization represents the look of the brand. This includes colors, typography, symbols and anything that graphically depicts the identity of brands. In the examples for breast cancer, the color pink and the pink ribbon would be considered part of the logo. Indeed, many organizations have adopted colors and ribbons as part of their identity (e.g. red ribbons for AIDS awareness). Wristbands are also a tangible way of identifying the brand (e.g. the Lance Armstrong Foundation and yellow bands).

The verbal expression of the brand includes the name, key messages, tone of voice and positioning statement (Sargeant & Ford, 2007). The most obvious aspect of a brand is the brand name of the organization, program or product. This is an area where some organizations struggle as they attempt to convey their mission and stand out from similar organizations as well. Consider breast cancer as a cause sector. A few examples:

- The Pink Agenda
- National Breast Cancer Foundation
- American Cancer Society
- Breastcancer.org
- Living Beyond Breast Cancer
- The Rose
- Breast Cancer Wellness
- Susan G. Komen for the Cure.

And many others – most with the color pink and the pink ribbon as part of their brand image. This makes it hard to stand out in the crowd. So choosing a name and brand that is memorable, and attempting to create some unique difference, is important to building an effective brand.

The slogan or tagline for the organization is the words or phrases that are said about the brand. For example, Nike has 'Just do it' but many nonprofits do not have memorable taglines. Nonprofits tend to use generic phrases or use words that are too broad and cannot be owned by one organization, such as 'breast cancer' or 'drop-out prevention'. Additionally, sometimes nonprofits are identified with people who are founders (Bill Gates for the Bill & Melinda Gates Foundation) or celebrities (Michael J. Fox for Parkinson's disease). As a result, the brand image of the person does reach over into the image of the organization (Andreasen & Kotler, 2008). Overall, the key to managing an effective brand image is consistency. The brand image needs to be conveyed to stakeholders consistently over an extended period of time in order to form not only an intellectual relationship with clients through knowledge and understanding of the organization does, but also an emotional bond.

One way to solidify the emotional bond is by developing a brand community. Recently, there has been added attention about building a brand community for nonprofits. Brand communities have long been a 'holy grail' of loyalty for many brands and a few – like Harley Davidson, Apple and Jeep – have been successful at engaging a large group of people who are completely passionate about their brand. In the for-profit context, this passion can lead to greater sales and positive word of mouth. According to Muniz and O'Guinn (2001), a brand community is defined as 'a specialized, non-geographically bound community, based on a structured set of social relationships among admirers of a brand' (p. 414). They referred to three key drivers of brand community:

- Consciousness of kind which refers to the bond that exists between a brand and customers;
- Shared rituals and traditions which refers to embedded symbols, events, celebrations and activities that are unique to the brand; and
- Moral responsibility, which refers to a shared duty among people.

So can't the same be said for advocates for nonprofits? The strong emotional connection between some people and the causes they care about may prove to be fertile ground for developing brand communities (Hassay & Peloza, 2009). This could lead to more engaged volunteers, a dedicated donor base, a broader donor base and positive word of mouth – especially through the use of social media. Indeed, there are good examples of brand communities. Think about the thousands of people who participate in Komen's Race for the Cure each year; or even more so, the dedication of those who walk 60 miles for three days for breast cancer. Think about the Young Professionals groups that many organizations develop in order to engage cause-minded Millennials. Some are developed around social media – whether Facebook groups or Twitter followers.

IMPORTANCE OF BRANDING FOR NONPROFITS

Branding can be as important to nonprofit organizations as it is for large for-profit companies. Indeed, many academic researchers are paying more attention to branding in the nonprofit context (Hankinson, 2000; Ritchie et al., 1998; Tapp, 1996). Many companies know that their brand is one of their biggest assets. The brand valuation is in the billions for companies such as Coca-Cola, Apple and Google, and to a nonprofit organization the brand image is perhaps its most important asset. There are several advantages to a strong brand. Firstly, brands enhance learning. A solid, positive brand image can be vital for nonprofits since it increases the level of awareness among stakeholders and gives them a strong identity and understanding of the organization's goals. Secondly, brands reduce risk. Donors and volunteers want to give their time and money to an organization that uses it effectively. This reduction of risk is even more important given the intangible nature of nonprofits, and most of this risk reduction comes in the form of enhanced trust. Thirdly, brands provide insurance. A strong brand can give nonprofits insurance against negative events that may damage an organization's reputation. Lastly, brands build loyalty and enable donors and volunteers to express their own identity through affiliation with the organization. Overall, branding aids in fundraising activities and helps to achieve the mission by garnering more volunteer support. Phillipa Hankinson (2000) states, 'Branded charity organizations are more likely to attract voluntary donations than unbranded charities whose cause and values may be less clearly defined and less well known. Brands allow donors to identify more closely with what the charity does and the values it represents' (p. 210).

Branding is also monetarily valuable to the organization. The top nonprofit brand in the US according to the 2010 Cone Nonprofit Power Brand 100 is the YMCA of the USA. This organization has a brand value of more than $6 billion, is the top-ranking nonprofit in terms of revenue and ranks number six on brand image. The YMCA outpaces the closest competitor by almost $2 billion. The organization started with a social mission and has become one of the largest sports and recreation facilities in 3000 communities; it makes most of its revenue from club memberships in these communities. YMCA benefits from the awareness of being a ubiquitous 'bricks and mortar' presence all over the country and yet still maintains a strong digital presence as well (www.coneinc.com). The American Cancer

Society was ranked as the nonprofit organization with the best brand image in the US. It stands out as the most personally relevant organization and has solidified its leadership with stakeholders, including patients, medical communities, the media and the community (www.coneinc.com). All of these big brands benefit from a large number of dedicated donors as well as other brand benefits.

SO WHY DON'T ALL NONPROFITS INVEST IN BRANDING?

Historically nonprofits have resisted marketing, branding, segmentation and positioning as being 'too commercial'. However, increasing competition from other organizations and the decreasing funding from governments has led many organizations to rely more on corporations, foundations and individuals for funding. What many nonprofits then find is that people cannot differentiate among all of the options for their donation dollars because they do not know what any of the organizations stand for. This weak emotional bond between donors or volunteers and the organization results in a nonprofit which must constantly find new donors or volunteers to keep it sustainable. There are several reasons why branding can be more difficult for nonprofits than other organizations.

The Nature of the Target Audience

Nonprofits typically have clients or beneficiaries of their programs or services, their donors and their volunteers who have different relationships with organizations and who all need different messages. Sometimes they overlap; in other cases there is a difference between those who donate to a cause and those who benefit from that cause. For example, a person may donate to their local food bank but never need to go there to get food. In other instances, people may donate to a school and still reap the benefits if their children attend the school.

The Nature of Their Programs and Services

Many programs and services are intangible and difficult to explain. The need is either not readily apparent or perhaps too far away to resonate with the donor (which is especially true for international causes). And indeed some organizations feel that their organizations are too complex for branding (Voeth & Herbst, 2008). For example, museums, orchestras and libraries often find it difficult to market their services since they deal with higher-order needs. Contrarily, food banks and homeless shelters find it easier to promote their programs since they deal with basic needs. Sometimes the need is in a faraway place; it may be harder to convince Americans to support schools in Afghanistan when there are issues in the schools here. All compound the difficulty with branding.

The Nature of the Transaction

Oftentimes, the client does not pay for the service and instead a donor is making the financial contribution for that program to exist. The lack of direct exchange between the donor and recipient, and the recipient and the program, make it more difficult to develop a brand image for many organizations.

Cost and Skill Set Requirements of Branding

Many nonprofits do not have the advantage that large companies have, primarily the financial resources necessary to create a solid brand image. Additionally, most nonprofits, especially small and medium-sized nonprofits, do not have the staff size or expertise to develop a solid brand image.

Overall Perceptions

Generally, the public likes nonprofit organizations and see them as deserving and doing good things for the community. The public has a strong sense of what it means to be a nonprofit. Many organizations assume that they are distinctive simply due to the nature of what they do, and therefore do not see the real need for branding.

Many nonprofits do not feel that they have the expertise to build and nurture a brand while trying to achieve their mission. As a result, they tend not to explore the specific traits and personalities of their brands to determine why stakeholders choose to enter a relationship with their organization (Voeth & Herbst, 2008). This is problematic, since to the public nonprofits are seen as a 'bland, homogenous mass of well-being but similar organizations. This perception matters because individuals are motivated to offer higher levels of support and exhibit higher levels of loyalty to brands that are seen as differentiated. Without this differentiation, there is little loyalty or emotional bonding between donors and nonprofit organizations' (Sargeant & Ford, 2007, pp. 43–44).

Mini Case: Developing a New Nonprofit Brand: Slant 45

When it was announced that the 2011 National Football League's Super Bowl 45 would be held in Dallas, Texas, USA, at the newly built Dallas Cowboys stadium, the North Texas Super Bowl Host Committee knew that the experience needed to be about more than just football. Part of that experience was the creation of a 'movement' called Service Learning Adventures in North Texas (or SLANT 45) whose purpose was to engage local third through fifth graders to give back to the community. The idea was to get children to learn from their projects and leave a lasting impression on local communities. Children would decide where and how they wanted to give their time and talent, and adults would act as coaches and mentors to get it done. The goal was to get 20 000 school children to give 45 000 service hours over the year. The organization was developed in conjunction with a Dallas nonprofit called Big Thought and funded by Bank of America, the Gary Patterson Foundation, the Ted & Shannon Skokos Foundation as well as other funders.

Projects included a food drive by a baseball team that collected more than 1300 cans and $800 for the Tarrant County Food Bank. Students at one school raised money for Make A Wish. Other projects focused on cleaning up graffiti, promoting the dangers of pollution, conducting toy drives and clothing drives, beautifying parks and recreation centers, and helping sick children and the elderly. Overall, hundreds of projects were developed for local communities.

For their efforts, kids were able to attend a concert called Kids Bowl Bash at the American Airlines Center in Dallas featuring American Idol Jordin Sparks, Disney star Mitchel Musso and attended by honorary chairs former President George Bush and former First Lady Laura Bush. More than 15 000 children attended. There were guest appearances by Cowboy quarterback legends Roger Staubach (chairman of the Super Bowl committee) and Troy Aikman as well as Cowboy great Daryl Johnston who served as chairman of SLANT 45. One of the outcomes of the project was that school children reflected on their experience through art. Their artwork (including more than 1000 pieces) was on display at several locations including the Fort Worth Museum of Science and History. The display traveled to North Park Mall in Dallas and the DFW Airport Rental Car Center. There is also a SLANT movie, a documentary that depicts the efforts behind SLANT 45, which chronicled the program from the start from the perspective of five children.

While the goals were once thought large, children shattered them early on. More than 44 000 children participated before the Super Bowl and dedicated more than 445 815 hours to community service. 'This was a great way to showcase the power of children,' said Gigi Antoni of Big Thought. 'When I heard we were trying to get 20 000 kids, I was scared. It sounded really ambitious. But this took on energy of its own. It was a grassroots movement of kids. And raises the profile of what we do' (Munsil, 2010).

The organization hopes that SLANT will be a major aspect of future Super Bowls and is working with the Indianapolis 2012 committee and the New Orleans 2013 committee to adapt it to their communities. SLANT continues to exist in the Dallas–Fort Worth area but without the '45' and without the direction of Big Thought or the Super Bowl committee. But the experience was so positive for many participants that children wanted to continue to give back to the community – regardless of American football.

'We came up with SLANT 45 to give the Super Bowl a conscience,' said Bill Lively, president of the Super Bowl committee. 'We had boys and girls commit to performing service under the banner of football. And, of all of the things we've done, this is the project I am most proud of' (Alfano, 2010, 2011; Mongueau, 2011; Munsil, 2010).

Key to the successful branding effort were: (1) a unique name that resonated with the community; (2) a complete guide for mentors and coaches on how to go about developing these projects including a 'Official Playbook' and 'Coach's Playbook' as well as many online sources; (3) major grassroots efforts; (4) the right people behind the effort (including those working behind the scenes); and (5) strategic partnerships from a development perspective as well as a funding perspective.

DEVELOPING STRONG NONPROFIT BRANDS

Understanding brand images means understanding how better to leverage that brand image with corporations and other partners, potentially enhancing revenue. There are several qualities that exemplify a strong brand. The brand should be simple, be clear, be consistent, have a distinctive differentiation, deliver an inspirational and emotional promise, be portable, be engaging and be relevant. And someone should be in charge of it. Indeed, these attributes are especially important for nonprofit brands given the number of causes and the emotional attachment of causes (Adamson, 2008; Wymer & Grau, 2010).

The Brand Idea Should Be Simple

A simple idea should be the foundation for the mission and the vision as well as for the tagline on the website and other brand touch points. The simple brand idea should be media-neutral (or media-agnostic); that means that the idea should be applicable to all sorts of communication tactics. At the end of the day, the idea should be the driver for the communication. If it takes too long to explain, then it is too complicated to convey (Wymer and Grau, 2010).

The Brand Should Be Conveyed In a Clear and Consistent Voice

All aspects of communication should have the same 'voice' and come from a distinct personality. Marketers talk about brand personalities – conservative or fun-loving. Since there are so many nonprofits out there all disseminating similar messages about help, having a distinctive brand personality will help differentiate the brand relative to all of the noise (Wymer and Grau, 2010).

The Brand Must Be Distinctive and Show a Relevant Difference Vis-à-Vis the Competition

Many brands start with a functional benefit (e.g. give food to the poor) but quickly find that they need to move up the branding ladder to a more emotional benefit. This emotional connection comes especially easy for nonprofit organizations. In the US, St Jude's Children's Hospital is a leading authority on cancer and other diseases that typically strike children. When a child visits St Jude's, typically most of the care is paid for through donations. As such, the hospital has a unique and distinctive brand with little competition, and given that the hospital helps sick children, it is easier to raise funds than it is for some other causes. Having a distinctive image is important given the competitive landscape within many cause sectors (e.g. think how many organizations belong to the breast cancer cause sector and also use the pink ribbon as part of its identity). Having the ability to engage with others is important for nonprofit organizations as well, given the emotional attachment some donors have with the cause. The reality is that there are limited financial resources out there – whether from foundations, corporations, investors or individual donors. So it is vital that the nonprofit stands out from the crowd (Wymer and Grau, 2010).

A Nonprofit Brand Should Strive to Deliver an Inspirational and Emotional Promise

To a certain extent, nonprofits by their very nature are automatically endowed with a sense of inspiration: the idea of doing something good for others. And the most famous brands become famous due to evangelists – people who are influential and who speak about the great things about the brand. In this case, the best thing that nonprofits can do is to do what they say they are doing, and do it well. Indeed, donor relationships are partially built on word of mouth. We see that for many companies, reputations are made or broken on recommendations. The same is true for nonprofits (Wymer and Grau, 2010).

The Brand Should Be Portable

Portability deals with an organization's ability to expand its mission through either program expansion or geographic expansion. This is the idea of scalability – a concept that many nonprofit organizations really struggle with for a variety of reasons. If the organization's name is too narrow, this could limit portability. If it includes a specific geographic area, this makes it difficult as well. Most large organizations have managed to deal with the portability issue through using affiliates; for example, the United Way has affiliates throughout the United States to raise money locally and distribute money locally. Other organizations like Communities in Schools have been able to scale their model throughout the United States and into various communities (Wymer and Grau, 2010).

The Brand Should Be Engaging

This means that the ideas are compelling enough to spread organically through word of mouth or digitally. Seth Godin, author of several marketing books and a leading marketing blog (http://sethgodin.typepd.com/seths_blog), says that all organizations should strive to be 'remark-able'. In other words, nonprofit brands should try to do things to get other people to talk about them, to tell their story. The RED campaign to help end the AIDS suffering in Africa (www.joinred.com) is one example of an organization that is particularly engaging and uses unique ways to build relationships with donors (Wymer and Grau, 2010).

The Brand Should Be Relevant

This is based on the idea of social impact. At the end of the day, what impact does the organization have on the lives of its stakeholders? What would the world be like if the organization no longer existed? It is important to ensure that the organization is fulfilling its mission and providing a positive return on investment to volunteers and to donors. This information needs to be communicated effectively and the website can be a wonderful tool to accomplish that goal (Wymer and Grau, 2010).

Developing a strong brand can be accomplished. But it takes time and leadership; make sure someone is in charge. There needs to be a brand ambassador within the organization who will maintain the consistency and cohesiveness of the brand image. This could be the development director, marketing director or executive director, but it needs to be someone who is at a high level of decision-making. That said, make sure that the organization is educated about the brand. Make sure all staff members and volunteers comprehend what the brand means to the nonprofit and its stakeholders (Wymer and Grau, 2010).

BRAND EQUITY MODELS AND NONPROFIT ORGANIZATIONS

Understanding what drives brand equity is crucial to building strong nonprofit brands (Laidler-Kylander & Simonin, 2009). However, there are few models that exist (Haigh & Gilbert, 2005). Nonprofit organizations typically benefit from relatively high levels of trust from the public; this translates nicely into a measure of brand strength. But methods for measuring brand equity and its related constructs vary greatly and this disagreement, it is argued, is one reason why branding research for nonprofit organizations is in such a state of flux (Reynolds & Philips, 2005).

Understanding the different drivers of brand equity for nonprofits and for-profits is vital to developing a core model. Oster (1995) suggests that differences in nonprofits and for-profits lie in at least five major areas: organizational culture, human resources, collaboration, target audience variations and complexity, and importance of mission. These differences suggest that nonprofits can and should build their brands a little differently from for-profit companies.

Brand equity is defined as 'a set of brand assets and liabilities linked to a brand, its name and symbol that add to or subtract from the value provided by a product or service to that firm's customers' (Aaker, 1991). Assets and liabilities can be grouped into five categories: brand loyalty, name awareness, perceived quality, brand associations, and other (Aaker, 1991). Recently, researchers Laidler-Kylander and Simonin (2009) developed a model for international nonprofit organizations using a systems approach that found four key variables: consistency, focus, trust and partnerships. These four variables, when considered together, have the potential to impact brand equity.

Consistency is described as internal consistency, external consistency and the match between the two. Internal consistency includes operations within programs allowing the organization to generate best practices in their field. For example, a literacy program can have higher than expected outcomes due to the programmatic research that it is based upon and the tutors who are hired to implement the program. This internal consistency leads to success which then leads to expansion efforts. External consistency deals with the messages that are developed and disseminated to various stakeholders that lead to the ability to raise funds and increase advocacy and engagement. Ideally, the organization should strive to develop a clear and cohesive message and work to disseminate that message to the right people at the right time. The match between internal and external consistency deals with the how the organization manages these stakeholders and the degree of trust that is generated as a result of that match up. This increased trust then 'loops' back to impact the other variables: trust, partnerships and focus. It seems that consistency is the glue that holds the brand together (Laidler-Kylander & Simonin, 2009).

Focus is described as organizational or operational focus within the organization and is not found to be as prevalent in the for-profit context. However, given the relatively limited resources of many nonprofits, maintaining a strong and vigilant organizational focus is a key function of building brand equity for many nonprofits. Nonprofits should not try to be 'all things to all people' but try to do their part effectively. For example, education is a huge issue but there are many facets of it – teacher quality and effectiveness, drop-out prevention, literacy programs, math and science education and mentoring – all of which are valid answers to the problem but each are truly different. From the model, focus has a direct impact on brand equity and also helps the organization differentiate itself among other competitive organizations (Laidler-Kylander & Simonin, 2009).

Trust is a key variable in nonprofit organizations. From the model, it appears that increasing the differentiation and visibility of the organization leads to trust enhancement and increased brand equity (Laidler-Kylander & Simonin, 2009). This tends to reinforce the work from Sargeant and Ford (2007) discussed earlier about the importance of differentiation and positioning for nonprofit organizations.

Lastly, partnerships are important to building equity as well, and these partnerships include alliances with for-profit brands (e.g. cause related marketing programs) and alliances with other like-minded causes (e.g. various players within the education field). Indeed, collaboration is much more prevalent in nonprofit sectors than for-profit sectors, primarily because of the competitive emphasis of the latter. The model states that partnerships and relevance are closely aligned; that the more relevant an organization is, the more partners it can attract, which leads to greater brand equity. Partnerships can lead to more funds raised, greater differentiation and more positive brand image. However, too many partnerships can dilute the brand. In order to guide nonprofits organizations, Laidler-Kylander and Simonin (2009) make the recommendations to ensure that the organization can build brand equity, as shown in Table 6.1.

Variables	Recommendations
Consistency	Increase internal coordination between operations and messaging Concentrate external messaging to increase communication consistency
Focus	Strive for focus despite growing pains and fundraising demands Stick with the mission
Trust	Differentiate through strong positioning Increase visibility and awareness through external messaging Promote organizational integrity
Partnerships	Select partners that have a good fit with the organization Proactively manage these relationships

SUMMARY

Branding is obviously an important concept for nonprofits. A strong brand can lead to many benefits for nonprofit organizations, including greater awareness for the cause, more loyalty among donors and volunteers, greater differentiation among other causes (including competitive causes), and the ability to weather negative information should it occur. There are several larger nonprofits that seem to have a very strategic grasp on the art and science of building a strong brand.

However, many nonprofits find themselves with a superficial understanding of branding that is rooted in tactics as opposed to a strategic direction. As a result, there is still much work to be done. As discussed, issues like developing a 'values-based' brand image needs more research. The concept of brand equity and how it can be applied in the nonprofit sector also warrants additional attention. And how a small to medium-sized nonprofit can develop a strong brand image with minimal resources should be explored. But overall, it seems that the leaders in the nonprofit marketplace have finally allowed themselves to modify some of the principles of 'selling soap' to make its organizations more successful. And that, in the end, helps everyone.

REFERENCES

Aaker, D. (1991). *Managing Brand Equity: Capitalizing on the Value of a Brand Name*. New York: Free Press.

Adamson, A.P. (2008). *Brand Digital: Simple Ways Top Brands Succeed in the Digital World*. New York: Palgrave Macmillan.

Alfano, P. (2010). Generosity of North Texas children shattered all expectations for Super Bowl service program. *Fort Worth Star-Telegram*, December 16. www.star-telegram.com.

Alfano, P. (2011). SLANT 45 participants get a night to celebrate accomplishments. *Fort Worth Star Telegram*, January 12. www.star-telegram.com.

Andreasen, A.R. & Kotler, P. (2008). *Strategic Marketing for Nonprofit Organizations*, 7th edn. Upper Saddle River, NJ: Pearson Prentice Hall.

Bedbury, S. & Fenichell, S. (2002). *A New Brand World: Eight Principles for Achieving Brand Leadership in the 21st Century*. New York: Viking Press.

De Chernatony, L. & Dall'Olmo Riley, F. (1998). Defining a 'brand': beyond the literature with experts' interpretations. *Journal of Marketing Management*, 14(4–5), 417–433.

Haigh, D. & Gilbert, S. (2005). Valuing Not-for-Profit and charity brands – real insight or smoke and mirrors. *International Journal of Nonprofit and Voluntary Sector Marketing*, 10(2), 107–130.

Hankinson, P. (2000). Brand orientation in charity organizations: qualitative research into key charity sectors. *International Journal of Nonprofit and Voluntary Sector Marketing*, 5(3), 207–219.

Hassay, D.N. & Peloza, J. (2009). Building the charity brand community. *Journal of Nonprofit and Public Sector Marketing*, 21, 24–55.

Keller, K.L. (2008). *Building, Measuring, and Managing Brand Equity*, 3rd edn. Upper Saddle River, NJ: Pearson Prentice Hall.

Laidler-Kylander, N. & Simonin, B. (2009). How international nonprofits build brand equity. *International Journal of Nonprofit and Voluntary Sector Marketing*, 14 (February), 57–69.

Mongueau, L. (2011, June 12). SLANT 45 student service programs not in the end zone after Super Bowl. *Dallas Morning News*, www.dallasnews.com.

Muniz, A. & O'Guinn, T. (2001). Brand community. *Journal of Consumer Research*, 27(4), 412–432.

Munsil, L. (2010, July 29). SLANT 45 draws Dallas-area kids into SuperBowl projects. *Dallas Morning News*, www.dallasnews.com.

Oster, S.M. (1995). *Strategic Management for Nonprofit Organizations*. New York: Oxford University Press.

Reynolds, T.J. & Philips, C.B. (2005). In search of true brand equity measures: all markets ain't created equal. *Journal of Advertising Research*, 45(2), 171.

Ritchie, R.J.B., Swami, S. & Weinberg, C. (1998). A brand new world for non-profits. *International Journal of Nonprofit and Voluntary Sector Marketing*, 3(3), 209–217.

Sargeant, A. & Ford, J.B. (2007). The power of brands. *Stanford Social Innovation Review*, Winter, 40–47.

Stride, H. & Lee, S. (2007). No logo? No way. Branding in the non-profit sector. *Journal of Marketing Management*, 23(1–2), 107–122.

Tapp, A. (1996). Charity brands: a qualitative study of current practice. *Journal of Nonprofit and Public Sector Marketing*, 1(4), 327–336.

Venable, B.T., Rose, G.M., Bush, V.D. & Gilbert, F.W. (2005). The role of brand personality in charitable giving: an assessment and validation. *Journal of the Academy of Marketing Sciences*, 33(3), 295–312.

Voeth, M. & Herbst, U. (2008). The concept of brand personality as an instrument for advanced non-profit branding: an empirical analysis. *Journal of Nonprofit and Public Sector Marketing*, 19(1), 71–97.

Wymer, W. & Grau, S.L. (2010). *Connected Causes: Online Marketing Strategies for Nonprofit Organizations*. Chicago, IL: Lyceum Books.

7. Nonprofit brands and brand management

Nathalie Laidler-Kylander

INTRODUCTION[1]

Global nonprofit brands have been described as the world's new 'super brands' (Wootliff & Deri, 2001). They command unprecedented levels of trust, and their brand valuations are on a par with major international corporations (Laidler-Kylanderet al., 2007). The 2009 Edelman Trust Barometer reveals that nonprofits command greater trust than business, government, and media in all the regions surveyed, except for Asia Pacific: 'Around the world, nonprofits are the only institutions trusted by more than 50% of informed publics' (Edelman PR, 2009). Many nonprofits have become familiar brand names in households around the world and nonprofits have also become the darlings of brand consultants seeking to address, and sometimes fix, their corporate clients' reputational needs through corporate social responsibility. Cross-sector alliances and co-branding initiatives with nonprofits are often viewed as strategic options that generate positive brand image spillovers and enhance brand equity of large firms (Hoeffler & Keller, 2002; Lafferty, 2009; Eisingerich & Rubera, 2010).

While Judd (2004) and others have argued that nonprofits need strong brands just as much as corporations, relatively little work exists pertaining to nonprofit branding and brand management (cf. Laidler-Kylander & Simonin, 2009; Laidler-Kylander et al., 2007). While international nonprofits and their brands are growing in importance and stature, a number of researchers have noted that these same organizations display surprisingly limited brand management activities (Bishop, 2005; Ewing & Napoli, 2005; Nissim, 2004). In search of an explanation, Laidler-Kylander and Simonin (2009) point to five main differences between international nonprofits and their for-profit counterparts, which they suggest might drive nonprofit organizations both to build and to manage their brands somewhat differently than for-profit companies. Briefly, these are: the role of the mission;

the complexity of customers and stakeholders; decentralized and flat organizational structures; collaborative rather than competitive approaches; and different human resources and organizational cultures. Andreasen and Kotler (2002) add that these differences are often coupled with a unique marketing environment in which nonprofits operate. The lack of any explicit brand equity framework specifically designed for the management of nonprofit brands may be one of the reasons for the previously noted limited brand management activities by international nonprofit managers (Haigh & Gilbert, 2005).

DEFINING BRANDS AND BRANDING[2]

In the for-profit sector, Kotler describes a brand as 'a name, term, symbol or design, or a combination of them, which is intended to signify the goods or services of one seller or group of sellers and to differentiate them from those of competitors' (Kotler, 1984). Aaker defines a brand as one of the most important intangible assets of any business (Aaker, 1991) and Bedbury summarizes a brand as 'a psychological concept, held in the minds of the public'. A recent construct by Lencastre and Corte-Real (2010), helps to integrate the definitions above, and specifies three components to the anatomy of a brand: 'the identity sign itself; the marketing object to which the sign refers; and the market response to the sign' (Lencastre & Corte-Real, 2010). Brands are associated with tangible entities such as consumer product goods, places, organizations or people, and help identify and differentiate products and entities, as well as create trust with consumers. In fact, Morrison and Firmstone assert that 'brands function in the same way as trust by simplifying decision making and acting as summarized knowledge' (Morrison & Firmstone, 2000). Brand equity is a measure of the strength of consumers' attachment to the brand and for Aaker, brand equity is 'a set of brand assets and liabilities linked to a brand, its name and symbol, that add to or subtract from the value provided by a product or service to that firm's customers' (Aaker, 1996). These assets and liabilities can be grouped into five main categories or variables: brand loyalty, name awareness, perceived quality, brand associations and other assets (such as patents and trademarks), and can be thought of as the drivers and levers that strengthen brand equity.

NONPROFIT BRANDS

Recent studies by Edelman PR suggest that throughout the world, nonprofit organizations are considered more trustworthy by the general public, carry greater brand trust, and potentially greater brand equity, than all other types of organizations (Edelman PR, 2009). Nonprofit management articles extol the virtues of managing the nonprofit brand and the importance of brand equity for nonprofit organizations (Bosc, 2002; Brunham, 2002; Webster, 2002). Among the top three skills identified as critical for future leaders of nonprofits is the ability to 'build your organization's brand' (Brunham, 2002). Finally, experts such as Smillie consider that the building and nurturing of strong global brands is critical for the future survival of many of today's major international NGOs (Smillie, 1995).

Definitions of the brand and its role differ somewhat for nonprofit organizations. Cuesta defines a nonprofit brand as: 'the shared emotional perception participants and supporters hold in connection with the programs and services (that) a nonprofit offers', and adds that the 'nonprofit brand is a value chain that aligns an organization's mission to the results that the board, staff and volunteers create for participants and supporters' (Cuesta, 2003). Sargeant enriches the brand concept for the nonprofit context by stating that nonprofits brands 'are in essence, a promise to the public that an organization possesses certain features or will behave in certain ways' (Sargeant, 2009). Other authors add that brands are vital internal instruments for galvanizing nonprofit organizations and that the most important advantage a nonprofit has is its brand, defined as a name, symbol, logo, personality or promise that immediately tells the community and the world who you are (Birkin, 2003; Bosc, 2002; Laidler-Kylander et al., 2007). Sargeant and Ford, however, believe that 'strongly differentiated nonprofit brands are surprisingly rare', and that 'nonprofits are perceived as a bland homogenous mass of well-meaning but similar organizations with which donors find it hard to bond emotionally and financially' (Sargeant & Ford, 2007).

Many international nonprofit organizations agree that they rely on their brands for funding, ensuring the safety of their personnel in the field, providing internal cohesion and positioning the organization for potential partnerships (Quelch & Laidler-Kylander, 2005). According to Andreasen and Kotler, nonprofit brands 'imply certain information, convey certain emotions, and can even have their own personality' (Andreasen & Kotler, 2002). More recently, Sametz states that nonprofits and foundations alike can weather the recession and even prosper by strengthening their brands to help them diversify their fundraising sources (Sametz, 2009). However,

Deatherage reports that in her recent work 'with a fairly large and long-established (nonprofit) organization', only a few people within the organization understood what a brand is and what it can do for a nonprofit (Deatherage, 2009). This same author argues that a nonprofit's brand is tied, in the minds of brand audiences, to a particular cause and that in some ways, branding an organization is also about branding the associated cause (Deatherage, 2009). Hankinson suggests that for UK charities, the brand 'unifies the workforce around a common purpose; acts as a catalyst for change; and contributes to the professionalism of the sector' (Hankinson, 2005). She also notes that 'the internal brand should work in tandem with the external brand', which is equivalent to the management of consistency across all points of interaction. Other researchers have noted the protective role of the external brand for some international nonprofit organizations, particularly those organizations active in relief operations (Laidler-Kylanderet al., 2007). These same authors suggest that for Medecins Sans Frontieres, for example, the brand helps protect field workers, enabling the organization to implement its mission.

DIFFERENCES BETWEEN NONPROFIT AND FOR-PROFIT BRANDS

Are the definitions and roles that brand plays really so different between for-profit and nonprofit sectors? What are the similarities and what are the differences? Why does the role that nonprofit brands need to play for their organizations appear to be so much more complex and varied than what is expected or needed in the for-profit sector? If within the nonprofit organization few understand the role of the brand, how can nonprofit organizations effectively manage their brands? These are some of the critical questions that this section of this chapter seeks to address.

Some researchers have found that many nonprofits 'devote little time, energy and care to branding' (Nissim, 2004). Other authors suggest that many 'nonprofits do not effectively utilize and manage their brands' (Bishop, 2005). Ewing and Napoli agree. They are surprised that 'the concept of brand management has been largely overlooked' (Ewing & Napoli, 2005). Bishop concludes that in nonprofit organizations, 'brand management is neglected because marketing itself is seen as a limited range of activities, mainly concerned with fundraising' (Bishop, 2005). Initial field interviews with Amnesty International have revealed that although the organization has a brand with very high equity (based on the Edelman PR findings), executives profess that they 'don't do any branding' (Quelch &

Laidler-Kylander, 2005). Ritchie, Swami and Weinberg caution that branding can appear to be a source of risk to nonprofits. Specifically, they suggest that: 'nonprofit brands can seem commercial; require financial and human resources; and can magnify the impact of negative information about an organization' (Ritchie, Swami & Weinberg, 1999).

So is the perceived limited brand management by nonprofit organizations a result of poor understanding of the importance of brands and limited marketing knowledge, or do nonprofits actually actively engage in brand management but do so in a different way, using different terminology? Many nonprofit organizations have strong, well-recognized brands so nonprofit managers do expend energy and resources building brand equity (although they may not use this terminology). It is probable that the models they use are implicit and intuitive (mental models) that differ from the existing for-profit models of brand equity. Do nonprofit organizations shy away from adopting corporate brand building models for fear that this may upset certain constituents or stakeholders? Could it be that fundamental differences between nonprofits and for-profits drive the differences, making the unilateral adoption of a for-profit brand model by nonprofits unfeasible? To explore this we turn to an analysis of the differences between for-profit and nonprofit actors.

Oster suggests that nonprofit organizations differ from their for-profit counterparts in at least five major areas: their organizational culture; their human resources; their collaborative rather than competitive approaches; the complexity of their customers; and the importance of mission (Oster, 1995). Compared to many international for-profit companies, international nonprofit organizations have highly decentralized organizational structures with low control by headquarters. This is coupled with little formal hierarchy, and a consensus-building culture valued by many individuals choosing to work for nonprofit organizations (Foreman, 1999; Quelch & Laidler-Kylander, 2005). Benz asserts that employees in nonprofit firm have long been viewed as 'intrinsically motivated', deriving non-financial rewards from their work (that may make up for wage differentials with the for-profit sector) (Benz, 2005). This same author's recent study confirms that job satisfaction ratings for employees in nonprofit organizations are higher than in for-profit organizations, and he concludes that nonprofits offer substantial non-pecuniary benefits. Liao, Foreman and Sargeant argue that 'competition has less relevance in the nonprofit arena', since demand for goods and services is 'insatiable'. These same authors add that the concept of collaboration between nonprofit organizations, even between those in competition for securing funds, is at least as important as competition (Liao, Foreman & Sargeant, 2000). Austin suggests that for nonprofit organizations, 'collaboration is becoming the rule', and that 'collaboration is taking place both between nonprofits and between nonprofit and businesses' (Austin, 2000). Some observers believe that nonprofit organizations are more complex to manage than for-profits, due in large part to the broader spectrum of stakeholders and brand audiences (Letts, Ryan & Grossman, 1999) and Ritchie, Swami and Weinberg identify four key brand publics: clients, donors, volunteers and government (Ritchie, Swami & Weinberg, 1999). In addition, nonprofits can be viewed as having upstream activities focused on fundraising, and downstream activities focused on program implementation (Letts, Ryan & Grossman, 1999). A single brand must therefore encompass both sets of activities and address all stakeholders. Because a disconnect exists between the purchaser and user of a nonprofit organization's product or services, purchasers (donors) must rely on their trust in the nonprofit's ability to carry out its mission successfully (Laidler-Kylander et al., 2007). Donor trust is therefore critical and 'brands facilitate the development of trust between a nonprofit and its constituencies' (Ritchie, Swami & Weinberg, 1999). Finally, nonprofits are mission-driven organizations. They lack the common objective shared by for-profit companies, that of making a profit. Instead, nonprofit organizations strive to implement a social mission and this mission becomes both a goal and a rallying cry. Oster argues that the mission in nonprofits creates trust among clients and donors, acts as an organizational boundary, motivates staff and helps in performance evaluations (Oster, 1995). What impact do these five fundamental differences between for-profits and nonprofits have on both the role of their brands and on brand management activities? Which of these differences might make brand management easier or harder for nonprofit organizations? Could some of these differences, such as collaborative nature, provide nonprofits with a competitive advantage in the future?

BRAND EQUITY MODELS

Many for-profit brand equity models exist where brand equity is a measure of brand strength from the perspective of the consumer. Common components of these brand equity models include consumer awareness, loyalty, consumer relationships and the positive consumer perceptions of the brand. Very little however has been written to date specifically about the factors or variables that drive the brand equity in international nonprofit organizations (Haigh and Gilbert, 2005). Laidler-Kylander and Simonin derived a brand equity model for international nonprofits using a system dynamics approach coupled with constant comparison. Using focus groups to elicit the mental models of managers in five large international nonprofit organizations, these authors propose a brand equity model composed of four key variables: trust, focus, partnerships and consistency (Laidler-Kylander & Simonin, 2009). Initial research also suggests that different types of international nonprofit organizations, depending on their organizational focus, may have some inherent differences that might warrant different brand equity models (Laidler-Kylander et al., 2007). Some of these differences include: different donor characteristics, purchase decisions and involvement; brand ownership differences; and varying criteria for organizational success and brand trust. Other researchers conclude that characteristics of accountability, for example, vary with type of nonprofit, and offer three different categories of nonprofit organizations: membership organizations, service organizations and network organizations (Ebrahim, 2003). In the for-profit sector, for example, different brand equity models for service companies have been proposed on the basis of inherent differences between the selling of services and products (Berry, 2000). Brand valuation is also starting to appear in the nonprofit field (Laidler-Kylander et al., 2007) and Haigh and Gilbert suggest that the process of valuing nonprofit brands can 'provide greater understanding and appreciation' of the brand itself and that the process of valuation is as important as the outcome (Haigh & Gilbert, 2005).

It would seem therefore that for nonprofits, brands and the role that brands play differ from the traditional scope and definitions found in the for-profit sector. Brands in the nonprofit sector must play a greater number of roles throughout the 'value chain' and engage a broader array of brand audiences. Given the differences between for-profits and nonprofits, the activities and models used to manage brands and build brand equity also differ, and nonprofit managers may rely on more implicit models that do not include traditional brand terminology. Laidler-Kylander and Simonin propose an empirical model that suggests that nonprofit brand equity may be driven by factors such as focus, consistency, trust and partnerships, rather than constructs of loyalty and awareness, which are found at the heart of many for-profit brand equity models (Laidler-Kylander & Simonin, 2009). For these authors, trust is particularly important because there is often disconnect between the buyers (donors) and users (recipients) of the product or service being provided by the nonprofit organization. Therefore both buyers and users make decisions to participate on the basis of the perceived trustworthiness of a particular nonprofit organization. Anything that erodes that trust, reduces brand equity. A nonprofit with a tight operational focus will more clearly stand for something specific in the minds of multiple audiences, and provides a brand with visibility and clarity, both of which enhance brand equity. Consistency between operations and communications as well as consistency in both over time helps build brand awareness and recognition. Finally, the corporations and nonprofits that a nonprofit organization decides to partner with impact, by association, how different audiences perceive that organization's own brand.

As brand management has increased amongst nonprofits, so too have brand protection activities. While strong brands are typically built slowly and over time, with substantial monetary investments, a brand can be easily destroyed. As indicated by Laider-Kylander, Quelch and Simonin: 'the negative impacts of scandals and criticisms, association with undesirable corporations, or simply the dilution of the brand through too many partnerships can significantly weaken a brand and substantially reduce its value' (Laider-Kylander et al., 2007). While such statements support the need for some level of brand protectionism within an organization, they may also promote 'brand narcissism' and increased risk aversion.

Recent scandals in the nonprofit sector have highlighted the manner in which brand can magnify negative information about an organization (Ritchie, Swami & Weinberg, 1999). For example, publicity surrounding the misuse of funds by the American Red Cross in 2001 had a negative impact on the fundraising ability of other Red Cross societies worldwide. Another such instance occurred in the United States in 1992, when it was found that the president of the United Way of America had engaged in nepotism, used charitable donations to finance a free-spending lifestyle, and transferred funds to spin-off organizations in which he and other officials had financial interests (Ritchie, Swami & Weinberg, 1999). Declines in contributions were as high as 20 percent in some local affiliates, despite the fact that each office was independent and separately incorporated.

If a nonprofit's brand enables the alignment of an organization's mission to the results that the board, staff and volunteers create for participants and supporters (Cuesta, 2003), then brand management activities that strengthen this alignment and implementation of mission should result in increased brand equity. On the other hand, brand management activities that either cause a misalignment, or reduce the organization's ability to implement its mission, may result in a decrease in brand equity. Perhaps two kinds of brand management activities co-exist for nonprofit organizations: activities that focus on increasing brand equity through alignment and mission implementation; and brand-protecting activities that seek to reduce the risk to this same brand equity. Do the brand-protecting activities impose limits on a nonprofit's ability to take risk and stretch the organization? What are the other potential downsides or detrimental aspects of traditional brand management activities?

IMPORTANCE OF INTERNAL BRANDING

Internal branding is emerging as 'one of the hottest topics in marketing today' (Bobula, 2005). In research conducted in 2007 on the drivers of brand equity in large international nonprofit organizations, study participants defined the internal brand as a 'mirror', or 'the essence of the organization, shaping our ideas and beliefs' (Laidler-Kylander, 2007). These definitions of a brand's role fit the three criteria of internal branding defined by Bergstrom, Blumenthal and Crothers: (1) communicating the brand effectively to the employees; (2) convincing them of its relevance; and (3) successfully linking every job in the organization to the delivery of the brand essence (Bergstrom, Blumenthal & Crothers, 2002). In addition, the proposal by Hankinson that internal branding 'unifies the workforce around a common purpose' echoes those definitions captured by Laidler-Kylander's research described above (Hankinson, 2005).

An important theme from the internal branding literature is that of consistency between the internal and external brand (Aurand, Gorchels & Bishop, 2005; Bergstrom, Blumenthal & Crothers, 2002; Burmann & Zeplin, 2005; Davies & Chun, 2002). Burmann and Zeplin state that the strength of a brand is 'determined by the consistency of the different brand identity components which ensures that the gaps between desired and actual brand identity and the outside perception remain small' (Burmann & Zeplin, 2005). In addition, Vallaster notes the importance in internal branding lies in creating a 'coherent brand understanding among employees from different cultural backgrounds'. She argues that the 'internal brand building process becomes more complex as global organizations increasingly employ a multicultural workforce' (Vallaster, 2004).

With respect to internal branding, international nonprofit organizations may be ahead of the curve since they seem to have accepted and embraced the importance of internal branding, whereas it is still emerging in the for-profit arena. It is also possible that the greater importance of internal branding for nonprofits is a direct reflection of the differences between nonprofits and for-profits, as highlighted earlier in the chapter. Specifically, the often decentralized organizational structures, consensus-building culture and motivational needs of nonprofit employees suggest that the role of the brand internally is as important, if not more important, than the external role (Foreman, 1999).

FUTURE MODELS OF NONPROFIT BRANDING[3]

A recent 18-month study by the Hauser Center at the Harvard Kennedy School, funded by a grant from the Rockefeller Foundation, provides a new framework for nonprofit practitioners to help understand the role of their brands and how they might better manage this asset (Kylander & Stone, 2012). These authors suggest that the dominant brand paradigm typical in nonprofit organizations a decade ago, which focused on communications and fundraising, is being replaced by a broader, more strategic concept of brand which contributes to an organization's mission and theory of change, as well as playing an internal role in expressing an organization's core values. These same authors advance a framework consisting of a role of brand cycle and the 'Brand IDEA'.

Role of Brand Cycle

Kylander and Stone (2012) suggest that the role of brand is to advance the nonprofit organization's strategy and that the management of brand is nested within an organization's strategy, which is in turn, nested within an organization's mission and values. Internally, the brand embodies the identity of the organization capturing both mission and values. Externally, the brand reflects the image held in the minds of the organization's multiple external stakeholders. A nonprofit brand is most powerful when the organization's values and mission are aligned with its brand identity, and when this internal identity is in turn aligned with the external image. Organizations with strong alignment among mission, values and brand identity on the one hand, and brand identity and brand image on the other, are able to establish a clear, distinct, consistent and credible position in the minds of both internal and external stakeholders. Internally, the result of strong alignment and clear positioning is cohesion among diverse internal constituencies. Externally, the result is greater trust among multiple audiences: including partners, beneficiaries, participants and donors. Internally, a strong brand identity means having a clear sense of who the organization is, what it does and why this is important. When an organization's employees and volunteers across functional areas and geographies all embrace a common brand identity, it creates organizational cohesion, builds focus and reinforces shared values. Externally, the importance of brand creating trust is familiar enough. Because nonprofit organizations rely on establishing trust with many external audiences, including partners of all kinds, doing what you say you do (alignment between identity and image) is critically important. Both internal cohesion (akin to the concept 'consistency' in Laidler-Kylander and Simonin, 2009) and high levels of external trust contribute to building greater organizational capacity and fueling social impact. A cohesive organization makes more efficient and focused use of existing resources and external trust attracts additional talent, financing, and authority. This increase in organizational capacity is directly related to an organization's ability to have enhanced social impact. By leveraging the trust of partners, beneficiaries and policy-makers among others, an organization is in a better position to effectively implement its mission objectives.

The Nonprofit Brand Idea

Flowing from the Role of Brand Cycle described above, Kylander and Stone propose four principles captured in the nonprofit brand IDEA: brand integrity, brand democracy, brand ethics, and brand affinity. Brand integrity means that the brand is aligned with, and bonded to, the mission of the organization and that the brand identity is aligned with the brand image. To be clear, the word 'integrity' here is used in the sense of structural integrity, not moral integrity. Internally, a brand with high structural integrity connects the mission to the identity of the organization, giving members, staff, volunteers, trustees, and others a common sense of why the organization does what it does, and why it matters in the world. Externally, a brand with high structural integrity captures the mission in its public image, and deploys that image in service of its mission at every step of a clearly articulated strategy.

Brand democracy means that the nonprofit organization trusts its members, staff, participants and volunteers to communicate their own clear understanding of the organization's core identity and be its brand advocates. The need to exert control on how the brand is presented and portrayed in order to exercise consistency is largely eliminated and replaced with brand democracy in which every employee and volunteer becomes an effective brand ambassador. With the rise in social media, brand control becomes increasingly difficult, if not impossible, and the concept of brand democracy extends beyond the traditional boundaries of the organization, which become increasingly porous, to include anyone blogging or tweeting about a particular organization. For brand democracy to work effectively, an organization must have organizational cohesion driven by a strong brand identity. Brand democracy, however, is not brand anarchy. Each organization can establish the limits or parameters on its brand, but the space within these limits can be large, and individuals as well as regional offices can be encouraged to use that space creatively, learning from each other with the head office celebrating especially creative or effective original brand images, slogans, or other representations.

Brand ethics means that the brand itself and the way in which the brand is deployed reflects the core values of the organization. Just as brand integrity aligns and cements the brand with mission, brand ethics aligns both the brand identity and the brand image with the core values and culture of the organization. Brand ethics appear in a double role: the establishment of an ethical brand, and the ethical use of brand.

Finally, brand affinity means that the brand is a good team player. It works well alongside other brands, sharing space and credit generously, promoting collective over individual interests. Such a brand attracts partners and collaborators, for it lends value to the partnerships without exploiting them. An organization with high brand affinity has shaped and managed its brand so that it combines smoothly and generously with its partners, collaborators and coalition members. Indeed, nonprofit organizations with the highest brand affinity actually promote the brands of their partners as much or more than they promote their own brands. Although the concept here is focused principally on organization brands, brand affinity appears to be at work especially clearly in coalition and movement brands, where multiple organizations join in a common cause that will have its own image and identity. Organizations with ambitious, multifaceted or long-term social objectives usually have a clear understanding of their own limited internal capacity and their need for multiple partners to achieve these broad social goals. Such organizations can focus their brand on these broad social goals rather than their individual organizations, promoting collective over individual interests.

IMPLICATIONS FOR BRAND MANAGEMENT AND HUMAN RESOURCES

Alongside the human capital of employees and volunteers, the nonprofit's organizational brand may be its most critical asset. Yet in the nonprofit sector there lingers both a reticence towards brand management, and a limited understanding of the potential role that the brand can play within the organization. Given the differences between for-profit and nonprofit organizations, effective management of a nonprofit brand may require a slightly different approach. Many of these differences center around both the people and culture of nonprofit organizations, and the recent models and frameworks that have been advanced to help nonprofit practitioners manage their brands take these differences into account. The importance of the internal role that brands play in nonprofit organizations has been highlighted. Indeed, internal branding may be as important for nonprofit practitioners as external branding. Brand equity can be enhanced in the nonprofit sector by emphasizing factors such as trust, focus, consistency and partner selection and the Brand IDEA framework can be a helpful tool for managing the broader, more strategic role of nonprofit brands.

Creating Brand Integrity Using Brand Democracy

In practical terms, a starting point for many nonprofit brand managers is to ensure that brand identity is aligned both with the organization's mission and values, and with the image held by key external constituents. This can sometimes be quite challenging since operational activities often evolve over time and the stated mission or external perceptions of the brand might not keep up. WWF is a good example; although the brand and panda logo are very well known, the majority of the organization's current activities are predominantly focused on habitat preservation and pollution reduction, not species conservation, as many external stakeholders believe. A disconnect therefore exists between the brand identity and brand image. WWF is addressing this issue by emphasizing the critical connection between habitat preservation and species conservation in its communications.

Many brand managers can conduct an analysis of current brand identity and ascertain how well this fits with their stated mission and strategy, as well as existing brand identity. Brand identity combines what the organization actually does, and what employees and other internal stakeholders believe the organization stands for and why it is important. The brand image can be determined using market research tools such as focus groups, interviews or surveys, or simply by asking external stakeholders who come into contact with staff what they think the organization does and stands for. The goal of this analysis will be to develop greater clarity, focus and buy-in in terms of the organizational identity, and to help staff promote an image consistent with this identity, thereby increasing brand integrity. As Kylander and Stone also suggest, both the elucidation and the dissemination of the brand require a democratic approach, and high levels of internal involvement and participation. Brand managers should be sure to poll internal stakeholders, and provide discussion forums and training opportunities around both the role of the brand on the one hand, and the individual organization's own brand identity on the other. It is important to have some degree of visual consistency in communicating the brand, but it is far more effective when employees discuss the organization's brand in personal and individual ways that create a consistent image. The benefit of a strong internal brand, as Brown notes (Brown, 2010), is that it guides decision-making and helps frame how internal stakeholders approach everything they do, including interacting with external stakeholders, thereby increasing efficiency and reducing the risk to brand equity. The strong internal brand, developed and communicated by internal constituents, helps create a focused, consistent external brand that is highly aligned with the internal brand, and results in greater brand trust externally. Interestingly, with the rise in importance and use of social media and communications, the distinction between internal and external stakeholders becomes somewhat blurred and the organizational boundaries increasingly porous.[4] The result is that a broader spectrum of individuals, including members or movement participants, can be included in this democratic approach to brand management. The Girl Effect brand, developed by the Nike Foundation in 2008 to promote development programs for adolescents, is an example of an open source brand, originally designed to influence key decision-makers in the development space, which has morphed into a movement with close to 1 million organizational and individual 'champions'. The challenge now facing the Nike Foundation and its key partners is how to integrate these 'champions' in the evolution of the Girl Effect brand, in order to maximize the positive impact for adolescent girls worldwide.

Leveraging Brand Ethics To Promote Brand Affinity

A democratically developed and communicated brand is anchored in the values and ethics of internal constituents and draws from the organization's mission and the values it espouses. For many nonprofits, the mission that drives the organization is unattainable without the cooperation and help of other organizations, governments and corporations. To be successful, nonprofit organizations need to develop partnerships and promote support for their theory of change. Indeed, the number and scope of partnerships (including cross-sector partnerships), coalitions and movements that nonprofits participate in has increased substantially between 2000 and 2005 (Global Corporate Citizenship Initiative, 2005). As previously noted, a brand with high brand affinity works well with other brands, and shares space and credit generously, promoting collective over individual interests. Nonprofit managers can attract key partners and collaborators by exploring and defining how joint value can be created and derived from partnerships. They can ask themselves and their staff which players in both the nonprofit sector, as well as business and governmental sectors, the organization might effectively partner with to further its mission and goals. How, specifically, can these organizations help further the mission and how can the nonprofit organization add value to that potential partner? Going back to the example of WWF, the organization establishes partnerships with large corporations and strives to help these partners change their environmental practices and lower their emissions levels. This key strategy helps WWF reduce pollution, and helps credibly position partnering companies as environmentally conscious. Nonprofit managers can shape and managed the brand so that the nonprofit combines smoothly and generously with its partners, collaborators and coalition members. Brand affinity appears to be at work especially clearly in coalition and movement brands, where multiple organizations join together in a common cause that emerges with its own image and identity and enhances the brand equity of all its members.

FINAL THOUGHTS

A brand does not belong to an organization or its management. A brand is a concept held in the minds of all stakeholders, both internal and external. The role of the brand for nonprofits is critical in every aspect of its operations, from funding to recruiting employees and volunteers, establishing partnerships, and delivering its products and services. All along the theory of change of an organization, the brand plays a role in garnering resources (human and financial), establishing credibility and trust, and enabling effective deployment of operations and the attainment of goals. A brand serves to create cohesion internally and trust externally. Every employee, volunteer, member and supporter becomes a nonprofit's brand ambassador. A nonprofit manager's task is to: ensure that brand is rooted in the organization's culture, values and ethics; promote integrity between mission, values, identity and image; implement a democratic approach to both the development and communication of the brand; and use the brand to build partnerships and coalitions that most effectively further the organization's social mission and overall objectives.

NOTES

1. The author would like to thank and acknowledge Dr Bernard Simonin, co-author and mentor, whose work is reflected in this chapter.
2. Much of this section emanates from work done at the Harvard Kennedy School's Hauser Center on the Role of Brand, sponsored by the Rockefeller Foundation in 2011.
3. Much of this section draws on Kylander and Stone (2012).
4. For more on this see Scearce, Kasper and McLeod Grant (2010).

REFERENCES

Aaker, D. (1991). *Managing Brand Equity*. New York: Free Press.
Aaker, D. (1996). *Building Strong Brands*. New York: Free Press.

Andreasen, A. & Kotler, P. (2002). *Strategic Marketing for Nonprofit Organizations*, 6th edn. Upper Saddle River, NJ: Prentice-Hall.

Aurand, Timothy W., Gorchels, Linda & Bishop, Terrence R. (2005). Human resource management's role in internal branding: an opportunity for cross-functional brand message synergy. *Journal of Product and Brand Management*, 14(3), 163–169.

Austin, James (2000). Strategic collaboration between nonprofits and businesses. *Nonprofit and Voluntary Sector Quarterly*, 29, 69–97.

Bedbury, Scott (2002). *A New Brand World*, New York: Viking Press.

Benz, Matthias (2005). Not for the profit, but for the satisfaction? – evidence on worker well-being in non-profit firms. *International Review for Social Sciences*, 88(2), 155–176.

Bergstrom, Alan, Blumenthal, Danielle & Crothers, Scott (2002). Why internal branding matters: the case of Saab. *Corporate Reputation Review*, 2(3), 133–142.

Berry, Leonard (2000). Cultivating service brand equity. *Journal of the Academy of Marketing Science*, 29(1), 128–37.

Birkin, Michael (2003). Nonprofit brands: let the word go forth. Onphilanthropy.com, http://www.onphilanthropy.com/site/News2?page=NewsArticle&id=6288, accessed November 2005.

Bishop, D. (2005). Not-for-profit brands: why are many under-utilized by their owners? Paper presented at the 2nd Australian Nonprofit and Social Marketing Conference, September 22–23, Melbourne, Australia.

Bobula, Jessica (2005). Internal branding becomes a hot topic for b-to-b. *B to B*, 90(11), 6.

Bosc, Joyce (2002). Brands: they need to work just as hard as you do! *Nonprofit World*, 20(1), 29–31.

Brown, W. (2010). Strategic management. In Renz, D.O., Herman, R.D. & Associates, *The Jossey Bass Handbook of Nonprofit Leadership and Management*, 3rd edn. San Francisco, CA: Jossey Bass, pp. 207–209.

Brunham, K. (2002). What skills will nonprofit leaders need in the future? *Nonprofit World*, 20(3), 33–36.

Burmann, C. and Zeplin, S. (2005). Building brand commitment: a behavioral approach to internal brand management. *Journal of Brand Management*, 12, 279–300.

Cuesta, Carlo (2003). Building the nonprofit brand from the inside out. Creation in Common LLC, at http://www.creationincommon.com.

Davies, G. and Chun, R. (2002). Gaps between the internal and external perceptions of the corporate brand. *Corporate Reputation Review*, 5(2–3), 144–158.

Deatherage, J. (2009). The importance of nonprofit branding. *Philanthropy Journal*, July 24.

Ebrahim, Alnoor (2003). Making sense of accountability: conceptual perspectives for northern and southern nonprofits. *Nonprofit Management and Leadership*, 14(2), 191–212.

Edelman PR (2009). Edelman Trust Barometer. http://www.edelman.com/trust/2009/.

Eisingerich, A.B. & Rubera, G. (2010). Drivers of brand commitment: a cross-national investigation. *Journal of International Marketing*, 18, 64–79.

Ewing, M. & Napoli, J. (2005). Developing and validating a multidimensional nonprofit brand orientation scale. *Journal of Business Research*, 58(6), 841–853.

Foreman, Karen (1999). Evolving global structures and the challenges facing international relief and development organizations. *Nonprofit and Voluntary Sector Quarterly*, 28, 178–197.

Global Corporate Citizenship Initiative (2005). Partnering for success. Harvard Kennedy School, presented at the World Economic Forum, January.

Haigh, D. & Gilbert, S. (2005). Valuing not-for-profit and charity brands – real insight or just smoke and mirrors. *International Journal of Nonprofit and Voluntary Sector Marketing*, 10(2), 107–130.

Hankinson, Philippa (2005). The internal brand in leading UK charities. *Journal of Product and Brand Management*, 13(2–3), 84.

Hoeffler, S. & Keller, K.L. (2002). Building brand equity through corporate societal marketing. *Journal of Public Policy and Marketing*, 21(1), 78–89.

Kotler, P. (1984). *Marketing Management*, Englewood Cliffs, NJ: Prentice Hall.

Kylander, N. and Stone, C. (2012). The role of brand in the nonprofit sector. *Stanford Social Innovation Review*, Spring.

Judd, N. (2004). On branding: building and maintaining your organization's brand in an AMC. *Association Management*, 56(7), 17–19.

Lafferty, B. (2009). Selecting the right cause partners for the right reasons: the role of importance and fit in cause-brand alliances. *Psychology and Marketing*, 26(4), 359.

Laidler-Kylander, N. (2007). Brand equity in international nonprofit organizations: a system dynamics approach. Doctoral dissertation.

Laidler-Kylander, N., Quelch, J.A. & Simonin, B.L. (2007). Building and valuing global brands in the nonprofit sector. *Nonprofit Management and Leadership*, 17(3), 253–277.

Laidler-Kylander, N. & Simonin, B. (2009). How international nonprofits build brand equity. *International Journal of Nonprofit and Voluntary Sector Marketing*, 14(1), 57–69.

Lencastre, P. & Corte-Real, A. (2010). One, two, three: a practical brand anatomy. *Journal of Brand Management*, 17, 399–412.

Letts, Christine W., Ryan, William P. & Grossman, Allen (1999). *High Performance Nonprofit Organizations: Managing Upstream For Greater Impact*. New York: John Wiley & Sons.

Liao, Mei-Na, Foreman, Susan & Sargeant, Adrian (2000). Market versus social orientation in the nonprofit context. *International Journal of Nonprofit and Voluntary Sector Marketing*, 6(3), 254–268.

Morrison, D.E. & Firmstone, J. (2000). The social function of trust and implications for e-commerce. *International Journal of Advertising*, 19(5), 32–57.

Nissim, B. (2004). Nonprofit branding: unveiling the essentials. http://www.guidestar.org/DisplayArticle.do?articleId=833, accessed January 2006.

Oster, Sharon M. (1995). *Strategic Management for Nonprofit Organizations*. New York: Oxford University Press.

Quelch, John & Laidler-Kylander, N. (2005). *The New Global Brands: Managing Non-Government Organizations in the 21st Century*. Toronto: Southwestern Publishing Company.

Ritchie, R., Swami, S. & Weinberg, C. (1999). A brand new world for nonprofits. *International Journal of Nonprofit and Voluntary Sector Marketing*, 4(1), 26–42.

Sametz (2009). Brand new day. *Boston Business Journal.* http://www.bizjournals.com/boston/stories/2009/03/30/story15.html?page=all.

Sargeant, A. (2009). *Marketing management for nonprofit organizations*, 3rd edn. Oxford, Oxford University Press.

Sargeant, Adrian & Ford, John B. (2007). The power of brands. *Stanford Social Innovation Review*, 5(1), 40–48.

Scearce, D., Kasper, G. & McLeod Grant, H. (2010). Working Wikily. *Stanford Social Innovation Review*, Summer.

Smillie, Ian (1995). *The Alms Bazaar: Altruism Under Fire: Non-Profit Organizations and International Development.* Ottawa: International Development Research Centre.

Vallaster, Christine (2004). Internal brand building in multicultural organisations: a roadmap towards action. *Qualitative Market Research*, 7(2), 100–113.

Webster, K. (2002). Branding the nonprofit. The Canterbury Group Ltd. http://zunia.org/uploads/media/knowledge/Non_prof.pdf.

Wootliff, J. & Deri, C. (2001). NGOs: the new super brands. *Corporate Reputation Review*, 4(2), 157–66.

8. Enhancing learning and skill development among paid staff and volunteers in nonprofit organizations

Jeannette Blackmar and Kelly LeRoux

Investment in human capital is essential to achieving high-performing nonprofit organizations. As Rodriquez et al. (2002, p. 309) concisely put it, 'High-performing people are critical for high-performing organizations.' A skilled workforce is critical in meeting the continuously complex demands placed on the nonprofit sector from myriad stakeholders. For example, due in part to the economic downturn in the United States (US), the nonprofit sector faces rising demands for services such as food banks, homeless shelters, counseling, emergency assistance, and family support services. Coupled with dramatic increases in an aging US population (US Department of Health and Human Services, 2011), nonprofits are experiencing greater demands for services than ever before, especially in the areas of health, human services and housing. Finally, in a performance-driven era, nonprofits are held to be increasingly accountable by donors (West, 2010a), regulatory agencies, funding entities, and the public. Combined, these multifaceted challenges require nonprofit managers and administrators to be equipped with specialized skills (Tierney, 2006). In its 'State of the Nonprofit Industry Survey', Blackbaud (2004) identified top management challenges reported by 1319 professionals as securing funding, ensuring program growth, driving board effectiveness, retaining staff, mission awareness and keeping pace with technology.

Moreover, nonprofit organizations today are embedded in the twenty-first century's knowledge-based economy where a 'high-knowledge, multi-skilled workforce is the most important competitive resource available to organizations today' (ASTD Public Policy Council, 2003, p. 6; Murphy and Garavan, 2009, p. 3). In addition to an up-to-date technically savvy workforce, a strong workforce must be able 'to learn quickly, adapt to change, communicate effectively, and foster interpersonal relationships' (Rodriquez et al., 2002, p. 310; ASTD Public Policy Council, 2003). The demand for such a workforce places 'human resource skill development through continuous employee training at center stage' (McMullen and Schellenberg, 2003, p. 6). Important, too, is viewing human capital holistically. This requires considerations of having not only enough people, but highly skilled and talented employees as well as volunteers, and placed in the right positions (Collins, 2002; Bryan, Joyce and Weiss, 2006). Yet, a distressing finding reported by the ASTD Public Policy Council (2003, p. 6) is that: 'At the heart of the human capital challenge facing organizations today, is the fact that skilled and knowledgeable workers are fast becoming an endangered species.'

Based on Paul Light's research, nonprofits leaders should be encouraged by the fact that nonprofit sector benefits from employees who are more committed, more motivated and more skilled on average than employees in both the for-profit and government sectors (Light, 2002). However, this glee may be subdued by the further finding that nonprofit organizations lagged in their ability and efforts to support a skilled and dedicated workforce (Light, 2002). In a call for nonprofit organizations to proactively support their workforce, Light cautions: 'Gone are the days when the nonprofit sector could count on a steady stream of new recruits willing to accept the stress, burnout, and the persistent lack of resources that come with a nonprofit job.' Despite an abundance of empirical research indicating training is a wise investment (Aguinis and Kraiger, 2009; Gault, 2010; Lowe and Schellenberg, 2001; McMullen and Schellenberg, 2003), many nonprofit organizations do not provide training, or integrate it fully with organizational management activities, or provide training on a continual basis for all their employees and volunteers. Furthermore, staff and volunteer training is often one of the first activities cut from the budget in the face of economic hardship or uncertainty. In some regards it appears that limited resources provide the reason for nonprofits to excuse the absence of training without taking 'into account the financial impacts of not having a training program' (Gault, 2010). Specifically, 31 percent of the nonprofits in Light's study indicated that organizations rarely or sometimes provide access to training (Light, 2002, p. 9). More recently, Bonner and Obergas (2009, p. 4) report in their study of 36 leaders of nonprofit human service entities that 'most nonprofits have not budgeted adequately or intentionally for professional development of their staff'.

It is critical that the nonprofit sector – both its organizations and scholars – prioritize human resources management, and specifically human resources development, in practice, empirical research and theory. This is critical as a multitude of workforce challenges directly threaten to undermine nonprofit capacity and, thus, effectiveness. These workforce challenges include turnover and vacancy, recruitment and retention, and 'leadership deficit'. Moreover, the culturally diverse workforce of today demands nonprofits 'work towards a future where inclusiveness is an intentional strategy' (HR Council for the Voluntary & Non-profit Sector, 2009, p. 7). Thus, an organizational challenge is how to create a culture that embraces inclusivity, going beyond cultural diversity to include sexual orientation, age, gender and disability (HR Council for the Voluntary & Non-profit Sector, 2009). Interestingly, the demographic realities point to both intergenerational leadership challenges with an influx of a new generation of workers, the Millennials, as well as the shrinking availability of nonprofit leaders.

The importance of having a skilled nonprofit workforce is made even more pronounced by the emerging leadership gap in the nonprofit sector. A number of scholars have pointed to a leadership crisis in the nonprofit sector (Schmitz and Stroup, 2005; Sims and Trager, 2009; Tierney, 2006) directly related to both the growth of the sector and retirement – or nearing retirement – of baby boomers (Halpern, 2006). Essentially, the supply of leaders is shrinking but the demand is ever-growing. As Tierney (2006, p. 9) describes, 'our leadership needs, it seems, are unprecedented'. The leadership deficit is intertwined with the ability (or lack thereof) of nonprofits to attract, train and nurture staff to prepare them for leadership positions (Schmitz and Stroup, 2005). A compounding factor is that the typical nonprofit organizational structure lacks opportunities for upward mobility. Schmitz and Stroup (2005) report that 'only 27% of nonprofit employees are satisfied with chances for advancement'. Therefore, there is the 'need to move out in order to move up' (Ban, Drahnak-Faller and Towers, 2003, p. 141). This is a drain of highly skilled and talented people. Importantly, Lobell and Connolly (2007) suggest that the nonprofit sector may have the benefit of better leaders than the for-profit sector. Their research points to the critical necessity of addressing the leadership deficit 'by exploring how we design and provide access to high-quality leadership development opportunities' (Lobell and Connolly, 2007, p. 24).

Further compounding issues contributing to the leadership crisis – as well as nonprofit staffing generally – is the lack of resources nonprofits have to dedicate to recruitment (Ban, Drahnak-Faller and Towers, 2003; Tierney, 2006) and the inability to 'attract, retain and advance those who are underrepresented in leadership, especially people of color' (Schmitz and Stroup, 2005). Tierney (2006, p. 31) reports:

> unlike businesses, most nonprofits cannot cultivate their own supply of future leaders. Successful companies routinely invest enormous amounts of time and money attracting talented junior managers and developing them into leaders. Most nonprofits (even larger ones) are too small to provide meaningful career

> development opportunities for their employees. Most cannot afford the huge investment in recruitment and human resources that such development requires – especially when boards, funders, and donors view such expenditures as wasteful overhead. Consequently, nonprofits have little option but to search outside their own organizations for new senior managers.

Resource scarcity is not limited to recruitment efforts but extends to an overall shortage of professional human resources management departments and/or personnel in nonprofit organizations (Ban, Drahnak-Faller and Towers, 2003; Halpern, 2006; Schmitz and Stroup, 2005). As Schmitz and Stroup (2005) report:

> Only 12 percent of nonprofit organizations have a dedicated staff member who focuses on personnel matters, and at 53 percent of nonprofit organizations, the executive director handles all human-resource duties. Only 10 percent of leaders of small organizations have received any human-resources training, yet even large organizations with human-resource departments face workforce challenges.

Without dedicated and professional human resource management expertise, it may be more difficult for nonprofit organizations to recruit, retain, and develop the skills and human capital potential of prospective employees and volunteers.

Each of the issues we have discussed thus far – including the rising demand for nonprofit services, increasing diversity of the nonprofit workforce, increasing competition for dedicated staff and volunteers, high turnover rates, the emerging leadership gap, and the critical link between human resources and organizational performance – points to the need for nonprofits to invest in the learning and skill development of their employees and volunteers. In this chapter, we examine the types of skills required for today's nonprofit workforce, as well as the various methods, both formal and informal, for enhancing the skills of nonprofit employees and volunteers. First, however, we turn to a discussion of training and the importance of its role in promoting skill development.

THE CRITICAL ROLE OF TRAINING IN SKILL DEVELOPMENT

While substantial literature has been focused on the nonprofit workforce (Halpern, 2006; Light, 2002), less attention is dedicated within the nonprofit scholarly literature on nonprofit training and development (but see Dolan, 2002; Garvey, 2009; Macduff, 2005; Pynes, 2009, pp. 308–335).

The one notable exception is nonprofit leadership development. In contrast, much research has been devoted to staff training in the fields of psychology, human resource management, human resource development (HRD) and knowledge management.

On the one hand, Dolan's (2002, p. 289) exploratory research findings indicate that training could be designed to meet the generic needs of the sector, as he found 'a lack of any significant association between training needs and those variables (such as organization type, size, source of resources) typically used to differentiate among organizations'. However, empirical research focused on key questions integral to nonprofit training and development is sorely needed. As recognized in human resource development literature and outlined by Pynes, there are five key questions related to nonprofit training and staff development: (1) 'How can we develop a comprehensive training plan to address the needs of managers … support staff, volunteers and board members?'(2) 'What methods can we use to assess our agency's training needs?' (3) 'How can we design and implement the training program?' (4) 'What training delivery methods will we use?' and (5) 'How will we demonstrate that the training budget was well spent?' (Pynes, 2009, p. 310). Nonprofit leaders and human resource personnel must carefully consider each of these questions as they plan for training and skill development activities and programs within their organizations.

First, we should begin with a definition of training. Training is a core component of the development function within human resources management that provides the workforce with opportunities to learn and develop skills (Klinger and Nalbandian, 2003). Reflecting a change in the focus on the process of training to a focus on the outcomes, training is often referred to as human resource development (Blanchard and Thacker, 2004). While commonly training and development are taken together, we focus here on staff [and volunteer] training. Training has been defined in numerous ways (Table 8.1).

Consistent amongst all of these definitions is the notion that training is a systematic, planned process that extends beyond the individual to impact positive change within the organization. While often contrasted with development, in that training focuses on learning related to current job tasks and responsibilities, it nonetheless impacts both job and organizational effectiveness. Thus, training must be aligned with performance, contributing to 'the long-term health of the organization. It positions us to meet change head-on. In fact, a well-developed workforce does not react to change – it creates change' (Fitzgerald, 1992, p. 81). In order for training to deliver on its promise as a tool for 'strengthening organizational effectiveness in the

Table 8.1

Author(s)	Training Definition
Fitzgerald (1992, p. 81)	'the acquisition of knowledge and skill for present tasks'; 'a tool to help individuals contribute to the organization and be successful in their current positions'; 'a means to an end'
Cascio (1988, p. 348)	'planned programs of organizational improvement through changes in skill, knowledge, attitude or social behavior'
Wexley and Latham (1981, p. 3)	'a planned effort by an organization to facilitate the learning of job-related behavior on the part of employees'
Aguinis and Kraiger (2009, p. 452)	'the systematic approach to affecting individuals' knowledge, skills, and attitudes in order to improve individual, team, and organizational effectiveness'
Willingham (2006)	'Training, on the other hand [contrasted to education], is a process that causes new habits, skills, attitudes, or behaviors to be formed. Getting people to automatically respond is the objective of training. Training involves behavior change'

face of continuous change', it must not be 'isolated from other organizational activities nor from an integrated human resources strategic plan' (HR Council for the Voluntary & Non-profit Sector, 2009). Additionally, the focus of training as a process is critical (Pynes, 2009). It emphasizes a comprehensive view of training that incorporates both inputs and outputs. Blanchard and Thacker (2004, p. 21) provide a framework of the training process that includes inputs (organizational needs, employee needs, budget, equipment and staff), process (analysis, design, method, implementation and evaluation) and outputs (knowledge, skills, attitudes, motivation and job performance).

However, even with the view of training as a process, the question of training effectiveness to organizational performance remains elusive. McMullen and Schellenberg (2003, p. 6) report a positive relationship between performance and training, namely in that training provides increased self-confidence and job satisfaction. Thus, training goes beyond the enhancement of skill-building but positively affects employee attitude. They write that training 'can also act as a signal that employers recognize that employees are faced with new skill demands and that they are committed to their employees – key factors affecting the quality of the employment relationship and ultimately productivity, morale, recruitment and retention (McMullen and Schellenberg, 2003, p. 46). Aguinis and Kraiger make explicit their recognition of the 'overwhelming evidence in favor of the benefits that training produces for individuals and teams, organizations and society (Aguinis and Kraiger, 2009, p. 467). These benefits relate directly to organizational performance such as improved quality and quantity of goods and services. But coupled with the direct enhancement of individual expertise and the technical skills are indirect benefits including less employee turnover, enhanced organizational reputation and building of social capital. In fact, Lowe and Schellenberg (2001) found that individuals who have adequate resources to do their jobs – defined as having the information, equipment, resources, and training they need to do their job well – have higher trust, commitment, better communications and more influence that individuals who lack these elements. They conclude that the quality of these employment relationships and organizational performance are 'organically linked' and mutually reinforcing (Lowe and Schellenberg, 2001, p. 15). This is supported by Aguinis and Kraiger (2009, p. 466) who suggest the 'benefits of training may have a cascading effect such that individual-level benefit affect team-level benefits, which in turn affect organizational and societal outcomes'.

As suggested by Kaufman and Guerra (2001), it is important that research focuses on the conditions for effective training that result in these benefits. In order to uncover these conditions, the instructional design model (Goldstein and Ford, 2002; Blanchard and Thacker, 2004) is useful to implement. The design model consists of five training process stages beginning with conducting a needs assessment, determining pre-training states and conditions, investigating training design, and delivery methods and evaluation. For example, Salas and Cannon-Bowers (2001, p. 477) emphasize that an individual's pre-training motivation, willingness, ability to learn, attitude and self-awareness are critical to enhance the benefits of training. Nahavandi (2012, p. 313), highlights the vital important of individual self-awareness in that 'participants must be aware of the need for change and specific areas they should address so that they are ready to change'. In addition, Nahavadi (2012, p. 313) emphasizes the need for challenging experiences, feedback and follow-up, the presence of role models and opportunities to practice.

Training also is susceptible to failure, or not providing desired benefits, if consideration of organizational culture is not integrated with training

(Bunch, 2007, 2009). Bunch (2007) indicates a paucity of research dedicated to the influence of organizational culture on training effectiveness. Bunch (2007, p. 157) observes:

> Training failure can be a manifestation of the values, beliefs, and assumptions shared by members of various levels of organizational culture. The disregard for sound practices is an immediate cause of failure but also a reflection of cultural barriers that can circumvent the best-designed program. Beliefs that training is simple, unimportant, or pointless generate behaviors such as employing incompetent trainers, rejecting the recommendations of competent trainers, discouraging transfer of learning to the job, and failing to recognize positive transfer.

Specifically, for reaping the benefits of training, an organization's culture must be one that values continuous learning (Gill, 2010; Nahavandi, 2012). Gill writes (2010, p. xii):

> A learning culture exists when an organization makes reflection, feedback, and sharing of knowledge part of the way it functions on a day-to-day basis. A nonprofit that has a learning culture is continuously learning from its own experience, which means it has the capacity for improvement and success. In this way, a culture of learning contributes to the overall capacity of the organization.

In fact, Sussman (2003, p. 22) highlights high-performing nonprofit organizations as ones that are 'voracious learners'.

We recognize the challenges and unique range of factors confronting individual nonprofit organizations to take training seriously by proactively integrating training into organizational capacity building, strategic planning and changing organizational culture. The difficulty of holistically implementing training may be due to lack of expertise, lack of specialized skills needed for training activities as there has been a 'devolution of HRD responsibilities' (Mcguire and Gubbins, 2010, p. 256). We now turn to a discussion of the essential skills needed in the nonprofit workplace, with particular emphasis on the skills required of nonprofits managers and leaders.

ESSENTIAL SKILLS FOR THE NONPROFIT WORKPLACE

It has been well established in the training literature that one of the most important steps organizations must take in training their employees and volunteers, is to conduct a needs assessment which entails a 'process of deciding who and what should be trained' (Salas and Cannon-Bowers,

2001, p. 245). It is critical to undergo a needs assessment in that there are a range of levels of who needs training in a nonprofit organization and what that training entails. In addition, due to the vast diversity of subsectors (arts and culture, human services, animal welfare and environmental protection, research institutes, advocacy organizations and so on) within the nonprofit sector – and variation even within subsectors – the skills that are required by nonprofit staff will differ at all levels within and across organizations. Therefore, the need for developing and implementing training will vary from one organization and one position to the next. However, there are some consistent training and development needs across all organizations within the nonprofit sector regardless of size, mission, or the particular role or position in question. For example, all nonprofit organizations should provide orientation training for new employees and volunteers, ongoing board training, human health and safety training, and diversity training. In addition, all nonprofit staff and volunteers require both 'hard' (i.e. technical) and 'soft' (i.e. interpersonal) skills. With this stated, however, specialized technical skill sets not only vary at different levels of the organization (executives, managers, clerical or technical) but also between subsectors. For example, staff at a nonprofit daycare center will need skills to promote positive child development effectively; staff at a nonprofit policy analysis institute will need research skills; staff at a mental health center will require skills to deliver effective treatment approaches.

Most of the research related to technical skill needs of nonprofit employees has been focused on the needs of management and executive-level personnel. A decade ago, Drew Dolan (2002) asked what the training needs of nonprofit administrators were and how these needs should be addressed. Dolan (2002) and Garvey (2009; which cites the research by O'Brian, 2008) identify the following practitioner-reported training needs: leadership, governance, financial management, fundraising, grant writing, marketing, volunteer administration, planning, cooperative ventures, communication, program evaluation and accounting. A study by the HR Council of the Voluntary & Non-profit Sector (n.d., p. 1) also includes board governance, grant seeking, proposal writing, fundraising, leadership, and core managerial skills including volunteer engagement and management. In addition, emerging areas of importance for skill development include succession planning and use of social media (HR Council for the Voluntary & Non-Profit Sector, 2009). Executive leadership skills and training continues to be in high demand as demonstrated by a vast and growing literature related to leadership development (Austin et al., 2011; Bonner and Obergas, 2009; Cornelius, Moyers and Bell, 2011; Enright, 2006; Hernez-Broome and Hughes, 2004; Sikka, Sauvage-Mar and Lobell, 2009; Williams, 2009).

One of the key issues in leadership development is the need for training dedicated to the acquisition of 'soft' skills.

In fact, acquisition of 'hard' skills and 'soft' skills are critical to all nonprofit employees and volunteers. Soft skills include interpersonal skills; communication skills; flexibility or ability to adapt to changing circumstances; skills for cooperation and collaboration within and across organizations (Romzek et al., 2012); skills for coping with stressful, challenging and traumatic events; and skills for coping with job-related problems and stress that lead to burnout. For example, employees and volunteers often experience the high costs of emotional labor when they work for a nonprofit that provides services in fields such as child welfare, homelessness, crisis counseling, emergency response or disaster relief. Nonprofits must provide training and resources for employees and volunteers to develop coping skills if they are to continue to meet these critical social challenges. Communication skills are another critical soft skill. Since nonprofits are public-serving organizations, all employees and volunteers must represent the organization well to clients, patrons, members and other stakeholders. Perhaps with the standard employment of cross-sector partnerships and collaborations in the delivery of goods and services, it is no surprise that Garvey (2009) reports a growing desire within the nonprofit sector for skills to enhance effective collaboration. Effective interorganizational and cross-sector partnerships require a repertoire of 'soft' skills in addition to communication, including negotiation, compromise, mediation, listening, and the ability to prioritize and balance multiple goals and objectives simultaneously.

In some ways, then, it becomes important to focus not only on skill needs but on competency needs. As Rodriquez et al. (2002, p. 310) have argued, 'Competencies such as interpersonal skills and teamwork can be as important as traditional knowledge, skills, and abilities'. The US Office of Personnel Management defines competencies as 'a measurable pattern of knowledge, skill, abilities, behaviors, and other characteristics that an individual needs to perform work roles or occupational functions successfully' (Rodriquez et al., 2002, p. 310), while Hay Group, Inc. (2003) defines it as 'an underlying characteristic of a person which enable them to deliver superior performance in a given job, role or situation'. In the existing nonprofit human resources literature, competencies are more commonly emphasized at the executive or manager level, but moving toward competency models for all staff may be beneficial. For example, the development and articulation of competencies can help to instill organizational norms related to performance and subtly communicate expectations of employees and volunteers. As Rodriquez et al. (2002, p. 322) suggest:

> the strategic use of competencies can also promote the desired culture of an organization – instead of focusing only on results [it] can focus on competencies to achieve the results. By identifying competencies or groups of competencies that are critical to the organization and placing them in a performance contract, an organization is communicating the way that business should be conducted.

There has been some discussion among nonprofit management education programs regarding the need to develop competencies for nonprofit managers and leaders (Rubin, Adamski and Block, 1989; Heimovics and Herman, 1989; Hall, 1994). These efforts focused on the determination of 'target competencies': the skills, knowledge and abilities necessary for effective nonprofit administration. These target competencies were developed and refined based on literature reviews, committee work, questionnaires, and discussions with academics and practitioners. Although the competencies developed by Hall were used to recommend the field's first competency-based curriculum, at Seattle University, the competency movement did not progress to the next phase, the evaluation of learning outcomes.

McMullen and Schellenburg (2003, p. 44) suggest that further research is needed to identify the skill sets needed within the nonprofit sector and how training can be used to meet those needs. Regardless of focusing on skills, competencies or training, however, determining the specific hard and soft skills required by a nonprofit organization may be met through conducting a needs assessment.

METHODS FOR ENHANCING SKILL DEVELOPMENT

There are a variety of methods, both formal and informal, employed by nonprofit organizations for enhancing the skill development of staff and volunteers. Formal methods generally consist of agency-sponsored training provided both inside and outside of the organization, as well as non-agency sponsored training such as nonprofit management education programs; while informal methods include activities such as mentoring, coaching and job rotation. We will examine each of these methods briefly in this section, beginning with the design and delivery of formal training.

Formal Methods of Skill Development

Considerations of training design and delivery are essential to ensuring that the benefits promised in theory by training actually manifest in those trained (Aguinis and Kraiger, 2009). Training design includes such elements as assuring inclusion of relevant information or concepts to be learned, the creation of opportunities for trainees to practice the skills, and providing feedback to trainees during and after practice (Salas and Cannon-Bowers, 2001, p. 481). In terms of design:

> benefits of training enhanced by applying theory-based learning principles such as encouraging trainees to organize the training content, making sure trainees expend effort in the acquisition of new skills, and providing trainees with an opportunity to make errors together with explicit instructions to encourage them to learn from those errors. (Aguinis and Kraiger, 2009, p. 463)

Essential in assessing training design is that employees and volunteers must have multiple ways to learn (Aguinis and Kraiger, 2009; Nahavandi, 2012). This is important because it has been argued that for training to be effective, we 'must engage in research on how individuals learn, not just the latest training fads' (Aguinis and Kraiger, 2009, p. 462). Furthermore, training design should include opportunities for learners to practice and learn from their mistakes as well as the successes. This builds self-efficacy which transfers back to the work environment (Nahavandi, 2012).

Training Delivery

Training may be implemented by formal or informal methods. Formal learning is generally internally sponsored by an organization but may also be offered outside the organization. Formal agency sponsored training includes orientations, apprenticeships, internships, job rotation, coaching, mentoring and teleconference or video training. Formal training received outside the organization includes nonprofit management education programs, conferences, workshops and seminars, lectures, online training and webinars. Agencies also integrate formal methods with informal agency-sponsored methods such as orientations, job instruction training, mentoring, internships, job rotation, coaching and e-learning. Each training method has strengths and weaknesses and it is often possible to combine multiple methods or adapt to fit participant needs (Austin et al., 2011). In fact, for training to be effective it is argued that multiple methods are the most effective means to reap the benefits of training due to different styles of adult learning. Studies on leadership development (Bonner and Obergas, 2009; Cornelius et al., 2011; Sikka et al., 2009) emphasize that there is no 'one-size-fits-all' approach. Bonner and Obergas's (2009) study on leadership development indicated that leaders in human service agencies learn best from a combination of personal experiences, a change in the scale or scope of the job, mistakes, mentoring and peer-to-peer sharing. Furthermore, Cornelius et al. (2011) in their *Daring to Lead* report, indicated that executives found coaching, peer networks and leadership programs very effective. In an executive position, these methods served to lessen the isolation often felt by leaders and enable time for reflection as well as opportunities for practice. Furthermore, integrating multiple methods was found to be important because each method reinforces learning in unexpected ways (Sikka et al., 2009).

Salas and Cannon-Bowers (2001, p. 481) report that organizations seek training methods that are cost-effective, content-valid, easy to use, engaging and technology-based. Dolan (2002) found that nonprofits were internally providing for much of their own training needs. For example, nonprofit organizations most commonly provide training in-house (51.3 percent) whereas almost 34 percent utilized other nonprofit organizations for training and 'nearly 30 percent indicated academic institutions provided some training' (Dolan, 2002, p. 286). In-house training is primarily the responsibility of supervisors and managers. Depending on size and capacity of the organization, training may be conducted by internal training staff who are formally part of human resources or personnel, or the organization may contract out to bring in someone with special expertise in a technical area. For example, hiring consultants or developing contracts with topic experts to impart knowledge and expertise to staff and volunteers is another formal method of promoting skill development. The consulting field has seen an increase in demand for services (La Piana Associates, Inc. and Fieldstone Alliance, n.d.; West, 2010b) especially training needs of specific skills such as social media.

Nonprofit management education programs are another common vehicle through which the skills of nonprofit employees are developed. Mirabella reports that in the US alone there are 292 colleges and universities providing coursework in nonprofit management topics, including 132 schools that offer a Master's degree with a concentration in nonprofit management, 168 schools offering undergraduate coursework related to nonprofits, and 73 schools with non-degree, continuing education programs designed to enhance the skills of current nonprofit workers (Mirabella, 2007). While colleges and universities thus play a critical role in promoting the skill development of the current and future nonprofit workforce, this type of classroom learning is most effective when simultaneously combined with some form of on-the-job training, whether in a paid or volunteer position, or via an internship or field placement experience.

Technology-delivered instruction is also growing as a preferred training delivery mechanism, particularly because it is deemed cost-effective, and this is almost always an important consideration for nonprofits. Consistent with growing trends in learning in business and university settings, it is well recognized that technology is having a dramatic impact on how training is delivered (Bell, 2007; Bellinger, 2007; McGuire and Gubbins, 2010; Salas and Cannon-Bowers, 2001; Welsh et al., 2003). The options are ever expanding, including video conferencing, Skype, webcasting, and online internet and intranet courses. In addition, social media such as YouTube, blogs and wikis can be constructed into an online learning environment (Toole, 2011). As Toole (2011, p. 32) states, 'Everything else in society is radically changing with the developing internet and associated technologies, and there is no logic in suggesting that education will not do the same.'

Informal Methods of Skill Development

McGuire and Gubbins (2010, p. 249) articulate a changing trend among training delivery methods with formal learning methods being supplanted by methods that are 'informal, situated, focused and experiential'. With the continuing rise in e-learning as both effective and cost-effective, this comes as no surprise. However McGuire and Gubbins (2010, p. 249) express reserve at 'branding formal learning as an outdated delivery mode' and argue that 'decisions on learning styles should be based upon sound evidence-based research'. Furthermore, Dolan's (2002) survey of 600 nonprofit directors indicated a preference for short-term training techniques such as half-day or day-long seminars. However, depending on the nature of the skill – such as diversity training – this may not be deemed adequate (Halpern, 2006). For example, diversity is not to be viewed as a 'problem to be overcome' but as a resource and a process (Rangarajan and Black, 2007; Soni, 2000, p. 405). Indeed, it is a process of becoming cultural competent rather than being culturally competent (Campinha-Bacote, 1994).

Recent literature points to the value of coaching, especially as an emerging tool for leadership development (Coan, 2003; Cornelius et al., 2011; Fischer and Beimers, 2009; Howard, Gislason and Kellogg, 2010; Joo, 2005; McCambridge, 2011; Wilson and Gislason, 2009). Gill (2010, p. 65) defines coaching generally as 'the process of facilitating self-awareness, learning and performance improvement of staff and volunteers, often on the job'. While similar to coaching, mentoring is part of a developmental relationship that provides individualized attention and feedback, but it is a more informal and long-term relationship (Nahavandi, 2012, p. 318). Joo (2005) also points out that mentors tend to be from within the organization, generally an individual in a senior position or with longevity within the organization, whereas a coach is brought in as a professional from outside the organization. Williams (2005, p. 3) points out numerous benefits to mentoring including knowledge-transfer, development of broad competencies and the ability to 'foster employee loyalty and commitment, improving morale while enriching organizational culture'. In fact, the need for executive coaching may arise due to insufficient dedication to executive transition planning in which 'the individuals who rise to the executive director position lack adequate preparation and supports for this new role' (Fischer and Beimers, 2009, p. 507). Given the need for succession planning and the emerging leadership crisis in the nonprofit sector that we discussed earlier, coaching and mentoring can be particularly useful strategies for developing the technical and leadership skills that current nonprofit employees will need in order to effectively lead existing organizations in the future.

THE FUTURE OF SKILL DEVELOPMENT EFFORTS IN NONPROFIT ORGANIZATIONS

Nonprofits are confronted with increasing demands for accountability and performance, both from their funding entities as well as the public. Having a skilled workforce is critical to nonprofit organizational performance today and will remain an essential ingredient for organizational success in the future. Efforts to promote skill development are not without challenges, including staff turnover, the time and expertise needed to train staff properly and, perhaps most importantly, cost. In finding ways to save money, nonprofits often turn first to their training and development budgets to make cuts. However, this is a mistake as the short-term decision to cut training can cause long-term problems. Gault (2010) has observed the irony that 'although employee training is recognized as a real cost to organizations, few take into account the financial impact of not having a training program'. Failing to invest in the skill development of employees and volunteers can have real consequences for nonprofits. Organizations that fail to invest in skill development for their staff and volunteers are destined to face higher rates of staff turnover, burnout and potentially problems of quality in service delivery. If quality suffers, so will an organization's reputation, from there it is only a matter of time before it faces financial consequences.

This chapter has highlighted a number of important considerations for designing and delivering effective training and skill development opportunities for nonprofit employees and volunteers. In sum, training process must be viewed from a holistic perspective. There is no single 'best' method to deliver training; in fact, organizations should strive to utilize multiple methods as there are multiple ways in which people learn. This is a case in which the ends – the mastery of the skill or task and transference of what is learned to the work environment – are more important than the means. Training continues to evolve 'to meet the challenges of satisfying current training needs, responding to emerging ones and developing cost-effective options for how, when and what training is delivered' (HR Council for the Voluntary & Non-Profit Sector, 2009). Nonprofit management programs and courses offered by post-secondary institutions will continue to grow in importance as a vehicle for enhancing the skills and meeting the training needs of current and future nonprofit employees, and will continue to play an important role in advancing the professionalism of the nonprofit workforce in general.

Training and other skill development initiatives within nonprofits should be embedded as a component of strategic human resources management, as they foster the creation and professionalization of dedicated human resources management within organizations. Ultimately, nonprofit leaders must approach the issue of skill development with an attitude that investment in human capital is critical to achieving high-performing organizations, create an organizational culture that supports continuous learning, and create a culture that views human capital as an asset, rather than a cost.

REFERENCES

Aguinis, H. & Kraiger, K. (2009). Benefits of training and development for individuals and teams, organizations, and society. *Annual Review in Psychology*, 60, 451–474.

ASTD Public Policy Council (2003). The human capital challenge. American Society for Training and Development.

Austin, Michael J., Regan, Kate, Samples, Mark W., Schwartz, Sara L. & Carnochan, Sarah (2011). Building managerial and organizational capacity in nonprofit human service organizations through a leadership development program. *Administration in Social Work*, 35(3), 258–281.

Ban, Carolyn, Drahnak-Faller, Alexic & Towers, Marcia (2003). Human resource challenges in human service and community development organizations: recruitment and retention of professional staff. *Review of Public Personnel Administration*, 23(2), 133–153.

Bell, Jane (2007). E-Learning: your flexible development friend? *Development and Learning in Organizations* 21(6), 7–9.

Bellinger, A. (2007). 'E-learning today and tomorrow'. *Training Journal*, April.

Blackbaud (2004). State of the Nonprofit Industry Survey. Charleston, SC: Blackbaud. http://www.blackbaud.com/files/resources/whitepapers/IA_SONI_Results_2004.pdf, accessed September 10, 2005.

Blanchard, P. Nick & Thacker, James W. (2004). *Effective Trainings: Systems, Strategies, and Practices*. Upper Saddle River, NJ: Pearson Prentice Hall.

Bonner, L. & Obergas, J. (2009). *Nonprofit Leadership Development: A Model for Identifying and Growing Leaders with the Nonprofit Sector*. Pittsburgh, PA: Looking Glass Institute.

Bryan, Lowell L., Joyce, Claudia I. & Wiess, Leigh M. (2006). Making a market in talent. *McKinsey Quarterly*, 2, 99–109.

Bunch, Kay (2007). Training failure as a consequence of organizational culture. *Human Resource Development Review*, 6, 142–163.

Bunch, Kay (2009). The influence of organizational culture on training effectiveness. In Hansenm, Carol D. & Lee, Yih-teen (eds), *The Cultural Context of Human Resource Development*. New York: Palgrave Macmillan, pp. 197–212.

Campinha-Bacote, Josepha (1994). Cultural competence in psychiatric mental health nursing. *Mental Health Nursing*, 2(1), 1–8.

Cascio, W.F. (1988). *Applied Psychology in Personnel Management*. Engelwood Cliffs: NJ: Prentice-Hall.

Coan, D. (2003). *Executive Coaching Project: Evaluation of Findings*. San Francisco, CA: CompassPoint Nonprofit Services.

Collins, Jim (2002). *Good to Great: Why some Companies Make the Leap ... and Others Don't*. New York: Harper Collins.

Cornelius, Marla, Moyers, Rick & Bell, Jeanne (2011). *Daring to Lead 2011: A National Study of Nonprofit Executive Leadership*. San Francisco, CA: Compass Point Nonprofit Services and the Meyer Foundation.

Dolan, Drew A. (2002). Training needs of administrators in the nonprofit sector: what are they and how should we address them? *Nonprofit Management and Leadership*, 12(3), 277–292.

Enright, Kathleen. P. (2006). *Investing in Leadership Volume 2: Inspiration and Ideas from Philanthropy's Latest Frontier.* Washington, DC: Grantmakers for Effective Organizations.

Fischer, Robert L. & Beimers, David (2009). 'Put me in, coach': a pilot evaluation of executive coaching in the nonprofit sector. *Nonprofit Management and Leadership*, 19(4), 507–522.

Fitzgerald, William (1992). Training versus Development. *Training and Development*. May, 81–84.

Garvey, David (2009). Nonprofit sector: workforce education needs and opportunities. *Continuing Higher Education Review*, 73, 114–124.

Gault, Kevin (2010). In a time of budget cuts, creativity is needed to train employees. *Chronicle of Philanthropy*, May 16.

Gill, Stephen J. (2010). *Developing a Learning Culture in Nonprofit Organizations*. Thousand Oaks, CA: SAGE Publications.

Goldstein, I.L. & Ford, J.K. (2002). *Training in Organizations*, 4th edn. Belmont, CA: Wadsworth.

Hall, Mary Stewart (1994). *Core Competencies for Effective Not-for-Profit Executives*. Seattle, WA: Seattle University.

Halpern, R. Patrick (2006). *Workforce Issues in the Nonprofit Sector: Generational Leadership Change and Diversity*. Kansas City, MO: American Humanics.

Hay Group (2003). Using competencies to identify high performers: an overview of the basics. Working Paper. Hay Group, Inc.

Heimovics, R.D. & Herman, R.D. (1989). The salient management skills: a conceptual framework for a curriculum for managers of nonprofit organizations. *American Review of Public Administration*, 19(4), 295–312.

Hernez-Broome, Gina & Hughes, Richard L. (2004). Leadership development: past, present, future. *Human Resources Planning*, 25(2), 34–32.

Howard, Kim Ammann, Gislason, Michelle & Kellogg, Virginia (2010). *Coaching and Philanthropy: An Action Guide for Grantmakers*. Washington, DC: Grantmakers for Effective Organizations and CompassPoint Nonprofit Services.

HR Council for the Voluntary & Non-profit Sector (2009). *Toward a Labour Force Strategy for Canada's Voluntary and Non-Profit Sector.* Accessed at *http://www.hrcouncil.ca/labour/strategy-study.cfm.*

HR Council for the Voluntary and Non-profit Sector (n.d.). Professional development in the the nonprofit sector – what's the demand? *Trends & Issues*, 1–3.

Joo, B. (2005). Executive coaching: a conceptual framework from an integrative review of practice and research. *Human Resource Development Review*, 4(4), 462–488.

Kaufman, Roger & Guerra I, Ingrid (2001). A perspective adjustment to add value to external clients (including society). *Human Resource Development Quarterly*, 12, 319–324.

Klinger, D.E. & Nalbandian, J. (2003). *Public Personnel Management: Contexts and Strategies*, 5th edn. Upper Saddle River, NJ: Prentice Hall.

La Piana Associates, Inc. & Fieldstone Alliance (n.d.). Professional development needs of consultants serving the nonprofit sector: findings of a survey of 322 consultants.

Light, Paul (2002). The content of their character: the state of the nonprofit workforce. *Nonprofit Quarterly*, 9(3), 6–16.

Lobell, Jean R. & Connolly, Paul M. (2007). Peak performance: nonprofit leaders rate highest in 360-degree reviews. *Nonprofit Quarterly*, 12–27.

Lowe, Graham & Schellenberg, Grant (2001). *What's a Good Job? The Importance of Employment Relationships*. CPRN Study W 105l. Ottawa: Canadian Policy Research Networks.

Macduff, Nancy (2005). Principles of training for volunteers and employees. In Herman, Robert D. & Associates (eds), *The Jossey-Bass Handbook of Nonprofit Leadership and Management*, 2nd edn. San Francisco, CA: Jossey-Bass, pp. 703–730.

McCambridge, Ruth (2011). Coaching as a capacity-building tool: an interview with Bill Ryan. *Nonprofit Quarterly*, 18(2), 24–29.

McGuire, D. & Gubbins, C. (2010). The slow death of formal learning: a polemic. *Human Resource Development Review*, 9(3) 249–265.

McMullen, Kathryn & Schellenberg, Grant (2003). Skills and training in the non-profit sector. CPRN Research Series on Human Resources in the Non-profit Sector, No. 3. Canadian Policy Research Networks.

Mirabella, Roseanne (2007). University-based educational programs in nonprofit management and philanthropic studies: a 10-year review and projections of future trends. *Nonprofit and Voluntary Sector Quarterly*, 36, 4.

Murphy, Aileen & Garavan, Thomas N. (2009). The adoption and diffusion of an NHRD standard: a conceptual framework. *Human Resource Development Review*, 8(1), 3–21.

Nahavandi, Afsaneh (2012). *The Art and Science of Leadership*, 6th edn. Upper Saddle River, NJ: Prentice Hall.

O'Brien, Anne (2008). *Training Needs of the Nonprofit Sector*. University of Utah. Salt Lake City, UT: Office of Professional Education.

Pynes, Joan E. (2009). *Human Resources Management for Public and Nonprofit Organizations: A Strategic Approach*. San Francisco, CA: Jossey-Bass.

Rodriquez, Donna, Patel, Rita, Bright, Andrea, Gregory, Donna & Gowing, Marilyn K. (2002). Developing competency models to promote integrated human resource practices. *Human Resource Management*, 41(3), 309–324.

Rangarajan, N. & Black, T. (2007). Exploring organizational barriers to diversity: a case study of the New York State Education Department. *Review of Public Personnel Management*, 27(3), 249–263.

Romzek, Barbara, LeRoux, Kelly & Blackmar, Jeannette (2012). A preliminary theory of informal accountability among network organizational actors. *Public Administration Review*, 72(3), 442–453.

Rubin, Hank, Adamski, Laura & Block, Stephen R. (1989). Toward a discipline of nonprofit administration: report from the Clarion Conference. *Nonprofit and Voluntary Sector Quarterly*, 18(3), 279–286.

Salas, E. & Cannon-Bowers, J.A. (2001). The science of training: a decade of progress. *Annual Review of Psychology*, 52, 471–499.

Schmitz, Paul & Stroup, Kala (2005). Building tomorrow's nonprofit work force. *Chronicle of Philanthropy*, July 21. http://www.publicallies.org/atf/cf/%7BFBE0137A-2CA6-4E0D-B229-54D5A098332C%7D/COP%207-21-05.pdf, accessed July 6, 2011.

Sikka, Mohan, Sauvage-Mar, Carolyn & Lobell, Jean (2009). What makes a difference in leadership? A view from the field. *Nonprofit Quarterly*, 16(4), 50–54.

Sims, David & Trager, Carol (2009). Finding leaders for America's nonprofits. Bridgespan Group.

Soni, V. (2000). A twenty-first-century reception for diversity in the public sector: a case study. *Public Administration Review*, 60(5), 395–408.

Sussman, C. (2003). Making change: how to build adaptive capacity. *Nonprofit Quarterly*, 10(4), 19–24. Tierney, Thomas J. (2006). The Leadership Deficit. *Stanford Social Innovation Review*, Summer, 26–35.

Toole, T. (2010). Social media: key tools for the future of work-based learning. *Development and Learning in Organizations*, 25(5), 31–34.

US Department of Health and Human Services (2011). Administration on Aging. Aging statistics. http://www.aoa.gov/AoARoot/Aging_Statistics/index.aspx, accessed 20 October 2011.

Welsh, E.T., Wanberg, C.R., Brown, K.G. & Simmering, M.J. (2003). E-learning: emerging uses, empirical results and future directions. *International Journal of Training Development*, 7, 245–258.

West, Maureen (2010a). Donors' demands for results and professional training programs fuel growth of consulting world. *Chronicle of Philanthropy*, 3 October.

West, Maureen (2010b). Nonprofits face a wealth of options as consulting field expands. *Chronicle of Philanthropy*, 3 October.

Wexley, K.N. & Latham, G.P. (1981). Developing and training human resources in organizations. Glenview, IL: Scott, Foresman & Company.

Williams, Ken (2005). *Mentoring the Next Generation of Nonprofit Leaders: A Practical Guide for Managers*. Washington, DC: AED Center for Leadership Development, Academy for Educational Development.

Williams, Ken (2009). *A Future of Leadership Development*. Washington, DC: AED Center for Leadership Development, Academy for Educational Development.

Willingham, R. (2006). Training versus Education. *Integrity*. http://www.clientdevelopmentinst.com/Attachments/Integrity%20Articles/White_Paper_Train_vs_Educ.pdf.

Wilson, Judith & Gislason, Michelle (2009). *Coaching Skills for Nonprofit Managers and Leaders: Developing People to Achieve Your Mission*. San Francisco, CA: Jossey-Bass.

9. Effectively leading a diverse nonprofit workforce

Joy Jones and Dail Fields

Prevailing uncertainties about global economic stability and growth challenge nonprofit organizations to make changes to ensure their survival and to cultivate required human capital, market share and diverse revenue streams. To compete for scarce resources, nonprofits will be required to become ever more strategic in the ways they accomplish their mission (Mesch, 2010). In addition, demographics of the available labor force are changing in many developed countries, with some suggesting there may be a shortage of leadership as the 'baby boomers' retire (Johnson, 2009). On a positive note, numerous university programs focused on nonprofit management have appeared with substantial enrollments suggesting a trend toward organizational professionalism that should not only change the culture of nonprofit organizations, but also correct inaccurate perception that working in nonprofits consists of informal activities done by amateurs (Mesch, 2010). Nonprofit leaders must focus on finding and developing employees with skills for innovation and flexibility in fulfilling a variety of roles and tasks while interfacing with staff and donors not only from domestic constituent groups, but also across international borders.

The data of the 2000 census removed any lingering doubts about shifts in demographics of the United States (US) labor market. The next and future generations may represent a changing demographic landscape including increased numbers of same-sex households, workers identifying themselves as multiracial, and increased representation of Latinos who now surpass African Americans as the largest minority segment of the US population. Overall, data suggest that nearly half of all new workers will be individuals traditionally classified as minorities; that is, women, people of color and ethnic minorities (McCuiston, Woolridge & Pierce, 2004). Leaders of nonprofits must be concerned about human resource strategies and practices that create commitment of diverse employees in order to serve successfully a diverse group of constituents. This diversity is occurring against a backdrop of sentiment in the US that may question the appropriateness of foreign workers and may be increasingly negative about the possible impacts of immigration (Tschirhart & Wise, 2007). While workers from diverse cultures may bring value to an organization through language skills, different approaches to problem solving, new work methods, and satisfaction of some stakeholder demands for diversity and multiculturalism, they may also increase management challenges (Tschirhart & Wise, 2007).

Working from the perspectives that effective nonprofit leaders are those that can adapt their behaviors effectively to meet the demands of changing conditions, including a workforce with more diverse work composition, this chapter focuses less on prescriptive approaches and more on the issues or variables that a nonprofit leader must consider when formulating their leadership strategy. Therefore in this chapter, we will discuss: (1) perspectives on workforce diversity and associated implications for nonprofit leaders; (2) how employee diversity may affect perceptions of a leader's behaviors and attributes; (3) how diversity may be reflected in specific communication tendencies of employees; and (4) how diagnostic thinking can be used to lead diverse employees more successfully within nonprofit settings.

PERSPECTIVES ON WORKFORCE DIVERSITY

The American workforce in general has been increasingly diversified as women, racial minorities, and immigrants from other countries and cultures have greater access to jobs. According to the 2000 US Census, the US population is 69.4 percent white, 12.7 percent African American, 12.6 percent Latino, 3.8 percent Asian, and 2.5 percent other races or ethnicities. Population projections predict greater growth in the non-white population groups, such that by 2050 approximately 30 percent of the US population will be composed of minorities. Other projections suggest that as early as 2025 minorities could compose as much as 32 percent of the US population with the fastest-growing minority cohorts being Latinos and Asians. These trends suggest the nonprofit sector must respond to the continued diversification of the US workforce by recruiting and retaining persons of color at all organizational levels.

Although there are over 1.5 million nonprofit organizations in the USA alone, the US Bureau of Labor Statistics, the classic source of workforce demographics by industry, offers little current data on nonprofit worker composition. Some studies indicate that the nonprofit sector employs a greater proportion of African Americans and a smaller proportion of

Latinos as compared to the public and private sectors (Halpern, 2006). Historically, the nonprofit labor force has contained approximately 67–70 percent women (Gibelman, 2000). Several reasons have been suggested for this pattern. Many of the activities associated with the nonprofit sector are in health and human services and tend to focus on female-dominated occupations, such as nursing, teaching, early childhood education, social work and day care. An alternative explanation is that males suffer a wage loss by working in the nonprofit sector compared to the for-profit sector, but women may not. Despite this relative dominance, the number of minorities – including women – in positions of power and influence (such as executive and leadership positions) in both philanthropic and nonprofit organizations could improve significantly. Other studies suggest a 'glass ceiling' is evidenced by disproportionate representation of men in upper-level management, whereas women are disproportionately represented at the direct-service and lower management levels. In addition, other evidence suggests that men earn higher salaries than women across hierarchical levels of nonprofit organizations (Gibelman, 2000). Overall lack of racial and ethnic diversity in nonprofit leadership can make the organizational culture alienating for persons of color (Halpern, 2006).

Research has produced little consistent information about the effects of diversity within organizations (Choi & Rainey, 2010; Kochan et al., 2003). Some studies have concluded that more heterogeneous work groups may consider more perspectives and produce higher-quality solutions than homogeneous groups. Information processing and decision-making theories suggest that diversity improves performance by contributing to higher-quality decisions and by taking advantage of a broader range of alternatives and new ideas (Cox, 1994). Some studies have found that work teams composed of people with different backgrounds tend to share more information and therefore perform better than more homogeneous teams. Although greater heterogeneity may reduce consensus in decision-making, this in turn may lead to consideration of more alternatives and thus improve problem solving (Choi & Rainey, 2010).

On the other hand, some research has reported a negative or insignificant relationship between diversity and organizational performance. Heterogeneous groups may experience problems in integration, coordination, motivation and conflict management, and have higher levels of dissatisfaction and turnover than more homogeneous groups. Consequently, diverse work groups may require more energy to accomplish tasks than homogeneous work groups. In some cases, individuals in more diverse groups can experience exclusion from decision-making processes (Choi & Rainey, 2010).

Some research in worker diversity holds that as diverse teams work together longer, teamwork and collaboration increase. The negative effects of surface-level diversity, such as demographic differences, may become less important the longer that groups of diverse people work together, as initial prejudices and stereotyping are replaced with task-oriented issues. Other views suggest that this viewpoint may be outmoded and that diversity integration efforts premised on the benefits of increased contact are destined for failure (Weisinger & Salipante, 2007) in part because differences in employee perspectives are subject to reduction through contact. These include differences in work ethic, expectations about workplace authority, views about work–life balance, and unfamiliarity with alternative work configurations such as virtual teams and strategic e-business partnerships.

As the implications of workforce diversity have received more rigorous attention by organizational researchers, some results suggest that the effects may vary according to the types of diversity. In a study of government agencies Choi and Rainey (2010) reported that racial diversity was associated with less social integration, more conflict and less cohesion in groups, consequently decreasing organizational performance. In contrast, higher levels of gender diversity increased perceived organizational performance. One possible interpretation is that gender diversity may be a less sensitive issue in work groups, as compared to racial diversity, and may require lower costs for conflict resolution or coordination. On the other hand, work groups with higher levels of racial diversity may experience more conflicts because of complicated differences arising from residual effects of racial injustice and related factors (Choi & Rainey, 2010).

Decades of research on the effects of diversity within teams and small groups indicate that diversity can have negative effects, as well as positive ones. Given the mixed viewpoints, a group of industry chief executives and human resource professionals commissioned a study to examine the relationships between gender and racial diversity and business performance (Kochan et al., 2003). Kochan et al. (2003) studied large for-profit companies and found that racial and gender diversity did not have the substantial positive effects on performance proposed by those espousing the more optimistic view of diversity, but also did not have the negative effect on group processes warned by those with a more pessimistic view. Most analyses yielded no negative effects on team processes at all, but when racial diversity was shown to have a negative effect, it was mitigated by training and development-focused initiatives. Gender diversity had either no effects or positive effects on team processes. There were few direct positive or negative effects of diversity on performance, either positive or negative. The findings suggest that context is crucial in determining the nature of diversity's impact on performance. Conditions that exacerbated racial diversity's negative effects on performance included a highly competitive context among teams. Finally, there was some promising evidence to suggest that, under certain conditions, racial diversity may even enhance performance, namely when organizations foster an environment that promotes learning from diversity. Choi and Rainey (2010) also found that active approaches to management of diversity within an organization led to more positive performance among employees within federal government agencies. Clearly, in an organizational setting, dismissing the importance of diversity may be detrimental to organizational success.

LEADERSHIP IMPLICATIONS OF DIVERSITY

There is clearly an imperative for nonprofit leaders to deliberately and proactively manage diversity within an organization. However, in a demographically diverse setting, leadership behaviors and actions may be subject to differences in interpretation, creating some possibly unanticipated complexity. This complexity can best be understood by considering the role of implicit leadership models (Johnson & Fields, 2010). Leadership characteristics, skills or behaviors will not automatically make a person a leader (Lord & Maher, 1991). Others must first perceive the person as a leader worthy of following. Eden and Leviatan (1975) found clear evidence that leadership factors reside in the mind of the follower. This study was not only the first to suggest that leadership is in the judgment of the follower, but also that followers use unconscious yet well-defined mental models in a process of identifying and interpreting another person as leader. The perception of a person as a leader is contingent on the fit between the potential leader's characteristics and an implicit conceptualization of the follower as to what a leader should be like. These internal mental models have been labeled implicit leadership theories or models (ILTs). Thus, it is critical for organizational members to understand ILTs. Indeed, understanding the linkage of follower perceptions and the leader–follower relationship has been recognized as crucial to the accomplishments or failure of leadership (Hollander & Offermann, 1990). In summary, ILTs are unconscious, individualized, well-defined internal representations of leadership from which a follower draws automatic and spontaneous conclusions about a person as a leader.

The GLOBE project investigated differences implicitly held about different types of leaders (business, military, political, and so on) across 62 cultures (House et al., 2004) and found that some aspects of leadership were shared across cultures (for instance, charismatic leadership) while others differed substantially between cultures. Additional evidence suggests that differences in cultural background and changing socio-economic status may manifest in different views about what makes a good leader. For example, in a study covering four countries, McDermott (2008) found significant differences in the preferences for numerous aspects of leadership of emerging professionals compared to middle managers surveyed earlier by the GLOBE study. Many of these differences may be attributable to changing social and economic conditions within the countries. For example, Israeli emerging professionals in 2008 compared to middle managers preferred leaders who can provide a stable environment by being more procedural and who are more humane-oriented (generous, compassionate, caring for people). These preferences may reflect the relative instability and militaristic tone present in the Israeli environment for an extended period. In the United States, emerging professionals indicated a greater preference for leaders who are administratively competent, autocratic, autonomous, decisive, modest and non-participative compared to middle managers. The economic, political and social environment in the United States has become more uncertain, and may account for the increased preferences for structure and direction from leaders expressed by emerging professionals. Both instances suggest that leadership preferences and interpretation of leader behaviors may be influenced by a wide range of variables that effective leaders must not only keep in mind, but also strive to understand.

Recent studies have illustrated how cultural backgrounds may impact the way that followers view leadership efforts. An example is a study comparing the perceived effectiveness of three aspects of leadership – service, humility and vision – between followers in Ghana and the US. First, respondents from Ghana reported that they experienced these leadership behaviors less frequently than did respondents from the USA. Ghanaian culture is characterized in part by higher levels of power distance compared to the USA. Power distance in a culture describes the extent to which there is separation between persons who have greater amounts of power and those with less (House et al., 2004). In high power distance settings, those in positions of power are viewed as being different types of people from those who are not (Hofstede, 2001). Thus, leader behaviors that center on humility and development of followers which are generally viewed positively by US followers may not be consistent with the norms inherent to the Ghanaian culture. In addition, although service and humility were related similarly in both cultures to judgments of leader effectiveness, vision had a significantly stronger relationship with leader effectiveness for Ghanaians. Because Ghanaian culture exhibits higher power distance in current practices, followers may have greater expectations that people in leadership roles will provide vision, foresight and direction for followers than their US counterparts. Followers in Ghanaian culture may view leaders who provide less vision as inadequate and ineffective. It is also important to note that when asked about how things should be in society, Ghanaians place much greater emphasis on uncertainty avoidance than Americans do. Thus, it is also possible that the value Ghanaians place on uncertainty avoidance manifests itself in a preference for leaders who provide vision. That is, vision may be viewed as a hedge against uncertainty by Ghanaians, and leaders who provide better vision are therefore perceived as being more effective. Clearly, these results illustrate that leader efforts to understand perceptions and values of followers in multicultural setting are critical to choices of leadership behaviors that may be more effective.

It is also critical for organizational leaders to be cognizant that some differences between groups in a diverse workforce may be much more significant. For example, a disagreement in the workplace that on the surface may appear to be a minor misunderstanding between two individuals can escalate if groups polarize and attribute the cause of the conflict to social identity tensions. This perspective is based on the social psychological premise that individuals base their self-concept in part from membership in a social group. Individuals classify themselves and others into categories or groups through a cognitive process that provides individuals with a systematic means of defining others for comparison purposes. Fundamental to these cognitive processes is the desire for one's in-group to have a positive evaluation relative to the out-group (Tajfel, 1979). The desire for each identity group to remain both distinctive and superior to others can lead to conflict. This is especially true in cases where social identities are based on attributes such as race or ethnicity, gender, religion or immigrant status. The degree to which there are current tensions as a result of historical conflict is referred to as intergroup anxiety (Stephan & Stephan, 1985).

The concept of 'faultlines' (hypothetical attributes that split a group into one of more subgroups) helps explain the effects of social identity differences and conflict in the workplace. Events that make social identity particularly salient have the potential to cause groups to polarize and negatively influence work (Chrobot-Mason, Ruderman, Weber & Ernst, 2009).

Leaders are faced with a considerable challenge when attempting to lead across social identity groups with a history of intergroup anxiety or conflict. Because organizational leaders are often members of the dominant social group and/or have attained status and power as a result of their position, they may have difficulty both recognizing and responding to triggers effectively. In an increasingly diverse workplace, members of groups with a history of conflict or tension often find themselves required to work together. Intergroup anxiety resulting from previous conflicts among groups may serve as a primer for future conflicts that emerge in the work context (Stephan & Stephan, 1985). For example, an event associated with everyday work life occurs, acting as a cue that one group may be devalued versus another group or discriminated against based on social identity. Such an event makes people vigilant about sensing whether social identity is a factor in the behavior of others. In groups with strong fault-lines, the possibility of a small event being perceived as threatening may be strong because the salience of group membership is high.

In a study covering employees in 16 countries, Chrobot-Mason et al. (2009) found evidence for the following four dominant types of events that may trigger group fault-lines: perceived differential treatment (e.g. greater pay raises or benefits to members of one group, but denied to others); different views on work–life balance (e.g. one group continually adjusts work to satisfy outside commitments while other groups view this as wrong); assimilation (e.g. an offsite meeting scheduled during a religious holiday); insults (e.g. employees of a minority group accused of stealing supplies). Interestingly, in this study the researchers found that nonprofit employees and managers were more willing than those in other organizations to discuss intergroup anxiety and fault-lines, perhaps because the nonprofits were more social justice-oriented.

COMMUNICATION AS A FOCAL TOPIC IN WORKFORCE DIVERSITY

Contingency models of leadership suggest that the relationship between leadership (i.e., both traits and behaviors) and leader effectiveness is contingent upon aspects of the situation (Fiedler, 1964). Although leaders often use standard communication practices rather than altering communication to fit specific situations, perceptions of communication competence and effectiveness are also contingent on the context (Davis, 1953). Communication is no longer viewed as a static and linear process but as a transactional, interdependent and circular process in which context permeates communication interactions. As Hall (1976) argued, communication is culture, and culture is communication. Therefore, in leading a diverse non-profit workforce, leaders must understand that demographic differences and communication are inextricably intertwined. In fact, demographic differences are embedded and reflected in all areas of organizational communication, including the influence process between leader and internal (e.g., employees), external (e.g., volunteers), special (e.g., governmental agencies) and intermediary (e.g., donors) audiences.

COMMUNICATION COMPETENCE AND DIVERSITY

Extending Barge's (1994) assertion that leadership is exercised through communication, Flauto (1999) argued that communication competence is a prerequisite for effective leadership. Communication competence involves 'the ability of the individual to demonstrate knowledge of the appropriate communicative behavior in a given situation' (Larson, Backlund, Redmond & Barbour, 1978, p. 16). A leader's ability to communicate appropriately and effectively provides a catalyst for organizations to transform goals and objectives into accomplishments (Rowley & Sherman, 2003). Previous research has identified the unique issues facing non-profit organizations when attempting to attract and retain members from diverse populations (Weisenger & Salipante, 2007). Certainly, leader communication competence is important in all organizational contexts; however, non-profit organizations present unique challenges for leaders. In the non-profit arena, communication must transpire between diverse members (e.g., paid versus volunteer) with a myriad of needs and purposes for entering the organization.

In a diverse workforce, communication competency requires that leaders recognize communication differences that result from relational demography within the organization. Tsui and O'Reilly (1989) used the term 'relational demography', 'to refer to the comparative demographic characteristics of dyads who are in a position to engage in regular interaction' (p. 403). Gerstner and Day (1997) stated, 'Demographic factors may not predict leader–member exchange quality but relational demography – the extent to which individuals are similar or dissimilar – may' (p. 3). In discussing demographic dissimilarity, Harrison, Price and Bell (1998) reported that there are two major categories of diversity: surface-level diversity and deep-level or perceived diversity. Harrison et al. argued that deep-level diversity (i.e., values, beliefs, and so on) might have a stronger impact on relationships than surface-level diversity. Ultimately, initial categorizations are based on surface-level demographics, but these perceptions change as deep-level information is obtained. However, if communication is ineffective or infrequent, perceptions may remain superficial. Therefore, leadership in a diverse workforce requires that leaders continuously work to bridge fault-lines which are often created by cultural diversity. Communication apprehension (CA) is one variable that may significantly decrease a leader's ability to bridge these cultural fault-lines.

COMMUNICATION APPREHENSION AND DIVERSITY

Based on Byrne's (1971) similarity-attraction paradigm, Green, Anderson and Shivers (1996) reported that relational demography might reduce communication and lead to greater social distance between dyads. CA has been found to increase social distance and decrease communication among diverse organizational members. Furthermore, empirical studies concerning demographic dissimilarity – such as educational dissimilarity and cultural dissimilarity – have suggested that when organizational members are dissimilar, communication-related anxiety increases. In addition, Buss (1980) posited that situational elements, such as diversity between communicators, may increase anxiety.

Despite interest in diverse workforce leadership, researchers have failed to examine the effects of CA. McCroskey (1977) defined communication apprehension 'as the fear or anxiety associated with either real or anticipated communication with another person or persons' (p. 98). Richmond (1984) explained that 'high CA people experience emotional distress during or anticipating communication, prefer to avoid communication, and are perceived by others and themselves as less competent, skilled, and successful' (p. 101). Therefore, CA may be a silent destroyer of functional leadership in a diverse workforce.

Causes of CA

Although CA is the most widely researched variable in interpersonal communication, relatively little progress has been made regarding etiological factors. Most contemporary communication theorists agree that both personality traits and situational aspects influence CA. Originally, CA was considered a characteristically stable personality trait (Beatty, Behnk & McCallum, 1978). However, further research indicated that a situational or 'state' CA orientation also exists. 'Trait apprehension' 'is a relatively enduring, personality type orientation toward a given mode of communication across a wide variety of contexts' (McCroskey, 1982, p. 147). In contrast, state apprehension is specific to a given communication situation. McCroskey (1982) reconceptualized the construct, placing CA on a continuum with state apprehension at one end and trait apprehension on the other end. Furthermore, McCroskey argued that as with all human behavior, CA must be viewed as the product of both personality characteristics and situational factors.

In researching etiological factors, Beatty, McCroskey and Heisel (1998) proposed a theory of CA anchored in the principles of psychobiology, labeling CA as a 'communibiological paradigm'. Ultimately, communibiologists believe that genetics are significantly more important in the development of communication behavior than learning processes and the environment. However, most CA theorists argue that CA originates through a dichotomous relationship of genetics and learned behavior, and even staunch advocates for communibiology acknowledge the role of environmental factors, social and cultural influences in the development of communication-related anxiety.

Influence of Culture on CA

Culture influences the way individuals communicate. For instance, unlike Western cultures, many non-Western cultures do not place as much importance on the frequency of communication (Olaniran and Roach, 1994). In researching the relationship between culture and communication frequency, Carducci and Zimbardo (1995) illustrated that only 30 percent of college-age students in Israel report being shy, versus 60 percent in Taiwan and Japan and 40 percent in the United States. Carducci and Zimbardo's study concluded that the largest predictors of shyness are cultural styles of assigning praise and blame to children. For instance, in Israel a child who attempts to accomplish a task is rewarded, regardless of the outcome. In contrast, if a child attempts something and succeeds, Japanese parents take the credit, but if the child fails, the child is responsible for the failure. Therefore, Carducci and Zimbardo reported that Asian students are less likely to speak in social settings than students from cultures in which trying is rewarded regardless of the result (e.g., Israel).

As with cross-cultural leadership, cross-cultural research on CA has most often been approached with an ethnocentric mindset. In other words, most research on CA has explored how the construct applies to the US culture. As Olaniran and Roach (1994) noted, though CA is a construct that is likely to occur in most cultures, 'it is also likely that different cultures perceive, manifest, and respond (reward/sanction) to CA differently' (p. 379). Therefore, CA may not only be increased when individuals communicate with those who are dissimilar, but CA may also be demonstrated and interpreted differently based on cultural orientation.

Effects of CA

Organizational members exchange information and model behavior through collaborative and assertive communication; however, individuals with high levels of CA frequently avoid communication, withdraw from communication or disrupt the communication of others (Cole & McCroskey, 2003). McCroskey and Richmond (1976) reported that the frequency of communication has a major impact on leaders' perceived credibility, perceived status and perceived leadership ability. Furthermore, individuals with high levels of CA are perceived as being less competent and less successful, requiring more training, and having difficulty establishing positive relationships with subordinates, supervisors and co-workers (Falcione, McCroskey & Daly, 1977; McCroskey & Richmond, 1979).

Research examining CA in organizational settings indicates that employees with high levels of CA migrate toward occupations that require less communication and usually do not hold management or supervisory positions. Researchers have found CA to be positively related to neuroticism (McCroskey, Heisel & Richmond, 2001) and negatively related to leader–member exchange (Madlock et al., 2007; Jones, 2009), quality and quantity of work (McCroskey, McCroskey & Richmond, 2005) and perceptions of leaders (McCroskey & Richmond, 1976). Therefore, in non-profit organizations, CA may be a threat to the development and retention of volunteers and paid employees.

As Flauto (1999) reported, a leader's vision becomes manifest through clear and effective communication. CA may drastically limit the frequency and efficiency of communicated messages, therefore limiting the leader's ability to produce positive organizational outcomes. The influence of CA may inhibit followers from expressing innovative ways of problem solving (e.g., as a result of intellectual stimulation) or articulating their individual needs (e.g., as a result of individualized consideration). Furthermore, the absence of communication is likely to promote perceptions of ineffective leadership by reducing members' confidence in the leader's vision or by inhibiting followers from understanding the leader's vision.

In addition to communicating a vision, the leader–member relationship is also determined through the frequency and quality of communication exchanges (Graen, Dansereau & Minami, 1972). Harvey et al. (2006) explained, 'A leader's ability to interact effectively with subordinates is generally held to be crucial in creating and maintaining an effective organization' (p. 747). Even the definition of communication embodies the importance of establishing relationships. As Fore (1987) noted, communication is 'the process in which relationships are established, maintained, modified, or terminated through an increase or reduction of meaning' (p. 2). Therefore, not surprisingly, in the only two studies conducted on CA and leader–member exchange theory (LMX) (Madlock et al., 2007; Jones, 2009), researchers found a negative relationship between CA and LMX. In other words, as CA increases, the quality of leader–member exchange decreases. Therefore, in order to increase the quality of interpersonal exchanges, leaders must learn to minimize and manage CA. Recognition and management of CA is especially important in a diverse workforce where crucial knowledge exchange creates trust and minimizes fault-lines between diverse members.

DIAGNOSTIC THINKING FOR LEADING IN A DIVERSE WORKFORCE

There is evidence that efforts by organizational leaders to manage effectively the differences that present difficulties in intergroup relationships lead to improved perceptions of the organization overall, especially among minority employees. For example, Choi & Rainey (2010) found that when federal government employees perceived that leaders managed racial diversity effectively, higher levels of racial diversity improved perceived organizational performance. In contrast, higher levels of racial diversity in agencies that were not successful in managing diversity significantly decreased perceptions of the agency's performance. In interviews with leaders of nonprofit organizations, McCuiston et al. (2004) found a consensus view that leading a diverse workforce is challenging for many of the reasons noted above, but that focusing attention on common goals is a strategy that may help diminish the effects of perceived and anticipated differences between social groups. Based on interview data, Weisinger and Salipante (2007) came to similar conclusions, finding that in a diverse workforce productive interaction included activities explicitly structured to recategorize workers with an organizational identity, not as members of social groups. Less productive interactions lacked structure and thus did not overcome social connections rooted in social identity groups. Engaging diverse workers in learning activities seemed to be particularly effective in limiting divisive effects of social identities and increasing perceived organizational membership.

Reflecting on detailed data they obtained from larger companies, Kochan et al. (2003) noted that since evidence is lacking to support that diversity is good or bad for organizational performance, strategies that can leverage benefits from diversity or mitigate its negative effects should be given priority. One such strategy requires that leaders focus on the development of group leadership and process skills that can facilitate opportunities for diverse workers to learn from one other how better to accomplish work objectives. Kochan et al. (2003) also advocate adoption of some basic analytic approaches that help organizations move beyond a typical focus on comparison of attitudes, performance and pay among different groups of employees, to questions such as the variables that lead more diverse work units to outperform work units that are more homogeneous.

Douglas, Ferris, Buckley and Gundlach (2003) suggest that leaders have a clear role in managing diversity not only at the organizational level by understanding and altering social and political processes, but also at the interpersonal level through development of relationships with members of various social identity groups. Although leadership style does make a difference in employee satisfaction and performance, the difference may not be related to what the leader does as much as to how the leader's actions are interpreted (Graen et al., 1972). Leader effectiveness largely relies on knowing when and how to articulate clear communication messages. For instance, a leader must provide a vision for the organization, and clearly communicate the vision throughout the organization (Flauto, 1999). However, clear communication requires not only articulating the vision, but also restructuring communication patterns and channels according to the specific receiver and context.

All communication interactions involve uncertainty and ambiguity, but uncertainty is greater when there are cultural differences between communicators (Devito, 2009). For instance, family means something very different to an individual from a collectivist culture than to someone from an individualist culture. In addition, the meaning of authority differs in high-power-distance and low-power-distance cultures. The adjustment principle in intercultural communication suggests that no two individuals share identical symbol systems. Devito (2009) posited that the art of intercultural communication is learning to understand the meaning behind diverse verbal and non-verbal symbols. However, many leaders place too much emphasis on self, approaching leadership from an ethnocentric mindset. Leading in a diverse workforce requires that leaders become other-oriented. In a like manner, the leader is also responsible for their learning concerning organizational members. Sharing information in intercultural groups will help reduce uncertainty, consequently increasing trust.

There is no better preparation for intercultural communication than learning about other cultures. Effective communication in a diverse workplace calls for an understanding of rules and customs of diverse cultures (also called accommodation theory; Giles, Mulac, Bradac & Johnson, 1987). Communication accommodation theory suggests that as individuals communicate they begin to mirror verbal and non-verbal communication behaviors. Accommodation allows communication patterns to become more homogeneous within the organizational culture. Therefore, although organizational members must recognize cross-cultural differences, these differences should serve as the basis for organizational learning, and members must use this learning to adapt their communication according to these differences.

NATURE OF THE TASK

As Eisenberg (1984) noted, contemporary communication theorists reject the view of an 'optimal model of communication ... in favor of a more rhetorical view of communicator as strategist' (p. 228). As with strategic communication, strategic leadership involves effectively maneuvering through various contexts and audiences and tailoring messages to diverse receivers. For instance, leaders must understand that information concerning task and job design must be communicated in a way that has meaning for a diverse population.

In high-context cultures (e.g., Mexico), oral agreements and personal relationships are extremely important (Hofstede, 2001). In contrast, in low-context cultures (e.g., United States), members place greater emphasis on written contracts and explicit information than on personal relationships (Devito, 2009). As a result of this cultural difference, members of high-context cultures have low tolerance for ambiguity and believe ambiguity results when social interactions are inefficient (Gudykunst, 1985). Devito noted that for members of high-context cultures, the directness of members of low-context cultures may seem rude or unnecessary. Alternatively, for members of low-context cultures, the ambiguity of members of high-context cultures may appear cold or dishonest (Devito, 2009). Therefore, leaders in a diverse non-profit workforce must learn to alter communication messages to fit the cultural communication patterns of unique members. Task instruction and job design may be more purposefully ambiguous for high-context members, but more specific and detailed for low-context members. Recognizing these cultural differences will also allow leaders to understand conflict that arises from relational demography.

Not only do task instructions and job design have to be altered to accommodate diverse members, but rewards may also have to be altered to fit the needs of diverse members. Chiang and Birtch (2005) noted that a difficult challenge for twenty-first century leaders is to identify rewards that lead to improved performance. Chiang and Birtch stated, 'As managers grapple with performance and motivation related issues, these may be further exacerbated by growing resource constraints, fierce competitive rivalry, harsh business climates, and entry into foreign markets' (p. 358). A reward's success is based largely on the ability to attract, retain and motivate employees. Eisenberg (1999) argued that due to discrepant cognitive, emotional and motivational patterns in collectivist (e.g. Japan) and individualist (e.g. US) cultures, various reward types may carry different meanings, as well as differing degrees of value and motivational impact. Reward preferences are largely shaped by individual needs, values and expectations, and reward effectiveness is greatly contingent on the perceived meaning of the receiver (Chiang and Birtch, 2005).

Previous empirical research indicated that collectivists tend to value non-financial rewards more than financial rewards. On the other hand, individualists tend to desire individual achievement, recognition and financial rewards. Although, some researchers suggest that the breadth and intensity of globalization is leading to 'convergence' of employee values, Chiang and Birtch (2005) reported that reward preference is largely influenced by the value systems inherent in different countries. However, individuals from similar cultures may also hold different reward preferences. Chiang and Birtch summarized their findings by explaining that 'while preferences for certain types of rewards remain relatively divergent, differences in preferences for both reward systems and the criteria by which rewards are allocated are diminishing as the forces of convergence take hold' (p. 357). For example, despite being an individualist culture, Hertzberg (1987) suggested that monetary rewards have very little motivational influence for employees in American organizations. Chiang and Birtch suggested that leaders should use the type–system–criterion (TSC) reward taxonomy as a tool for identifying which specific reward preferences are influenced by various contextual factors.

NATURE OF THE GROUP

In addition to the divergence–convergence debate, Devito (2009) argued that although most cultures have a dominant orientation, individualism and collectivism are not mutually exclusive tendencies. In the globalized world, leaders must understand how individual and collective tendencies influence organizational members; however, leaders must also learn the profiles of specific members in order to implement leadership behaviors that are contingent on the context.

Hofstede (2001) suggested, 'The strong feelings of desirability for individualism in the United States make it more difficult for Americans to understand that people in less individualistically oriented societies may want to resolve societal and organizational problems in other ways' (p. 213). For example, respondents from more individualistic cultures (which include both the US and Britain) may perceive that decisions made by individuals are usually of higher quality than decisions made by groups

(Hofstede, 2001). However, employees with collectivist tendencies may feel that decisions made by groups are more valuable to the organization than decisions made by the individual. In the collectivist orientation, individuals perceive personal goals as subordinate to the goals of the collective. Therefore, in organizations that consist of members with collectivist tendencies, small-group leadership may need to be shared or rotated. Members with individualist tendencies may feel motivated to compete for leadership in teams and groups. Furthermore, due to the importance of interpersonal relationships in high-context collectivist cultures, leaders will need to cultivate high-quality exchange relationships with collectivist organizational members. In contrast, members with individualistic tendencies may prefer that communication focus on the task rather than relationship building or pro-social messages.

LEADERSHIP APPROACH CHOICES

Situational Leadership

Leadership effectiveness may not be related to the style of leadership as much as how the leader's actions are interpreted (Graen, Dansereau & Minami, 1972). As contingency models of leadership suggest, the relationship between leadership style and leadership effectiveness is dependent upon aspects of the situation (Fiedler, 1964). For instance, Hersey and Blanchard's (1969) situational leadership theory posits that instead of using one type of leadership, successful leaders should change their leadership styles based on the specific task and the maturity of followers.

As with communication behaviors, leaders must adapt leadership behaviors to fit specific situations. The important issue in selecting a leadership style in a diverse workforce is that the chosen style promotes an atmosphere of trust and leverages the benefits of diversity. As Hersey and Blanchard (1969) argued, a 'best' style of leadership does not exist. Nevertheless, according to Floyd (2009), certain communication characteristics will allow leaders to behave competently and effectively in most situations. These communication characteristics include: (1) self-awareness, the awareness of personal behavior and how behavior affects others; (2) adaptability, the ability to assess what is appropriate and effective in a specific context; (3) empathy, the ability to be other-oriented and attempt to understand the thoughts and feelings of others; (4) cognitive complexity, the ability to consider a variety of explanations and to approach a problem in multiple ways; and (5) ethics, the ability to communicate honestly and to judge whether something is morally right or wrong.

Floyd's (2009) characteristics of communication competency suggest multiple approaches to leadership in a diverse non-profit workforce. Furthermore, despite the need to alter leadership to fit specific situations, servant leadership and transformational leadership are two approaches that may have broader appeal as they both encompass Floyd's standards. Ultimately, Floyd's standards of communication competency suggest the importance of leaders being other-oriented, ethical, empathic and adaptable. Therefore, as with competency in communication, competency in leadership requires that leaders put followers first while learning to direct communication toward the needs of individual followers.

Servant Leadership

According to Greenleaf (1977), servant leadership is a philosophy and practice of leadership in which leaders achieve results for their organization by giving priority to the needs of the followers they serve. Over the last few years, servant leadership has attracted vast attention from researchers and scholars. Barbuto and Wheeler (2006) posited that servant leadership consists of altruistic calling, wisdom, emotional healing, persuasive mapping and community stewardship.

Although there are numerous conceptualizations of the servant leadership construct, the dimensions provided by Barbuto and Wheeler (2006) and other researchers (e.g., Winston, 2004) relate to Floyd's (2009) characteristics of communication competency. This parallel between Floyd's standards and servant leadership dimensions indicates that implementing servant leadership behaviors may be beneficial in communicating and leading in a diverse workforce. House et al. (2004) suggested that differences between cultures might influence the perceived effectiveness of servant leadership. For instance, in collectivistic, high-power-distance cultures such as China, servant leadership behaviors may be perceived differently than in individualistic, low-power-distance cultures such as the United States (Hofstede, 2001; Hale & Fields, 2007). Although the various dimensions of servant leadership have not been rated as equally important, cross-cultural studies on servant leadership have suggested that servant leadership behaviours may be culturally universal (Hale & Fields, 2007; Sun & Wang, 2009). For instance, Hale and Fields reported that although vision had a significantly stronger relationship with leader effectiveness for Ghanaians than for Americans, both subsamples similarly equated service and humility with leader effectiveness. In a like manner, Barbuto and Wheeler's (2006) five-factor structure of servant leadership has been found to be valid and reliable in the Chinese context with fewer items than the original measure (Sun & Wang, 2009).

Transformational Leadership

Transformational leadership behaviors (i.e., individualized consideration, intellectual stimulation, idealized influence and inspirational motivation) may also be effective in leading diverse organizational members. Transformational behaviors help empower followers, making followers less dependent on the leader. Sosik, Godshalk and Yammarino (2004) explained:

> Both mentors and transformational leaders act as role models who encourage learning and development, and work to develop others' self-confidence, personal identity, and well-being. Thus, transformational leaders likely serve as mentors, and mentors likely exhibit various degrees of transformational leadership behavior. (p. 245)

The distinct difference between servant leadership and transformational leadership is that in transformational leadership the key focus is on the organization's goals, whereas in servant leadership the key focus is on the follower. According to Bass (1990), by demonstrating transformational leadership behaviors, organizational goals are achieved as followers 'transcend their own self-interests for the good of the group, organization, or society' (p. 53).

Transformational leaders work to empower organizational members, which is significant in leading a non-profit workforce in which volunteers may need intrinsic motivation to be committed to the organization. Furthermore, transformational leaders work to cultivate an organizational culture by giving attention to priorities and concerns, quickly reacting to crisis situations, wisely allocating rewards and clearly articulating the organization's vision (Yukl, 2006). Previous empirical studies on the effectiveness of transformational leadership in culturally diverse organizations found that the relationship between transformational leadership and employee satisfaction was significant among culturally diverse members. As with servant leadership, transformational leadership behaviors relate to Floyd's (2009) characteristics of communication competency. Therefore, transformational leadership behaviors may also be effective when leading a diverse non-profit workforce.

REFERENCES

Barbuto, J.E. & Wheeler, D.W. (2006). Scale development and construct clarification of servant leadership. *Group and Organization Management*, 31(3), 300–326.

Barge, J.K. (1994). *Leadership Communication Skills for Organizations and Groups*. New York: St Martin's Press.

Bass, B.M. (1990). *Bass & Stogdill's Handbook of Leadership: Theory, Research, & Managerial Applications*, 3rd edn. New York: Free Press.

Beatty, M.J., Behnke, R.R. & McCallum, K. (1978). Situational determinants of communication apprehension. *Communication Monographs*, 45, 187–191.

Beatty, M.J., McCroskey, J.C. & Heisel, A.D. (1998). Communication apprehension as temperamental expression: a communibiological paradigm. *Communication Monographs*, 65, 197–219.

Buss, A.H. (1980) *Self-Consciousness and Social Anxiety*. San Francisco, CA: W.H. Freeman.

Byrne, D. (1971). *The Attraction Paradigm*. New York: Academic Press.

Carducci, B.J. & Zimbardo, P.G. (1995). Are you shy? *Psychology Today*, 28(6), 34–78.

Chiang, F.T. & Birtch, T.A. (2005). A taxonomy of reward preference. *Journal of International Management*, 11, 357–375.

Choi, S. & Rainey, H.G. (2010). Managing diversity in US federal agencies: effects of diversity and diversity management on employee perceptions of organizational performance. *Public Administration Review*, 70(1), 109–121.

Chrobot-Mason, D., Ruderman, M.N., Weber, T.J. & Ernst, C. (2009). The challenge of leading on unstable ground: triggers that activate social identity faultlines. *Human Relations*, 62, 1763–1793.

Cole, J.G. & McCroskey, J.C. (2003). The association of perceived communication apprehension, shyness, and verbal aggression with perceptions of source credibility and affect in organizational and interpersonal context. *Communication Quarterly*, 5(1), 101–110.

Cox, T. (1994). *Cultural Diversity in Organizations: Theory, Research, and Practice*. San Francisco, CA: Berrett-Koehler.

Davis, K. (1953). Management communication and the grapevine. *Harvard Business Review*, September–October, 43–49.

Devito, J.A. (2009). *The Interpersonal Communication Book*, 12th edn. New York: Pearson.

Douglas, C., Ferris, G.R., Buckley, M.R. & Gundlach, M.J. (2003). A volume in LMX leadership: the series. In Graen, G. (ed.), *Dealing with Diversity*. Greenwich, CT: Information Age, pp. 59–90.

Eden, D. & Leviatan, U. (1975). Implicit leadership theory as a determinant of the factor structure underlying supervisory behavior scales. *Journal of Applied Psychology*, 60, 736–741.

Eisenberg, E.M. (1984). Ambiguity as strategy in organizational communication. *Communication Monographs*, 51, 227–242.

Eisenberg, J. (1999). How individualism-collectivism moderates the effects of rewards on creativity and innovation: a comparative review of practices in Japan and the US. *Creativity and Innovation Management*, 8(4), 251–261.

Falcione, R.L., McCroskey, J.C. & Daly, J.A. (1977). Job satisfaction as a function of employees' communication apprehension, self-esteem, and perceptions of their immediate supervisors. *Communication Yearbook*, 1, 363–376.

Fiedler, F. (1964). A contingency model of leadership effectiveness. In Berkowitz, L. (ed.), *Advances in Experimental Social Psychology, Vol. 1*. New York: Academic Press.

Flauto, F.J. (1999). Walking the talk: the relationship between leadership and communication competence. *Journal of Leadership Studies*, 6(1), 86–97.

Floyd, K. (2009). *Interpersonal Communication: The Whole Story*. New York: McGraw Hill.

Fore, W.F. (1987). *Television and Religion: The Shaping of Faith, Values, and Culture*. New Haven, CT: Augsburg Publishing House.

Gerstner, C.R. & Day, D.V. (1997). Meta-analytic review of leader–member exchange theory: correlations and constructs. *Journal of Applied Psychology*, 82, 837–844.

Gibelman, M. (2000). The nonprofit sector and gender discrimination: a preliminary investigation into the glass ceiling. *Nonprofit Management and Leadership*, 10(3), 251–269.

Giles, H., Mulac, A., Bradac, J. & Johnson, P. (1987). Speech accommodation theory: the first decade and beyond. *Communication Yearbook*, 10, 8–34.

Graen, G.B., Dansereau, F. & Minami, T. (1972). An empirical test of the man-in-the-middle hypothesis among executives in a hierarchical organization employing a unit-set analysis. *Organizational Behavior and Human Performance*, 8, 262–285.

Green, S.G., Anderson, S.E. & Shivers, S.L. (1996). Demographic and organizational influences on leader–member exchange and related work attitudes. *Organizational Behavior and Human Decision Processes*, 66(2), 203–214.

Greenleaf, R.K. (1977). *Servant Leadership: A Journey Into the Nature of Legitimate Power and Greatness*. New York: Paulist Press.

Gudykunst, W.B. (1985). The influence of cultural similarity, type of relationships, and self-monitoring on uncertainty reduction processes. *Communication Monographs*, 52, 203–217.

Hale, J.R. & Fields, D. (2007). Exploring servant leadership across cultures: a study of followers in Ghana and the USA. *Leadership*, 3(4), 397–417.

Hall, E.T. (1976). *Beyond Culture*. Garden City, NY: Anchor Press.

Halpern, R.P. (2006). *Workforce Issues in the Nonprofit Sector.* Washington, DC: American Humanics.

Harrison, D.A., Price, K.H. & Bell, M.P. (1998). Beyond relational demography: time, and the effects of surface-and deep-level diversity on work group cohesion. *Academy of Management Journal*, 41(1), 96–107.

Harvey, P., Martinko, M.J. & Douglas, S.C. (2006). Causal reasoning in dysfunctional leader–member interactions. *Journal of Managerial Psychology*, 21(8), 747–762.

Hersey, P. and Blanchard, K.H. (1969). *Management of Organizational Behavior – Utilizing Human Resources*. Upper Saddle River, NJ: Prentice Hall.

Hertzberg, F. (1987). One more time: how do you motivate employees? *Harvard Business Review*, 18(3), 1–16.

Hofstede, Geert (2001). *Culture's Consequences: Comparing Values, Behaviors, Institutions, and Organizations across Nations*, 2nd edn. Thousand Oaks, CA: SAGE.

Hollander, E.P. & Offermann, L.R. (1990). Power and leadership in organization: relationships in transition. *American Psychologist*, 45(2), 179.

House, R.J., Hanges, P.J., Javidan, M., Dorfman, P.W. & Gupta, V. (eds) (2004). *Culture, Leadership, and Organizations: The GLOBE Study of 62 Cultures*. Thousand Oaks, CA: Sage.

Johnson, B. & Fields, D. (2010). CAUTION! Implicit leadership theories at work. In F. Gandolfi (ed.), *Foundations of Contemporary Leadership*. Hamburg: Lambert Academic Publishing, pp. 55–82.

Johnson, J. (2009). The nonprofit leadership deficit: a case for more optimism. *Nonprofit Management and Leadership*, 19(3), 285–304.

Jones, J. (2009). Mediating effect of follower communication apprehension in the relationship between demographic dissimilarity and LMX. Conference Proceedings. North Eastern Association of Business, Economics, and Technology, Penn State University, State College, Pennsylvania, March.

Kochan, T., Bezrukova, K., Ely, R., Jackson, S., Joshi, A., Jehn, K., Leonard, J., Levine, D. & Thoman, D. (2003). The effects of diversity on business performance: report of the Diversity Research Network. *Human Resource Management*, 42(1), 3–21.

Larson, C.E., Backlund, P.M., Redmond, M.K. & Barbour, A. (1978). *Assessing communication competence*. Paper Presented at the annual meeting of the Speech Communication Association, Minneapolis, MN, April.

Lord, R.G. & Maher, K.J. (1991). *Leadership and Information Processing: Linking Perceptions and Performance*. Boston, MA: Unwin Hyman.

Madlock, P.E., Martin, M.M., Bogdan, L. & Ervin, M. (2007). The impact of communication traits on leader–member exchange. *Human Communication*, 10, 451–464.

McCroskey, J.C. (1977). Oral communication apprehension: a summary of recent theory and research. *Human Communication Research*, 31(1), 78–96.

McCroskey, J.C. (1982). *An Introduction to Rhetorical Communication*, 4th edn. Englewood Cliffs, NJ: Prentice Hall.

McCroskey, J.C., Heisel, A.D. & Richmond, V.P. (2001). Eysenck's big three and communication traits: three correlational studies. *Communication Monographs*, 68, 360–366.

McCroskey, J.C. & Richmond, V.P. (1976). The effects of communication apprehension on the perception of peers. *Western Speech Communication*, Winter, 14–21.

McCroskey, J.C. & Richmond, V.P. (1979). The impact of communication apprehension on individuals in organizations. *Communication Quarterly*, 27, 55–61.

McCroskey, L.L., McCroskey, J.C. & Richmond, V.P. (2004). Applying organizational orientations theory to employees of profit and non-profit organizations. *Communication Quarterly*, 53, 21–40.

McCuiston, V.E., Woolridge, B.R. & Pierce, C.K. (2004). Leading the diverse workforce: profit, prospects and progress. *Leadership & Organization Development Journal*, 25(1–2), 73–92.

McDermott, M. (2008). Culture and leadership in transition: comparing perceptions of cultural values, cultural practices, and leadership preferences across generations in Israel, South Africa, and the United States. Doctoral dissertation. Regent University, Virginia Beach, VA.

Mesch, D. (2010). Management of human resources in 2020: the outlook for nonprofit organizations. *Public Administration Review, Special Issue on the Future of Public Administration in 2020*, 70, S173–S174.

Olaniran, B.A. & Roach, K.D. (1994). Communication apprehension and classroom apprehension in Nigerian classrooms. *Communication Quarterly*, 42, 379–389.

Richmond, V.P. (1984). Implications of quietness: some facts and speculations. In Daly, J.A. & McCroskey, J.C. (eds), *Avoiding Communication*. Beverly Hills, CA: Sage, pp. 145–156.

Rowley, D.J. & Sherman, H. (2003). The special challenge of academic leadership. *Managerial Decision*, 41, 1058–1063.

Sosik, J.J., Godshalk, V.M. & Yammarino, F.J. (2004). Transformational leadership, learning goal orientation, and expectations for career success in mentor–protégé relationships: a multiple level of analysis paper. *Leadership Quarterly*, 15, 241–261.

Stephan, C.W. & Stephan, W.G. (1992). Reducing intercultural anxiety through intercultural contact. *International Journal of Intercultural Relations*, 16(1), 89–106.

Sun, J. & Wang, B. (2009). Servant leadership in China: conceptualization and measurement. *Global Leadership*, 5, 321–344.

Tajfel, H. and Turner, J.C. (1986). The social identity theory of inter-group behavior. In S. Worchel and L.W. Austin (eds), *Psychology of Intergroup Relations*. Chicago, IL: Nelson-Hall.

Tschirhart, M. & Wise, L. (2007). U.S. nonprofit organizations' demand for temporary foreign professionals. *Nonprofit Management and Leadership*, 18(2), 121–140.

Tsui, A.S. & O'Reilly, C.O. (1989). Beyond simple demographic effects: the importance of relational demography in superior–subordinate dyads. *Academy of Management Journal*, 32, 402–423.

Weisinger, J.Y. & Salipante, P.F. (2007). An expanded theory of pluralistic interactions in voluntary nonprofit organizations. *Nonprofit Management and Leadership*, 18(2), 157–173.

Winston, B.E. (2004). Servant leadership at Heritage Bible College: a single-case study, *Leadership and Organization Development Journal*, 25(7), 600–617.

Yukl, G. (2006). *Leadership in Organizations*, 6th edn. Upper Saddle River, NJ: Pearson Education.

10. Organizational change in nonprofit organizations: implications for human resource management

Thomas R. Packard

ORGANIZATIONAL CHANGE: CHALLENGES AND OPPORTUNITIES

Walter Philips, the CEO of San Diego Youth Services (SDYS), a highly regarded and highly successful human services organization in San Diego County in California, had led ongoing growth and innovation in the agency for over ten years, and recently concluded that the agency was facing new major challenges to which it would need to respond. The agency has been a major provider of comprehensive services at 14 locations for homeless, abused and at-risk youth and their families and communities, serving over 10 000 youth and their families per year with a budget of over $12 million and 197 staff. In spite of the agency's 40-plus years of outstanding service provision, challenges in the agency's environment required large-scale changes in the agency's operations.

Under Walter Philips's leadership, the agency launched a formal organizational change process to streamline management and decrease administrative costs, clarify the management structure and philosophy with respect to management of budgets and staff, and consolidate programs under divisions to increase integration and accountability. The agency's use of tactics of planned organizational change as discussed in this chapter enabled the agency to successfully create a new organizational structure, new job descriptions, a new system of team meetings, and new fiscal reports and procedures while maintaining high staff morale and continuity of service delivery.

The challenges that SDYS was facing are common in nonprofit organizations (NPOs). Needs and demands for organizational change, coming from the organization's environment, staff, clients and often from its own leaders, are so widespread as to be considered constants. As resources become scarcer, these challenges become more complicated. Funding cuts, increasing accountability requirements, and factors within the organization such as low morale, burnout and high turnover are among the realities affecting many nonprofit managers. Growing and even mature NPOs may need to develop their management skills and infrastructure further. Given the scope and intensity of these and other challenges and opportunities, NPOs need to find and implement new ways of working.

These challenges also present change opportunities. Program redesign, restructuring, developing program evaluation systems, enhancing diversity, and changing an obsolete or dysfunctional organizational culture can all help an organization to survive and even thrive during a very challenging time. Key challenges, needs and opportunities facing an organization are typically addressed by an executive and their staff using their existing talents, skills and energies to respond as well as they can. While notable successes have been reported in the literature and popular press, research and practice in the field of organizational change suggests that in many cases the conscious use of planned change processes can enhance prospects for successful change, and therefore organizational survival and growth, through the use of processes to enhance program and management capacities in order to deliver maximally effective services and to develop a highly competent and committed workforce.

Planned organizational change processes can be used to improve organizational outcomes or processes, or to develop innovative new programs or strategies. This typically involves making staff aware of the need for change and developing processes to enlist staff support and commitment. While some executives and managers, through their own personality characteristics and acquired skills, have created successful change, there are many other organizations where change efforts are not successful. It is also likely that in many organizations there are conditions which would warrant explicit organizational change, but the organization's leaders lack the awareness, skills or interest to address this need.

The purpose of this chapter is to review the needs and opportunities for organizational change in nonprofit organizations, and the ways a human resources (HR) professional can address these by serving as an internal organizational change agent or providing expert consulting to executives and staff who engage in organizational change activities. The chapter begins with an overview of some of the challenges facing nonprofit organizations, touching upon how planned organizational change processes can help. Next, the evolving role of the HR professional is discussed, setting the stage for a discussion of how an HR professional can assist the organization in using planned organizational change. After reviewing definitions of organizational change and the use of organizational change in NPOs, a model and process for planned organizational change is presented. This model can be used by an organization's executive on their own, or in combination with consultation and guidance from the organization's HR professional. The use of external consultants is also discussed. Common organizational change methods are reviewed, offering a menu of options for internal change leaders to consider using, based on their organization's unique circumstances. The chapter ends with a summary and implications for HR managers in NPOs.

THE BROADENING ROLE OF HUMAN RESOURCE MANAGEMENT

The role of HR professionals has broadened in recent decades, from an initial focus on strictly personnel functions such as recruiting, hiring, training, performance appraisal and discipline, to a newer conceptualization of strategic human resource management (SHRM). According to Pynes (2009), SHRM 'refers to the implementation of human resources activities, policies, and practices to make the necessary ongoing changes to support or improve the agency's operational and strategic objectives' (p. 31). Facilitating organizational change has been identified as one SHRM function in this new conceptualization.

Contemporary HR staff who in the past were heavily involved with overseeing and conducting staff training are now in many cases also fulfilling roles as internal organizational consultants or change agents who advise executive management or play a lead role in initiating and managing processes for improving the internal functioning of the organization. These can range from management development and leadership training to facilitation of problem-solving groups, to providing expertise, as one's training allows, in processes such as total quality management and organization development consulting.

For example, Balougen and Hope-Hailey (2004) have suggested that the HR system can function as a 'change lever' (p. 91), filling traditional HR functions and also providing organization development consulting, which will be discussed later. In a similar vein, Alfes et al. (2010) have described the current HR manager as a change agent, facilitating organizational change processes through activities such as staff surveys and organization-wide communication processes regarding organizational change. Many useful guidelines and tools that an HR professional can use to lead or facilitate organizational change are detailed in *The Essentials of Managing Change and Transition* (Harvard Business School, 2005).

The use of formal organizational change processes has been most used in medium-sized to large (or very large, even multinational) organizations, and will be presented here as it may be used in medium-sized to large nonprofits. Some specific techniques could be used by an individual manager in a very small organization, perhaps with assistance from an outside consultant.

ORGANIZATIONAL CHANGE: DEFINITIONS

The literature on organizational change addresses for-profit, nonprofit and governmental organizations. While the focus here is on nonprofits, knowledge from the other sectors will be used here as relevant and appropriate. Within the huge literature on organizational change, the focus here is on planned change implemented by managers as change agents or change leaders employing what Demers calls 'rational adaptation' approaches (Demers, 2007), which see managers as change agents who can assess their environments and other conditions and then purposefully drive change within their organizations, rather than on organizational change that happens to organizations such as when funding is cut or environmental conditions seem to dictate what change must occur. This latter dynamic, change which comes without intention from the organization's staff, can however be followed by purposeful, planned organizational change to deal with such negative changes affecting an organization. The focus here will be on change in NPOs, but this area of study extensively uses principles developed in other sectors.

ORGANIZATIONAL CHANGE IN NONPROFIT ORGANIZATIONS

While there is a growing literature on organizational change in the nonprofit sector (e.g., Brothers & Sherman, 2011; McWilliam & Ward-Griffin, 2006; Ramos, 2007) and in human service organizations (Austin, 2004; Proehl, 2001) as an important subset of nonprofits, much of it is based on individual case studies, often with minimal attention to theory and little detail on actual change tactics used. Such reports of organizational change initiatives suggest that, typically, they are initiated and managed by the organization's leaders, with little attention to the use of formal change management processes or techniques. However, most administrators have received little or no training in organizational change processes and models.

A related process, capacity building, has received extensive attention in NPOs. Defined as 'actions that improve nonprofit effectiveness' (Blumenthal, 2003, as cited in McNamara, n.d.), capacity building is primarily focused on the content of change as defined below: activities to improve organization effectiveness. The HR professional can play a valuable role in the organization by facilitating capacity building.

LEVELS AND DIMENSIONS OF ORGANIZATIONAL CHANGE

Organizations and staffs change in small ways, such as developing new procedures, perhaps without even considering that change is occurring. Beyond daily changes, there are three levels of increasing intensity of change. Costello (1994, as cited in Proehl, 2001) described these three levels of organizational change. Developmental change involves adjustments to existing operations or improving a skill, method or process that does not currently meet the organization's standard. This level of change is the least threatening to employees and the easiest to manage. Examples include simple problem solving, routine training and improving communications. Transitional change involves implementing something new and abandoning old ways of functioning. This move through a transitional period to a new future state requires patience and time. Examples include basic reorganizations, new technology systems and implementing a new program. The most extreme form of change is transformational change, which requires major shifts in vision, strategy, structure or systems. This might evolve out of necessity, for example as a result of major policy changes such as managed care or a shift to outcomes measurement or performance-based contracting required by funding organizations. The new state after such change involves a new culture, new beliefs and awareness of new possibilities. Examples here might include major changes in organizational strategy or programming.

For larger-scale changes, in which radical changes in the organization's culture or systems are required, the use of the process discussed below should enhance the prospects of the organization reaching its desired new state. Consultants may also be brought into any change process as appropriate.

One important distinction to be made about organizational change is to describe it based on the distinctions between change content and change process. Change content, according to Anderson and Ackerman Anderson (2011), looks at 'what in the organization needs to change, such as structure, systems, business processes, technology, products, or services' (p. 52).

In a similar conceptualization, Armenakis and Bedeian (1999) include in change content the diagnostic models used to identify targets of change. Change process includes, according to Armenakis and Bedeian, the phases of change, including what is referred to below as change tactics. Similarly, Anderson and Ackerman Anderson see the change process as the ways in which the content changes will be planned, designed and implemented. They add a third element to their model: people, which refers to 'the human dynamics of change, including individual mind-set and behavior as well as collective culture' (p. 52).

A planned change initiative typically begins by identifying the need or opportunity, often through an organization's executive assessing the organization's external and internal conditions. External conditions include changing priorities or demands from the organization's funders or other stakeholders, threats such as decreases in funding, and new opportunities for the organization based on identified community needs. Internal conditions could include program quality or the need to adopt more evidence-based models, the need for enhanced cultural competence, management process issues such as an inadequate performance measurement system, or significant morale issues with staff.

After some amount of assessment, the organization's leaders (typically upper management staff) identify the content of the change needed to address the contextual factors. This may range from addressing funding cuts or restructuring, to creating new service delivery systems, or even implementing a strategic planning process. Then, attention is given to the process of change: the selection of strategies and tactics used by change leaders to implement the change content identified, leading to the hoped-for organizational improvements which will better address the external and internal factors which precipitated the need for change. The change process, of course, needs to pay significant attention to the people factors discussed by Anderson and Ackerman Anderson.

PLANNED ORGANIZATIONAL CHANGE

After a brief review of reasons that organizational change efforts often fail, I will review a model for implementing organizational change which can be used by an executive, perhaps with consultation from the HR professional. This model can also involve the use of consultation technologies and methods described later.

The role of an organization's executive is now commonly considered to include change management. Eadie (2006), in discussing the need for innovation in NPOs, has asserted that the 'chief executive as effective change leader must be a visionary, not only capable of thinking of the organization in terms of long-run purposes and ends, he or she also must be strongly committed to a collaborative approach to fashioning the vision that creatively draws upon the knowledge, expertise, and experience of board and staff members' (p. 38). To underline the importance of a formal change process, we will look briefly at why so many planned change efforts fail.

WHY ORGANIZATIONAL CHANGE EFFORTS OFTEN FAIL

Because substantive organizational change often confronts indifference or resistance and leads to discomfort or stress on the part of employees, it is not surprising that many change efforts fail. Many initiatives fail because they are introduced in an authoritarian way. Kotter (1996) found several commonalities in failed change efforts:

1. Allowing too much complacency: change agents need to establish a high level of urgency to motivate staff to want change.
2. Failing to create a sufficiently powerful guiding coalition: key leaders need to support the change effort publicly.
3. Underestimating the power of vision: 'vision plays a key role in producing useful change by helping to direct, align, and inspire actions on the part of large numbers of people' (p. 7).
4. Undercommunicating the vision: people need to see clearly that the benefits to them will outweigh the costs, and they need to see their leaders behaving consistently with their stated intentions and values.
5. Permitting obstacles to block the new vision: a change vision can be stalled by existing systems such as organizational structure and rewards systems that are not in alignment with the change.
6. Failing to create short-term wins: staff need to see some quick successes to combat complacency or discouragement.
7. Declaring victory too soon: large-scale change, usually involving culture change, takes years to accomplish fully.
8. Neglecting to anchor changes firmly in the corporate culture: the results of change need to be visibly connected to improved organizational performance, and new behaviors and systems need to be based on the new norms and values.

The change model described next is intended to address factors that may lead to failed efforts, and it is based on the key elements of successful change models covered in the literature.

A MODEL OF ORGANIZATIONAL CHANGE

The model of organizational change presented here is appropriate for transitional and transformational change as described above. A leader may initiate an organizational change process to meet a particular need or goal, such as moving the organization from a process-oriented to an outcomes-oriented culture, implementing an evidence-based practice, or addressing significant funding cuts. This model is adapted from other models, particularly those of Proehl (2001), Fernandez and Rainey (2006), Lewis, Packard and Lewis (2012) and Palmer, Dunford and Akin (2009).

The model presented here is known as a 'phase' model, suggesting that organizational change is a process with distinct steps or phases. Within these phases, specific change tactics are blended into the steps to be taken to implement organizational change. A preliminary study of the use of these tactics (Packard, 2010) found statistically significant differences in the use of change tactics between successful and unsuccessful change processes.

Although the steps below are presented in a logical linear fashion, they may at times overlap or be addressed in a different sequence, based on specific organizational conditions. Throughout the process, change leaders should be alert to human factors, including staff resistance and their need to be informed of activities. Involving staff in the process should have a significant effect on creating staff commitment, as well as leading to better ideas and outcomes.

1. Assess the Present

A change initiative typically starts with a change leader such as the executive and their management team, and perhaps other staff, who need to develop a clear understanding of the problem, the need for change (the current state) and the desired outcome (the future state). This may involve gathering and assessing available data to focus the change. For example, in the case of SDYS introduced at the beginning of this chapter, Walter Philips saw the emerging downturn in the national economy leading to the possibility of a decrease in funding; and also noted within the agency some inefficiencies at the administrative level and some duplication of duties which, combined with a lack of coordination and integration between the programs within the agency, created conditions requiring significant change.

Next, the change leader or team can assess the scope of the change and determine the type of change needed. Transitional or transformational change would suggest the use of this change management process. Change leaders should also determine the extent to which important preconditions for change are present. In an NPO, a core level of management competence, clearly articulated humanistic values and a participative management philosophy would be desirable preconditions. Substantive change will be less likely with ineffective or authoritarian management, an excessively bureaucratic or political culture, or heavily conflictual management–staff relations. If these conditions exist, they should be the first targets for change and will require outside help. Other aspects of organizational readiness to consider are likely levels of support and enthusiasm for the change and the capabilities of staff (their skills and abilities).

The leader should also engage in some self-assessment. According to Burke (2011, p. 248), a change leader should have a tolerance for ambiguity, accept not being able to control everything, understand how feelings affect behavior and be open to shared decision-making.

2. Create a Sense of Urgency

The change leader will need to communicate clearly and persuasively the need, desire and urgency for the change. Staff may be both comfortable and happy with the status quo and feel that they are overworked enough as it is, and therefore may be disinclined to take on a significant change in the way they and their programs operate. At SDYS, Walter Philips attended many meetings, from the board to program staff, to articulate the need for the change.

A change formula (Beer, 1992, as cited in Proehl, 2001, p. 72) suggests that change can occur when: (1) there is dissatisfaction with the current state; (2) staff have a clear vision of an ideal future state of the organization; (3) there is a clear and feasible process for reaching the desired state; and (4) these factors considered together outweigh the perceived costs of changing. From an employee's point of view, costs of change can include changes in employees' sense of competence, power or status, workplace relationships, rewards, and identity or roles. Therefore, the change leader can create conditions for change by creating dissatisfaction with the status quo, providing a clear and compelling vision for the new state, and establishing and using an effective and efficient process that minimizes the 'costs' to participants.

The change leader can use data to show that if a change is not made, the organization and staff will suffer undesirable consequences, such as loss of clients, loss of funding, a decrease in service quality or productivity, or a serious morale problem. Problems can range from new directives from funders, funding cutbacks or expectations for improved services, to low staff morale, burnout or inadequate management systems. As much as possible, existing data should be used to demonstrate the urgency for change.

3. Clarify the Change Imperative

In addition to articulating fully the problem needing attention, the vision for success – outcomes for the change – need to be clearly communicated. There needs to be a clear and specific plan for how the change initiative will be implemented, including a basic strategy, who will be involved, and planned activities and persons accountable for them. The plan should also describe how any additional data will be collected and analyzed, and the use of task forces and other change processes. The time frame for the project and available resources (especially staff time and any necessary financial support) should be noted. At SDYS, Walter Philips used the meetings discussed above to clarify the change imperative: to reduce administrative overheads, consolidate administrative and management positions, and re-organize programs into more appropriate bundles of services.

4. Ensure Support and Address Resistance

Throughout the process, change leaders will need continuously to show support for the process and anticipate and address resistance. Top management, such as the organization's executive, and perhaps the board, should formally show support for the process.

Resistance will need to be thoughtfully addressed. As Proehl (2001) summarized, people resist for three possible reasons: not knowing about the change, not being able to change or not being willing to change. Those who do not know about the change can be influenced by change leaders communicating the who, what, when, why and how of the change, and by getting them involved in the process. Those who feel unable to change can be educated regarding the new knowledge and skills that will be needed during and after the change. This might involve training in problem-solving methods, new management skills, team building or conflict management. A small number of staff may be unwilling to change. Their concerns should be recognized and addressed through feedback and coaching, showing how they may benefit. Rewards and performance management may be used as needed.

At SDYS, Walter Philips and his management team clearly and regularly showed their support for this process. Resistance was an especially difficult area, with even some of the key leaders in the organization being resistant to the change. He personally spent time meeting with each of these individuals as well as with staff throughout the organization to discuss the changes, to go over the reasons why the changes were necessary, and to be very clear about his expectations for them as they went through the change process.

5. Develop an Action System

The executive or top management team cannot accomplish large-scale change alone. Building a broad-based action system with designated responsibility for implementing and overseeing the change initiative serves several functions. If many staff members are involved, multiple talents can be brought to bear to address the challenges and tasks ahead. Spreading the workload can help ensure that the additional demands of change do not significantly disrupt ongoing work. Additionally, getting staff members involved can increase their sense of ownership of the results.

A large-scale change initiative can be guided and overseen by a 'change coalition' (Kotter, 1996) such as an organizational change steering committee that has representatives from all key stakeholder groups in the organization, including different levels of the hierarchy (from executives to line staff), different program and administrative areas, and labor organization representation if appropriate. Most members of the organization must consider this group legitimate.

Specific roles should be delineated. The CEO or other executive can serve as a sponsor, who demonstrates organizational commitment to the process and ensures that necessary resources (especially including staff time) are allocated. The key staff person responsible for day-to-day operation of the initiative, perhaps the HR manager, can serve as a champion who not only oversees implementation but also provides ongoing energy and focus for staff. There will probably be multiple change agents who are responsible for implementation at the unit or team level. They may be task force or problem-solving group chairs, facilitators or external consultants.

Many other staff should be involved as task force or committee members or involved in data collection and analysis and the design and implementation of new systems or processes. Employees from various management and staff levels should be invited to participate based on their relevant knowledge and skills. People with credibility in the organization, formal or informal power, and particular interest in the problem should be especially considered. People who are directly affected by the problem are particularly important for inclusion.

Finally, organizational systems need to be set up to ensure effective functioning of the process. This includes structural arrangements, such as the reporting relationships of the various committees and task forces, and communication processes to ensure that all staff members are aware of what is happening. Newsletters, email bulletins, all-staff meetings and reports at regular unit meetings should all be used on an ongoing basis. Communication systems for all the involved groups to coordinate with each other and several mechanisms for communicating progress on the initiative should be developed. Consultant and writer John Kotter (1996) has said that when it comes to organizational change, 'you cannot overcommunicate'. Messages about the need for change and what is being done need to be ongoing and frequent.

The action system in the SDYS change process primarily consisted of the upper management team, where most of the changes would need to take place. Middle managers such as program directors were talked with on numerous occasions.

6. Implement the Plan for Change

After the situation is analyzed, people are involved and change management processes are in place, strategies and processes can be initiated to implement the change. Problem-solving groups, going by various names such as task forces or action teams, are always needed in planned organizational change. Sometimes problem-solving groups use TQM techniques such as workflow or process analysis and cause-and-effect diagrams. Change efforts should usually include the analysis of existing organizational performance data to identify where quality, efficiency and effectiveness improvements need to be made. Additional data may be gathered as needed. Employee attitude surveys (Burke, 2011) are a very useful way to develop a deeper understanding of employee concerns and needs, and perhaps to assess the current culture and climate of the organization. Survey results can provide guidance for issues to address and strategies for ensuring staff commitment to the process.

For organization-wide change, sometimes business process reengineering (described below) is used to identify workflow and coordination improvement opportunities and eliminate processes that do not add value. Organization redesign, if necessary, should include not only traditional restructuring but also changes in decision-making and communication processes across organizational functions. Workshops using trained facilitators for team building, role clarification, conflict management and other concerns can often augment the change effort.

An action planning system including tasks, persons responsible and timelines should be used to track progress. Project activities should be revised as appropriate based on new information or changing conditions. Proehl (2001) recommends 'acting quickly and revising frequently' (p. 169), identifying opportunities for short-term successes so that staff can see tangible results from their efforts. When a new system is designed, procedures will need to be written and a staff training program developed.

It is important that adequate resources in terms of staff time and any necessary financial and technological support are made available. There should be widespread participation of staff in the change process, but staff should not be overtaxed.

7. Evaluate, Institutionalize and Celebrate

Any changes made should be evaluated to ensure success, and they also need to be institutionalized. Staff will need to be retrained, and training for new staff should reflect the new system. Job descriptions and performance appraisal systems may need to be modified to support the new systems. Implementation of new systems should be monitored, with further adjustments made as needed. Changes and successes should be celebrated in ways consistent with the organization's culture. Special events can be held when major milestones are met, and smaller successes can be rewarded and celebrated in staff meetings and other arenas.

At SDYS, the results of the change were institutionalized through incorporation into agency policies and procedures. These included a new organizational structure, new team meetings processes, new job titles and descriptions, new supervision lines of authority, and new fiscal reports and procedures. New marketing materials were developed to reflect the changes.

USE OF CONSULTANTS

The process just outlined is a complex one, and may be made more manageable with the use of consultants. Such consultants could be internal to the organization; with, for example, the HR manager providing guidance on the process and perhaps serving as a coach to executives. In situations in which an administrator or the organization does not have the knowledge or skills to respond to a particular need for change, external consultants can help by providing expertise in specific organizational change methods. The information here should help the executive or HR manager know what to expect and how to deal with the particular consultation process being used, so that an administrator wanting to initiate change requiring outside expertise will have some ideas on where to begin.

Types of Consultation

Yankey and Willen (2006) describe two broad types of consultation. The expert model involves a content expert, such as a specialist in program evaluation, who applies specific expertise to address a goal that the organization identifies. Organizational change typically involves the other type, a process model, in which the consultant is in more of a facilitator role, using expertise in change management processes but not giving expert advice on what an organization should do to solve its problem, except by suggesting change technologies to use.

Consultants and clients should thoughtfully consider the needs of the situation and arrange for the best approach. The expert model can be used, for example, if a program has identified a specialized need such as training on work with incest victims or automating an information system. The organization can then solicit consultants with the needed expertise. For complicated situations ranging from poor morale to funding crises, process skills will likely be needed because there will be no easy 'right' answer. Ideally, a consultant would have both process skills and expertise in selected areas. For example, in a funding crisis, process skills would be needed to help the client organization sort things out, identify issues and consider actions; expertise skills in areas such as strategic planning, budgeting, cost analysis and fund development would be valuable as well.

Selecting and Using Consultants

Yankey and Willen (2006) provide useful guidelines for selecting and using consultants as well as guidelines for making the consultation useful. To find a consultant, managers can ask managers in other organizations about consultants they have used or can contact relevant foundations, funding organizations, or professional associations. Internet searches can be especially useful here. A consultant being considered based on such a search should be asked to provide references from former clients.

Yankey and Willen (2006, p. 414) suggest that consultant interviews should cover not only consultant expertise and prior work but also these characteristics:

- honesty about their capabilities;
- compatibility with the organization;
- beliefs and values regarding organizational development;
- personality fit;
- motivations;
- ethics; and
- appreciation for confidentiality.

There should be clarity regarding the consultation goals, reflected both in the request for proposals, if one is used, and in the contract with the consultant chosen. A contract should outline responsible parties and their roles, the problem and goal, individuals and/or units or programs to be involved, consultant 'deliverables' (for example, a report, recommendations, services provided), ground rules, fees and a schedule.

A few commonly used consultation approaches to enhance organizational performance will be mentioned here. These are used more frequently in for-profit businesses, which usually have greater resources available for consultation. However, many are becoming more common in NPOs.

Some Common Consultation Technologies

Organization development

Organization development (OD) (French & Bell, 1999) has been one of the most common consultation methods in business and industry and is being increasingly used in NPOs. In OD, the consultant and the client organization jointly assess an organization's change needs and develop an action plan for addressing them. Organization development represents Yankey and Willen's 'process' model, although OD consultants often provide technical expertise in areas such as strategic planning, re-engineering, and total quality management, which vary on the 'process' to 'expert' continuum.

To change the way an organization solves its problems, the OD consultant may use interventions including:

- group process interventions such as team building, problem-solving sessions and role clarification sessions;
- training programs designed to enhance organizational skills using educational strategies such as simulations and structured experiences;
- survey feedback, or the gathering and sharing of diagnostic data about the organization and its current norms and processes;
- action research, which involves broad participation in the development of change strategies based on structured research and behavioral science technologies; and
- changes in organizational structure based on group agreement about suggested alterations.

The key to defining an intervention as OD is not the specific strategy used but the roles of the consultant and staff that might be affected by a change. This assumes that the organization and its members must have some control over the change process. Also, regardless of specific consultation activities, an effective OD consultant will follow clear procedures that include problem identification, contracting, assessment, planning, intervention, and evaluation.

In many situations, the assessment process leads not to training or group process interventions but to changes in organizational systems. If members of an organization are actively involved in the process, they are likely to be as actively involved in supporting the implementation of solutions.

Action research

Action research is a core technology of organization development. As its name implies, action research involves first gathering data on a problem (a research phase), and then action: the implementation of a change initiative. The next cycle of research involves gathering data on results, analyzing the data and making adjustments or planning new activities. Continuing with new activities constitutes another cycle of action, followed by another research phase of data collection.

Appreciative inquiry

A recent approach to organizational change that offers an option to traditional action research is appreciative inquiry. It involves 'the discovery of what gives "life" to a living system when it is most effective, alive, and constructively capable in ecological, economic, and human terms' (Cooperrider, Whitney & Stavros, 2003, p. 3). This innovative approach emphasizes asking positive questions to reveal the positive elements of an organization in order to help achieve its ideal future.

Business process re-engineering (BPR)

BPR, sometimes referred to as simply re-engineering, reached fad status in the business and government sectors in the 1990s. It has been defined as 'a fundamental rethinking and radical redesign of business processes to achieve dramatic improvements in critical contemporary measures of performance such as cost, quality, capital, service, and speed' (Hammer & Champy, 1993, as cited in Grobman, 2008, p. 297).

Re-engineering typically involves a thorough examination of the whole organization, focusing on structures and processes. The current organization is assessed, and a new, ideal organization is proposed that eliminates all processes that do not add value for customers. Re-engineering is sometimes seen as a euphemism for downsizing, and a common result of re-engineering is the elimination of management layers and positions. When positions are eliminated, an organization should do everything possible to retain employees in still-needed positions.

Total quality management (TQM)

TQM is an organization-wide philosophy and process of continuous improvements in quality by focusing on the control of variation to satisfy customer requirements, including top management support and employee participation and teamwork (Grobman, 2008, pp. 295–296). As contrasted with re-engineering, TQM focuses on the line worker level rather than the larger administrative systems and structures. TQM uses structured problem-solving methods to analyze work processes, eliminate unnecessary steps and improve quality.

Management analysis

Management analysis is a generic term involving expert analysis and audits of management structures, goals and objectives, and processes including organization charts, staff utilization, coordination mechanisms, roles and responsibilities, and work methods to improve efficiency and reduce costs. Recommendations often include reorganization, consolidation, downsizing or rightsizing and, in government settings, sometimes privatization. This is a clear example of Yankey and Willen's 'expert' model, although some management analysts attempt to include employees in analysis of findings and preparation of recommendations in order to have 'buy-in'.

Learning organizations and organizational learning

Organizational learning can be seen as organizational change to the extent that it involves having the organization create a new culture, which is focused on ongoing learning for organizational improvement. Definitions of these terms and the distinctions between them are still evolving. In the simplest terms, a learning organization is an organization that is 'skilled at creating, acquiring, and transferring knowledge, and at modifying its behavior to reflect new knowledge and insights' (Garvin, 1998, as cited in Austin & Hopkins, 2004, p. 11); and organizational learning is 'the process of improving actions through better knowledge and understanding' (Fiol & Lyles, 1985, as cited in Austin & Hopkins, 2004, p. 12).

SUMMARY AND IMPLICATIONS FOR HUMAN RESOURCE MANAGEMENT

A word of clarification is warranted here. Siegal and Stearn (2010) have criticized major organizational change initiatives which spend too much time preparing for a major transformation, often failing to achieve desired results. Their approach, 'results-driven change management' consists of clearly stating the purpose of the change effort, assigning several groups to work toward achieving rapid results, sharing learning from these initial successes with others in the organization, and applying this new knowledge to further change management activities. The change process described here, which focuses on change tactics rather than specific change methods, could be used within a strategy of expecting the achievement of quick, as well as long-term, results.

Given the challenges facing NPOs, the conscious use of planned organizational change tactics and methods should enable an organization to adapt, grow and thrive more proactively and effectively. The organization's executive can function as a change leader, clearly articulating the need for change and providing both a vision for an improved state of the organization and clear processes which can be used to get to the new desired state. The organization's HR professional can play a valuable role by providing consultation and advice to change leaders or serving in a change leader role, and can facilitate the use of external consultants as needed. An HR professional can add significant value to the organization by providing expert knowledge and skills regarding change tactics and methods, helping the organization to more effectively fulfill its mission.

ACKNOWLEDGEMENT

Some of this material is adapted from Chapter 11 of *Management of Human Service Programs, 5th ed.* (2012) by Lewis, J., Packard, T., and Lewis, M., Belmont, CA: Brooks/Cole Cengage Learning.

REFERENCES

Alfes, K., Truss, C. & Gill, J. (2010). The HR manager as change agent: evidence from the public sector. *Journal of Change Management*, 10(1), 109–127.

Anderson, D. & Ackerman Anderson, L. (2011). Conscious change leadership: achieving breakthrough results. *Leader to Leader*, 62, 51–59.

Armenakis, A. and Bedeian, A. (1999). Organizational change: a review of theory and research in the 1990s. *Journal of Management*, 25(3), 293–315.

Austin, M. (Ed.). (2004). *Changing Welfare Services: Case Studies of Local Welfare Reform Programs*. New York: Haworth Press.

Austin, M. & Hopkins, K. (2004). Defining the learning organization. In Austin, M. & Hopkins, K. (eds), *Supervision as Collaboration in the Human Services: Building a Learning Culture*. Thousand Oaks, CA: Sage, pp. 11–18.

Balougen, J. & Hope-Hailey, V. (2004). *Exploring Strategic Change*, 2nd edn. Harlow: FT Prentice Hall.

Brothers, J. & Sherman, A. (2011). *Building Nonprofit Capacity: A Guide to Managing Change through Organizational Lifecycles*. San Francisco, CA: Jossey-Bass.

Burke, W. (2011). *Organization Change: Theory and Practice*. 3rd edn. Thousand Oaks, CA: Sage Publications.

Cooperrider, D., Whitney, D. & Stavros, J. (eds) (2003). *Appreciative Inquiry Handbook: The First in a Series of AI Workbooks for Leaders of Change*. San Francisco, CA: Berrett-Koehler Publishers.

Demers, C. (2007). *Organizational Change Theories*. Thousand Oaks, CA: Sage Publications.

Eadie, D. (2006). Building the capacity to lead innovation. In Edwards, R. & Yankey, J. (eds), *Effectively Managing Nonprofit Organizations*. Washington, DC: NASW Press, pp. 29–46.

Fernandez, S. & Rainey, H. (2006). Managing successful organizational change in the public sector. *Public Administration Review*, March–April, 168–176.

French, W. & Bell, C. (1999). *Organization Development: Behavioral Science Interventions for Organization Improvement*, 6th edn. Englewood Cliffs, NJ: Prentice-Hall.

Grobman, G. (2008). *The Nonprofit Handbook,* 5th edn. Harrisburg, PA: White Hat Communications.

Harvard Business School (2005). *The Essentials of Managing Change and Transition*. Boston: Harvard Business School Publishing Corporation.

Kotter, J. (1996). *Leading Change*. Boston, MA: Harvard Business School Press.

Lewis, J., Packard, T. & Lewis, M. (2012). *Management of Human Service Programs*, 5th edn. Belmont, CA: Thompson/Brooks Cole.

McNamara, C. (N.D.). Free Management Library. *Capacity Building (Nonprofit)*. http://managementhelp.org/organizationalperformance/nonprofits/capacity-building.htm, accessed November 30, 2011.

McWilliam, C. & Ward-Griffin, C. (2006). Implementing organizational change in health and social services. *Journal of Organizational Change Management*, 19(2), 119–135.

Packard, T. (2010). *Organizational Change in Human Services Organizations: Comparing Successful and Unsuccessful Interventions*. Association for Research on Nonprofit Organizations and Voluntary Action Annual Conference, Alexandria, VA, November.

Palmer, I., Dunford, R. & Akin, G. (2009). *Managing Organizational Change: A Multiple Perspectives Approach*, 2nd edn. Boston, MA: McGraw-Hill Irwin.

Proehl, R. (2001). *Organizational Change in the Human Services*. Thousand Oaks, CA: Sage Publications.

Pynes, J. (2009). *Human Resource Management for Public and Nonprofit Organizations*, 3rd edn. San Francisco, CA: Jossey-Bass.

Ramos, C.M. (2007). Organizational change in a human service agency. *Consulting Psychology Journal: Practice and Research*, 59(1), 41–53.

Siegal, W. & Stearn, J. (2010). Beat the change management trap: your organization is more ready to change than you think, *Leader to Leader*, 55, 37–44.

Yankey, J. & Willen, C. (2006). Consulting with nonprofit organizations. In Edwards, R. & Yankey, J. (eds), *Effectively Managing Nonprofit Organizations*. Washington, DC: NASW Press, pp. 407–428.

PART III

Developing human resource management skills

11. University-based education programs in nonprofit management and philanthropic studies: current state of the field and future directions

Roseanne Mirabella and Mary McDonald

In response to the knowledge needs of those administering programs in the third sector, there has been a well-documented expansion of nonprofit, non-governmental and philanthropy education programs in universities and colleges globally (Wish & Mirabella, 1998a, 1998b; Mirabella & Wish, 2000; Mirabella, 2007; Mirabella, Gemelli, Malcolm & Berger, 2007). This chapter presents the most recent data available on these education programs, compiled through an electronic database accessible through the internet, and will report on census trends, provide a comparative perspective, and conclude with critical observations on the nascent field as it is developing.

The lead author has been tracking and mapping the growth of the nonprofit management education field in the United States since 1996 by type of program, graduate, undergraduate, continuing education, noncredit and online course offerings, and this research is ongoing. There are currently over 325 universities and colleges across the United States offering courses in nonprofit management and philanthropy. This longitudinal study reveals how programs in the field have changed over time, including differences in distribution across program and degree type, significant modifications in curricular content, and emerging programmatic forms.

METHODOLOGY

The original census of programs in the United States was launched in the mid-1990s through a mail survey of schools and universities known to have nonprofit management education programs. This was immediately supplemented by a mailing to schools accredited by the Association to Advance

Collegiate Schools of Business (AACSB) and the National Association of Schools of Public Affairs and Administration (NASPAA). Several years later, realizing the oversight of not seeking out social work programs in our database, a concerted effort was made to add these programs as well.

As web-based resources became more readily available, the collection of data was automated and maintained on the web (http://academic.shu.edu/npo/). We also developed the capability to have representatives of these academic degree programs update their information using a password provided by the lead author. The proposed changes are placed in a 'holding bin' until reviewed and verified. Following verification the revised information is posted on the university's individual page. For this update, an electronic message was sent to all of the universities in the database, as well as to several professional listservs for nonprofit scholars. Revisions to current listings were submitted by university representatives. In addition, a global review of emails and website links was conducted and corrections were made as necessary.

CENSUS OF PROGRAMS IN THE UNITED STATES

There continues to be an increase in the number of nonprofit management education programs (NMEs) offered by college and universities in the United States. Table 11.1 summarizes the growth in programs by type. The number of universities offering courses online has increased dramatically since 2002, from 10 to 62, or 520 percent. The number of universities offering NME undergraduate courses has doubled in the 15 years to 2011, to 136. Although the number of institutions has only grown by 67 percent during this time, the number of programs being offered has more than doubled. We continue to see a smaller number of universities offering multiple programs. For example, Arizona State offers an undergraduate program, a master's degree program, and professional development courses. The University of Washington offers courses through program in public administration, as well as through the social work programs. The line graphs in Figure 11.1 illustrate the growth in programs by type as well as the overall growth.

In 1996, there were 66 colleges and universities with at least one undergraduate course in nonprofit management. By 2006, this number had increased by more than three-quarters to 117, increasing another 16 percent since then to 136 in 2011 (Table 11.2). An increasing number of these programs offer a concentration (three or more courses) in nonprofit management. There were 26 undergraduate programs with a nonprofit concentration in 1996, increasing to 61 and 97 in 2006 and 2011, respectively.

Table 11.1 Growth in Nonprofit Management Education Programs, 1996–2011

	1996	2002	2006	2011	% increase (1996–2011)
Universities offering NME undergraduate courses	66	86	117	136	106
Universities offering NME graduate courses	128	155	161	239	87
Universities offering NME noncredit courses	51	72	75	89	75
Universities offering NME continuing education courses	39	57	56	74	90
Universities offering NME online courses	[a]	10	17	62	520[b]
Number of institutions	179	253	238	265	67
Number of programs	284	380	426	600	111

[a] Data not available; [b] 2002–2011

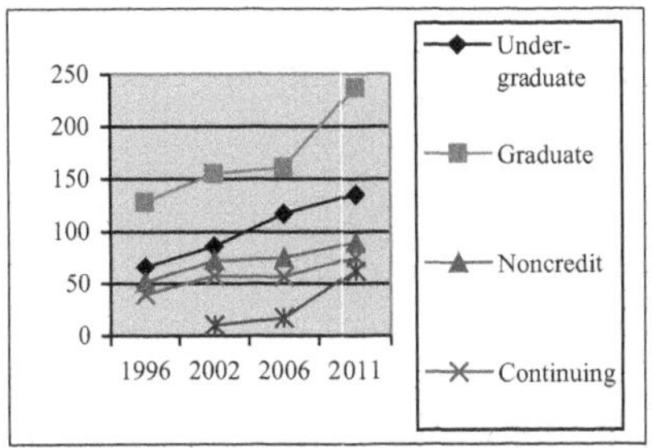

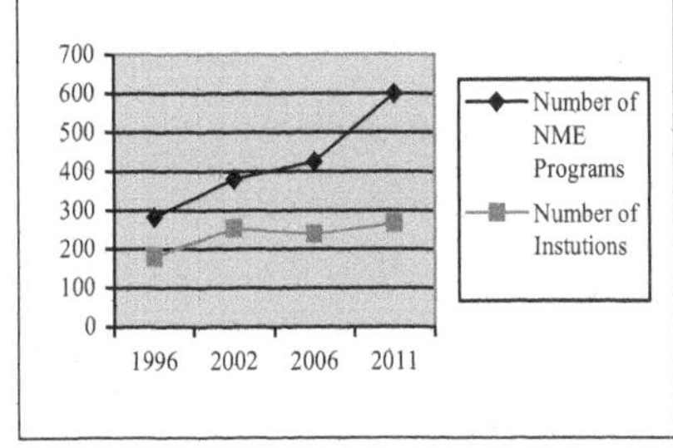

Figure 11.1 Growth in NME Programs (1996–2011)

As can be seen from Table 11.1, the number of universities offering graduate courses has increased from 128 to 239 or 87 percent. NME courses are most frequently found in a graduate program, either with one or two electives as part of a Master's degree program, with three or more courses within a program, or as a concentration within a graduate degree program (Table 11.3). These data are also shown graphically (Figure 11.2). From the line graph, we can see that the number of universities offering graduate courses in all three categories continues to increase.

Table 11.2 Undergraduate nonprofit management education programs by year

	1996	2006	2011
Universities Offering NPM Undergraduate Courses	66	117	136
Universities Offering NPM Undergraduate Concentration	26	61	97

Table 11.3 Graduate Programs in NME by year, 1996–2011

	1996	2006	2011
Universities offering NME graduate courses	128	161	239
Universities offering three or more graduate courses in NME	82	126	201
Universities offering a graduate concentration in NME	[a]	105	156

[a] Data not available

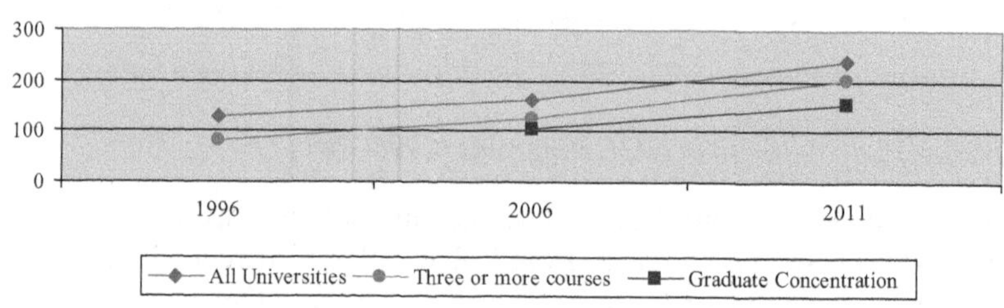

Figure 11.2 Growth in NME Graduate Programs (1996–2011)

THE GRADUATE CONCENTRATION IN NONPROFIT MANAGEMENT

In this section, we examine the nonprofit management programs that have a stated concentration in nonprofit management. These programs advertise this option on the university website and in promotional materials. First we take a look at the institutional location of the programs with a concentration in nonprofit management (Table 11.4). While colleges of arts and sciences continue to hold steady as the most likely places to find these programs, they showed a slight decrease (4 percent) over the five years to 2011. Business schools have declined as a percentage of the total (36 percent), as have schools of business and public administration (38 percent). In the next section we discuss the trend towards development of social entrepreneurship programs, a curriculum primarily found in a school of business. This may account, in part, for the decline in nonprofit management programs within this academic setting. There was an increase in the number of programs offering a concentration in nonprofit management located in another colleges or schools, from 22 in 2006 to 29 in 2011. Included in this group are graduate or professional schools, other colleges and interdisciplinary programs. The largest increases in the number of programs offering a concentration in nonprofit management have occurred among schools of public affairs and administration (200 percent) and schools of social work (186 percent).

Table 11.4 Institutional Location of NME Graduate Concentration, 2006–2011

School or College	2006	2011	% Increase (Decrease)
Arts & Sciences	48	46	*(4%)*
Business	22	14	*(36%)*
Business & Public Administration	13	8	*(38%)*
Public Affairs & Administration	13	39	*200%*
Social Work	7	20	*186%*
Other College or School	22	29	*32%*
Total	**105**	**156**	

Table 11.5 shows the change in regional location of graduate programs in nonprofit management education over the 15 years to 2011. The Northeast now leads the nation with the largest number of nonprofit programs, comprising 34 percent of all universities with three or more courses and 31 percent of all universities with a concentration. Although in the past the Midwest had more nonprofit programs than any other region in both categories, its proportion has declined to 24 percent of the programs with three or more courses and 26 percent of programs with concentrations. This represents a 25 percent and 28 percent decline, respectively, since 2006. As the proportion of programs in the Midwest has declined, the number in the South has increased in both categories, with 21 percent of the programs offering three or more courses and 24 percent offering a concentration in nonprofit management. The number of nonprofit management programs in the West has remained about the same during this time period, with slight increases in both categories.

Table 11.5 Regional Location of NME Graduate Programs, 1996–2011

	1996 (%)	2006 (%)		2011 (%)	
		Three or more courses	Concentration	Three or more courses	Concentration
Northeast [a]	27	31	30	34	31
Midwest [b]	29	32	36	24	26
South [c]	16	17	17	21	24
West [d]	18	20	17	21	19
Total (n)	82	126	105	201	156

a Includes Connecticut, Washington DC, Massachusetts, Maryland, Maine, New Hampshire, New Jersey, New York, Pennsylvania, Rhode Island, and Vermont.
b Includes Illinois, Indiana, Michigan, Minnesota, Missouri, Nebraska, South Dakota, and Wisconsin.
c Includes Alabama, Arkansas, Florida, Georgia, Kentucky, Louisiana, North Carolina, South Carolina, Tennessee, Virginia, and West Virginia.
d Includes Arizona, California, Colorado, Montana, Oregon, Texas, Utah and Washington.

Graduate programs in nonprofit management make available a variety of certificates to their students. Of the 126 certificates offered, more than 70 percent are certificates in nonprofit management and 13 percent are certificates in the leadership of nonprofit organizations. Combined with certificates in fundraising (6 percent), these three certificates account for over 90 percent of all certificates offered. Among those certificates in the remaining 10 percent are certificates in community studies, marketing, philanthropy, social entrepreneurship and volunteer management. Included in this last category (volunteer management) are certificates in volunteer program management and volunteer and community resource management.

Drawing on previous work in this area establishing functional categories for understanding nonprofit management courses (Mirabella, 2007; Mirabella & Wish, 2000, 1999; Young, 1987), Table 11.6 summarizes the curricular elements of the various nonprofit programs by function. Although the absolute number of nonprofit courses being offered across the country has increased in all categories, it is interesting to look at the comparative rate of growth. Similar to findings in previous studies, inside management functions continue to dominate the curricular offerings with almost 50 percent of all courses. Courses in a variety of nonprofit management skills make up the vast majority of courses in this group including courses in nonprofit management and leadership, governance, program evaluation, information technology, and organization theory and development. The percentage of courses offered in this subcategory has grown as well. In the past, internal management skills accounted for about one-quarter of all courses offered, while today they account for one-third of all nonprofit courses. The number of courses in both financial management and human resource management has increased in the 15 years to 2011; however the rate of growth for both of these subcategories has been slower than all other course categories. The two subcategories in the boundary spanning function – legal issues and strategic planning – increased as well, though both represent a smaller percentage of all courses than in previous years (3 percent and 4 percent, respectively).

There are some interesting changes to take note of in the category of courses comprising the outside functions of nonprofit organizations. Firstly, courses in advocacy, public policy and community organizing continue to increase. Included in this category are courses in public lobbying and advocacy, organizing for social justice, community organizing and political participation, coalition building, and government and nonprofit sector relationships. There is a relatively new subcategory of courses in the advocacy category, the content of which is focused on creating social change. While some of these courses are more descriptive with a focus on

Table 11.6 Frequency of Courses by Function and Year, 1996–2011

	1996 (%)	2006 (%)	2011 (%)	Percentage Increase (1996–2011)
Outside function				
Philanthropy and the third sector	9	13	10	255
Advocacy, public policy, and community organizing	10	15	12	300
Fundraising	15	14	17	280
Marketing and public relations	7	6	5	151
Boundary spanning				
Legal issues	4	4	3	167
Strategic planning	6	3	4	138
Inside function				
Internal management skills	26	25	33	327
Financial management	13	9	9	132
Human resource management	10	12	6	96
Total (n)	*526*	*1,136*	*1,749*	

the relationship between public policy and social change, others are concerned with creating change, including strategic management of policy change and strategic approaches for global social impact. Although the absolute number of advocacy, public policy and community organizing courses in this area has increased 300 percent, they fell as a proportion of all courses offered in 2011. Moving to the philanthropy and the third sector category, our census shows that courses in philanthropy, civil society and foundations of the nonprofit sector have increased in the 15 years to 2011, although similar to the advocacy category their percentage of the total number of courses presently offered has decreased as well. Although the 2006 census found fundraising as the third most frequent type of course offered, in the 2011 census it regains the number two position that it held previously, with 17 percent of all courses in this subcategory. About two-thirds of the courses in this category are the fundraising courses historically found in these programs, including resource development, grant writing, capital and endowment campaigns, endowment management and annual and major gifts. The other third of the courses in this category are those related to a more recent trend in the field, the development and adoption of courses and programs in social entrepreneurship. Among the social entrepreneurship courses in this category are courses in the nonprofit enterprise, principles and practices of social entrepreneurship, the rise of social entrepreneurs, and social entrepreneurship and social innovation. The development of social enterprise and entrepreneurship programs will be discussed more fully in the section on recent developments in the field.

Managing Staff and Volunteers: Courses in Human Resource Management

There are almost 100 courses in the various aspects of human resource management offered through nonprofit management education programs in the United States. Almost half of these courses are generic human resource management courses for both public and nonprofit managers, primarily offered through public administration and social work programs. About half of the remaining courses (27 percent) focus exclusively on human resource management in nonprofit organizations, while the remaining courses (25 percent) are concerned with the management of volunteers. In this section, major components of the current human resources curriculum available through nonprofit management education programs are highlighted.

The data for this portion of the chapter are drawn from a research project being conducted by the authors who are undertaking a comprehensive review of the syllabi of graduate programs in nonprofit management education, including a review of course goals, content areas, required readings, assignments and faculty characteristics. The programs included in the study are those leading to a Master's degree offered by 27 of the institutional members of the National Academic Centers Council (NACC). NACC was founded in 1991 by leaders of university-based nonprofit academic programs who wanted to share information and ideas to strengthen their programs and advance the field of philanthropic and nonprofit sector education within their institutions and beyond. These findings report on the analysis of courses within 27 of the 50 NACC member programs for which complete syllabi were available. Syllabi were collected from NACC programs for all courses, including required core and competency courses, required and elective new public management (NPM) concentration courses, and general electives. The results presented here are based on an analysis of the required course offerings in human resource management of 27 NACC institutions for which we have a complete dataset.[1] This represents more than two-thirds of the NACC membership institutions with academic graduate courses in nonprofit management. The weekly content of each required course was coded according to the 16 elements of NACC's curricular guidelines (see Appendix). The coding was done by subcategory of each element with element totals calculated from the subcategories. Each weekly unit in the schedule was coded by topic discussed, utilizing assigned readings as an aid in coding. For example, the content of various volumes was examined, when necessary, for assistance in determining weekly content.

Of the 16 curricular categories promulgated by NACC, one (#13) is primarily concerned with nonprofit human resource management. Included within this category are four sub-elements:

1. Human resource issues within both formal and informal nonprofit organizations and how human resource issues in nonprofit organizations are different from the experience in public and for-profit organizations.
2. The role, value and dynamics of volunteerism in carrying out the work and fulfilling the missions of nonprofit organizations.
3. Issues of supervision and human resource management systems and practices relevant to both paid and unpaid employees.
4. The dimensions and dynamics of individual and organizational diversity within the nonprofit sector and their implications for effective human resource management (http://www.naccouncil.org/pdf/GradCG07.pdf).

Of the 236 class sessions in human resource management coded, about one-quarter were concerned with the first sub-element, that is, general issues in human resource management, including the differences and similarities between management in the public and nonprofit sector. About 20 percent of the coursework focused on the second sub-element, the role of volunteers in nonprofit organizations. The third sub-element, issues related to supervision and management systems in human resources, accounted for the largest portion of class sessions with more than 40 percent devoted to these conversations. Finally, a little more than 10 percent of class sessions were devoted to a discussion of diversity and its implication for managing human resources in the sector.

The Burning NME Issue Today

Although there were many changes in this census of programs from previous updates, perhaps the most dramatic of these is the increase in the number of graduate-level social entrepreneurship courses offered in the United States. The historical census of nonprofit management education courses maintained by Seton Hall University included only four courses in social entrepreneurship in 1998, increasing to 21 and 26 in 2002 and 2006, respectively. Today there are almost 100 social entrepreneurship courses offered. Most of these courses are offered as singleton courses within the nonprofit management Master's degree program. However, some are included as part of a concentration in social entrepreneurship or a complete master's degree in social entrepreneurship.

In our review of graduate education programs with a social entrepreneurship emphasis, we found 20 such programs in the United States. The majority of social entrepreneurship programs are located in a business school (65 percent), most leading to the MBA, one leading to an MBA in Nonprofit Management (Brandeis University), another to the Master of Arts in Social Entrepreneurship (Northwest University), and a third type, the MBA with a Minor in Social Innovation (Brigham Young University). Of the remaining 35 percent, five of these programs are located within a school of public affairs, administration or management. Most in this group lead to the Master of Public Administration degree, though the American University awards the Master of Arts in Social Enterprise and the New School University the Master of Science in Nonprofit Management. The remaining two universities are located in universities with a religious affiliation: the program in Social Entrepreneurship and Change at Pepperdine University, and the emphasis in social entrepreneurship at Trinity International University. Pepperdine University awards a Master of Arts in Social Entrepreneurship and Change, while Trinity International University includes its social entrepreneurship program as a concentration within the Master of Arts in Cultural Engagement.

More than half of the universities with concentrations in social entrepreneurship have created a separate program or institute to house both the coursework and other activities centered on social enterprise and entrepreneurship. For example, the Social Enterprise at Kellogg (SEEK) program at Northwestern University has a curriculum designed for 'global leaders ... in the service of social development and change' (http://www.kellogg.northwestern.edu/academic/seek/). Perhaps one of the most well-known centers is Duke University's Center for the Advancement of Social Entrepreneurship (CASE) which 'promotes the entrepreneurial pursuit of social impact through the thoughtful adaptation of business expertise' (http://www.caseatduke.org/). It is interesting to note that all of the centers or institutes developed for this purpose are housed within a business school setting.

Using historical data from 1998, we can trace the change in these programs over time, from a program in nonprofit management to a social entrepreneurship program. One example of this is the business program at Dartmouth University. In 2002, Dartmouth offered two courses, a course in Nonprofit Management I and another in Nonprofit Management II. By 2006, these had morphed into Entrepreneurship in the Social Sector I and Entrepreneurship in the Social Sector II. Another would be the program within the F.W. Olin Graduate School of Business at Babson College. In 1998 and 2002, the sole course offering was a course entitled Management of Not-for-Profit Organizations. There were no listings for Babson in the 2006 update. In 2011 they had a newly developed initiative within the Arthur M. Blank Center and offered one course in Socially Responsible Entrepreneurship. These changes appear to represent a pattern in the business schools and perhaps the replacement of nonprofit courses with courses narrowed to a social entrepreneurship emphasis.

The *Chronicle of Philanthropy* recently listed the top ten buzzwords of the past decade and, not surprisingly, social entrepreneurs top the list (Bernholz, 2011). There is evidence of the impact of the social entrepreneurship movement in the inventory of courses now included in the census. There are 18 courses centered on social impact and innovation, from strategic approaches to social impact to leading innovation and change. The curriculum focuses on what differentiates the entrepreneurial leader from other leaders of nonprofit organizations. Through cases, films, projects and current-day examples, students become familiar with successful entrepreneurs of the day, those that use innovative techniques to meet societal needs. Students are also introduced to various models for earned income and identifying innovative opportunities for organizational growth. One syllabus, for its course on managing innovations, asserts the critical nature of this curricular offering: 'The ability to manage innovation and change in organizations is essential in the increasingly turbulent environments. This course aims to enhance students' understanding of innovation processes in organization and how to manage such processes effectively' (University of Georgia, School of Social Work, http://ssw.uga.edu:8091/plone/current-students/mnpo-students/mnpo-syllabi1/7423.Innovations.Jaskyte.2008.pdf, accessed 10 March 2011). A more complete treatment of the development of social entrepreneurship within nonprofit management programs can be found in Mirabella and Young 2012.

FINAL THOUGHTS

It is interesting that social entrepreneurship education is developing rapidly, in diverse institutional settings, without a great deal of solid grounding in the long-term efficacy of this approach. At present, there is little empirical evidence to warrant such a broad embrace of social entrepreneurs and their methods. For example, Lounsbury and Strang posit that 'the key empirical cases are the success stories of particular individuals and organizations around the world that are identified as "social entrepreneurs"' (2009, p. 73). In other words, we have embraced the social entrepreneurship approach for widespread adoption based on the past success of individual entrepreneurs, even though there is scant evidence that collectively social entrepreneurship as an approach is making a marked, systematic difference; rather, the social entrepreneurship logic has been widely embraced based on individual success stories. Yet it is the curricular trend that at present appears to have the most momentum.

In his recent work on *Driving Social Change*, Paul Light (2011) provides direction for solving what he describes as the 'world's toughest problems' through the inclusion of several drivers, one of which is social entrepreneurship. He maintains that each of four drivers is necessary for 'social breakthroughs' in solving the tough issues of the day, and recognizes social entrepreneurship as one of several important drivers. This excerpt from the introduction to his work explains the role of each driver in the policy process and the importance of defining problems before adopting solutions. He also cautions that the choice of driver is directly related to and follows from examination of the type of problem to be solved, not the popularity of the particular driver:

> However, social breakthrough is not a synonym for social entrepreneurship or innovation. Rather, it is the destination of all social action, and involves a cycle of engagement that can act as a map for deploying resources and energy. Although a breakthrough can come from the new combinations of ideas that underpin innovation (social entrepreneurship), it can also come from the aggressive defense, delivery, and expansion of past breakthroughs (social safekeeping), careful research on trends and solutions (social exploring), and the unrelenting demand for change embedded in social networks (social advocacy). The choice of one driver over another depends entirely on the problem to be solved, not the popularity of a particular approach. The urgent threat comes first, while the choice of a particular driver for achieving impact comes second. Form follows function, path follows purpose, and driver follows destination, not vice versa. (Light, 2011, pp. 3–4)

Light has outlined for us an approach to addressing social problems that recognizes the need for a complete tool box of drivers to address complicated social issues successfully. He provides an approach to social action that begins with an understanding of the problem to be addressed and development of solutions based on careful research and empirical evidence (social exploring), without resorting to a policy logic based on anecdotal success stories. In addition, Light recognizes the importance of protecting already established breakthroughs from aggressive attacks as these are vital sources and creators of social capital (p. 71). Solving the urgent threats ahead 'lies in both creating and protecting the world's great breakthroughs' (p. 149).

In short, addressing the world's deepest needs requires a broader approach and a more balanced embrace of the various tools currently available to solve our most pressing problems: social entrepreneurship, social safekeeping, social exploring and social advocacy. The development of social entrepreneurship curricula in nonprofit management programs is not inconsistent with this broader approach but it is only one component of a wider array of curricular upgrades that need to be made. Although social entrepreneurship is currently in vogue, Light cautions us not to disregard the other drivers which are just as critical in bringing about social change. In the future, our educational programs for those who will lead and manage nonprofits and other forms of social purpose organization must include coursework to prepare students for all potential roles they might be called upon to play, including roles as social entrepreneurs, social safekeepers, social explorers and social advocates.

NOTE

1. Data collection is ongoing. As syllabi sets are completed, universities are added to the analysis.

APPENDIX: NACC CURRICULAR ELEMENTS

1.0 Comparative Perspectives on the Nonprofit Sector, Voluntary Action and Philanthropy
2.0 Scope and Significance of the Nonprofit Sector, Voluntary Action and Philanthropy
3.0 History and Theories of the Nonprofit Sector, Voluntary Action and Philanthropy
4.0 Ethics and Values
5.0 Nonprofit Governance and Leadership

6.0 Public Policy, Advocacy and Social Change
7.0 Nonprofit Law
8.0 Nonprofit Economics
9.0 Nonprofit Finance
10.0 Fundraising and Development
11.0 Financial Management and Accountability
12.0 Leadership, Organization and Management
13.0 Nonprofit Human Resource Management
14.0 Nonprofit Marketing
15.0 Information Technology and Management
16.0 Assessment, Evaluation and Decision-Making Methods

REFERENCES

Bernholz, Lucy (2011). Philanthropies 10 favorite buzzwords of the decade show how nonprofits are changing. *Chronicle of Philanthropy*, http://philanthropy.com/article/Philanthropys-Buzzwords-of/125795/?sid=&utm_source=&utm_medium=en, accessed February 24, 2011.

Light, Paul (2011). *Driving Social Change: How to Solve the World's Toughest Problems*. Hoboken, NJ: Wiley.

Lounsbury, Michael & Strang, David (2009). Social entrepreneurship: success stories and logic construction. In Hammack, D. and Heydemann, S. (eds), *Globalization, Philanthropy, and Civil Society*. Indianapolis, IN: Indiana University Press, pp. 71–94.

Mirabella, Roseanne (2007). University-based educational programs in nonprofit management and philanthropic studies: a 10-year review and projections of future trends. *Nonprofit and Voluntary Sector Quarterly*, 36(4), 11s–27s.

Mirabella, Roseanne M., Gemelli, Giuliana, Malcolm, Margy-Jean & Berger, Bagriel (2007). Nonprofit and philanthropic studies: international overview of the field in Africa, Canada, Latin America, Asia, the Pacific, and Europe. *Nonprofit and Voluntary Sector Quarterly*, 36(4), 110s–135s.

Mirabella, Roseanne M. & Naomi B. Wish (1999). Educational impact of graduate nonprofit degree programs: perspectives of multiple stakeholders, research report. *Nonprofit Management and Leadership*, 9(3), 329–340.

Mirabella, Roseanne M. & Wish, Naomi B. (2000), Graduate Department of Public and Healthcare Administration, the 'best place' debate: a comparison of graduate education programs for nonprofit managers. *Public Administration Review*, 60(3), 219–229.

Mirabella, Roseanne & Young, Dennis R. (2012). The development of education for social entrepreneurship and nonprofit management: Diverging or converging paths? *Nonprofit Management and Leadership*, 23:1, pp. 43–57.

Wish, Naomi B. & Mirabella, Roseanne M. (1998a). Curricular variations in nonprofit management graduate programs, research report. *Nonprofit Management and Leadership*, 9(1), 99–110.

Wish, Naomi B. & Mirabella, Roseanne M. (1998b). Nonprofit management education: current offerings and practices in university-based programs. In

O'Neill, Michael & Fletcher, Kathleen (eds), *Nonprofit Management Education: US and World Perspectives*, Westport, CT: Praeger, pp. 13–22.

Young, Dennis R. (1987). Executive leadership in nonprofit organizations. In Powell, Walter W. (ed.), *The Nonprofit Sector: A Research Handbook*. New Haven: Yale University Press, pp. 167–179.

Index